Why
Freud
Fainted

Why
Freud
Fainted

SAMUEL

ROSENBERG

The Bobbs-Merrill Company, Inc.
Indianapolis/New York

The author gratefully acknowledges the permission of the publishers to reprint excerpts from the following:

The Collected Works of C. G. Jung, ed. Herbert Read, Michael Fordham, Gerhard Adler, William McGuire; trans. R. F. C. Hull. Vol. 5, *Symbols of Transformation* copyright © 1956 by Princeton University Press. Excerpts reprinted by permission of Princeton University Press.

Paper 10, "Medusa's Head," in *The Collected Papers of Sigmund Freud*, edited by Ernest Jones, M.D., Volume 5, edited by James Strachey, published by Basic Books, Inc. by arrangement with The Hogarth Press Ltd. and The Institute of Psycho-Analysis, London.

The Interpretation of Dreams, by Sigmund Freud, translated from the German and edited by James Strachey, published in the United States by Basic Books, Inc., Publishers, New York, by arrangement with George Allen & Unwin Ltd. and The Hogarth Press, Ltd., London.

The Life and Work of Sigmund Freud, Volume I, by Ernest Jones, M.D., © 1953 by Ernest Jones, Basic Books, Inc., Publishers, New York.

The Life and Work of Sigmund Freud, Volume III, by Ernest Jones, M.D., © 1957 by Ernest Jones, Basic Books, Inc., Publishers, New York.

Memories, Dreams, Reflections, by C. G. Jung, recorded and edited by Aniela Jaffe, translated by Richard and Clara Winston. Copyright © 1962, 1963 by Random House, Inc. Reprinted by permission of Pantheon Books, a Division of Random House, Inc.

A Psycho-Analytic Dialogue: The Letters of Sigmund Freud and Karl Abraham, 1907–1926, edited by Hilda C. Abraham and Ernst L. Freud, translated by Bernard Marsh and Hilda C. Abraham, © Hilda C. Abraham and Ernst L. Freud 1965, Basic Books, Inc., Publishers, New York.

Copyright © 1978 by Samuel Rosenberg

Published by The Bobbs-Merrill Company, Inc.
Indianapolis   New York

Designed by Jacques Chazaud
Manufactured in the United States of America

First printing

Library of Congress Cataloging in Publication Data

Rosenberg, Samuel.
Why Freud fainted.

1. Freud, Sigmund, 1856–1939.   2. Psychoanalysis and literature.   I. Title
BF173.F85R68   813'.5'4   77-25141
ISBN 0-672-52206-3

*For our beloved brother
Jerome Rosenberg,
musician and teacher*

Contents

PART ONE

The Sigmund Freud Reenactment Syndrome

The task which was imposed upon me in the dream of carrying out a dissection of *my own body* was thus my self-analysis.
—Sigmund Freud, *The Interpretation of Dreams*, 1900

. . . wrote over every square inch of the only foolscap available, *his own body* . . . thereby, he said, reflecting his own person . . . transaccidented through slow fires of consciousness into a dividual chaos, common to all flesh, human only, mortal . . .
—James Joyce, *Finnegans Wake*, 1939

1

The entry in my travel notebook reads: "December 1. Aboard Swissair's flight to Zurich and Vienna. It is 3 A.M. Though I've been up since five yesterday morning, I remain wide awake. All around me in this huge darkened plane the hundred or so passengers are asleep, some stretched out on the rows of empty seats. Even the stewardesses are snoozing prettily in the back row of this high-flying, jet-propelled, multimilliondollar flophouse.

"This scene reminds me—must be mental fatigue—of the surreal scene in *Moby Dick:* Melville's astonishing description of the ill-fated *Pequod's* fo'c'sle as an underground burial crypt where, 'in triangular oaken vaults' (hammocks!), the sleeping sailors lie 'in chiselled muteness' like stone effigies of medieval 'kings and counsellors.' What a splendid morbid imagination!

"I scold myself: Melville deployed this necromantic image as a dramatic anticipation of the death of the entire crew, drowned when the great white whale rammed their boats and then the *Pequod* itself. Only Ishmael lived to tell the tale. But why have *I* foisted this guignol memory-scene upon myself and this congregation of innocent economy-class travelers? Maybe I'm a necrophile too. But more likely this morbid association arises from my subconscious fear of flying, compounded by the excited prospect of entering 'Freud's Vienna.' Vienna. Like the devastated, punished German cities I photographed after the war, Vienna is linked in my mind with the expulsion and extermination of hundreds of thousands of Jewish children, women, and men. Four of Freud's sisters were among them.

"A few minutes ago, as I sat with my nose pressed to the window, looking down at the moonlit cloud-blanket stretching from horizon to horizon—it looks like a vast bowl of yogurt—my thoughts wandered among images associated with fear of flying, plane crashes, and untimely death. Suddenly I remembered the 'Freudian' comedy that occurred when I worked as a playreader for a Broadway producer. One morning he asked his secretary and me to witness his last will and testament. He explained unhappily that the 'great' Sam Goldwyn, to whom he was trying to sell the play he'd just produced, had phoned from Hollywood 'last night' and ordered him to attend a meeting 'tomorrow night.' When he told Goldwyn that he was afraid to fly and would arrive by train later in the week, Goldwyn had grossly and loudly insulted him and threatened to cancel the deal if he missed the meeting. (He did not, I regret to say, tell my boss that he would 'include him out.')

"After we signed the document (without being permitted to read it), this scared, humiliated man said to me, 'Wait a minute. I want to talk to you.' After his secretary left he paced the floor for a few minutes and said, 'You psychoanalyze every book and script you read, so maybe you can analyze the nightmare I had last night.'

"After a long pause he continued: 'Sam, you remember the Allen Tate adaptation of *The Turn of the Screw*, the play I turned down last week? Well, in my nightmare Allen Tate appeared like the ghost of Quint. But not so silent. He shouted at me, threatened me, screamed at me, demanding that I produce his play. I kept on rejecting the play and giving my reasons all night long. I woke in a cold sweat and with a terrific headache. Now why should such an ordinary situation as turning down a play turn into a terrible nightmare? Waddya make of it, Sam?'

"After thinking, 'This is small retribution for the way this man treats his actors and employees: a nightmare-inflicting sonofabitch has nightmares,' I assumed a Viennese accent and answered, 'Dis iss a verrry interrresting drrrream you are telling me. Of cuss only a very expensive high-class psychoanalyst could explain the unique inner meaning of such a nightmare. He would probably ask you why you turned down Henry James's ghost story about evil children and a possibly insane governess. But there is one detail in what Freud would call the "manifest content," or top layer of your dream, that we *can* talk about. It's the name of your dream-persecutor: Allen Tate. You know Yiddish. What does "Tate" mean in Yiddish?'

" 'It means *death* or *dead.*'

" 'Right. And "alle" or "allen tate" means *all are dead.* Isn't that what usually happens when a plane crashes?'

" 'So?'

" 'So here's one possible interpretation of your nightmare. You are mortally afraid of flying and decide to take a train instead. But the great producer Goldwyn, a fellow Jew, phones you. He not only forces you to fly at the risk of your life, but humiliates you when you try to explain your fears. You then go to sleep and dream that a man whose name means in Yiddish "all are dead" demands that you produce his version of the Henry James story in which the dead return to haunt innocent children. The dream is a good example of the way the unconscious mind works: a subconscious fear of death or failure is dramatized in a disguised, symbolic, condensed manner. It may be that in your dream Allen Tate is a disguised Sam Goldwyn. [Pause.] Or: *you* are Allen Tate, screaming at Goldwyn, also a producer, because *he threatened to turn you and your play down.* Sometimes *all* the characters in a dream are fractions of the dreamer's psyche.'

"My employer laughed and said, 'I'll buy interpretation number two. I did have some nasty death wishes toward Goldwyn before I fell asleep. All to take effect *after* he produced my play, of course.' "

2

Indeed, dreams are so closely related to linguistic expression that Ferenczi (1910) has remarked that every tongue has its own dream language.
—Freud, *The Interpretation of Dreams*

My improvised pun-interpretation of the Allen Tate nightmare was based on many similar interpretations I'd read in Freud's various writings about dream mechanisms. One example: In a footnote in his "dream-book" Freud wrote: "The nicest instance of a dream-interpretation which has reached us from ancient times is based on a play upon words. It is told by Artemidorus (Book IV, Chapter 24): 'I think that Aristander gave a most happy interpretation to Alexander (the Great) of Macedon when he surrounded Tyre (*tvros*) and was besieging it but was feeling uneasy and disturbed because of the length of time the siege was taking. Alexander dreamt that he saw a satyr (*satyros*) dancing on his shield. Aristander happened to be . . . in attendance on the king during his Syrian campaign. By dividing the word for satyr into *sa* and *tyros*, meaning "Tyre is thine," he encouraged Alexander to press home the siege so that he became master of the city.' "

> SERENDIPITY, from *Serendip*, a former name for Ceylon, plus -ITY. A word coined by Horace Walpole, who says (in a letter to Horace Mann, January 28, 1754) that he had formed it upon the title of the fairy-tale "The Three Princes of Serendip," the heroes of which "were always making discoveries, by accidents and sagacity, of things they were not in quest of."
> —*Oxford Unabridged Dictionary*

As I sat in the seemingly motionless plane, nervously reviewing my reasons for making this costly trip to Vienna (what if nothing new turns up?), some memories of discoveries made in foreign places arrived to comfort and reassure. My Conan Doyle book,* I recalled, was triggered by three serendipitous encounters, one with a Japanese tourist on a Swiss train near Reichenbach Falls—the place where Doyle perversely drowned Sherlock Holmes and Professor Moriarty like unwanted kittens. (Ten years later he resurrected Holmes, but left the evil Professor in the drink. I often wonder why Doyle refused to fully revive Moriarty, one of the greatest of fictional characters.)

The second reassuring example was the discovery of the profound "Jacob allegory" in several Shakespeare plays, a still-continuing study ignited by a name shouted in an Italian street. While photographing a Venetian back-alley, I heard a woman call her son home: "*Iago! Vieni qui!*" ("Iago! Come here!") Later, in Rome, my multilingual friend Leon Cahan explained: "No, Sam, she wasn't calling her nice little boy a villain, not even lovingly. 'Iago,' the Italian and Spanish form of the Hebrew name 'Jacob' or 'Yaacob,' is a common name in Venice. Catholics revere the

---

Naked is the Best Disguise. Bobbs-Merrill, N.Y., 1974.

Biblical Jacob as 'Sant-iago,' as in San*tiago* de Compostela, the Spanish shrine to which medieval pilgrims walked from all parts of Europe."

Later, after some months of tracing the Iago-Jacob images through his plays, I found that Shakespeare, an advanced Bible hermeneutist, used his knowledge of the God-manipulated good-and-evil Jacob toward the creation of his murderous heroes and villains: Iago, Shylock, Iachimo, Brutus, Macbeth, Hamlet, and others. As I think of the "Jacob allegory" found in many Shakespeare plays, it becomes related to the bitter words spoken in *King Lear:* "As flies to wanton boys, are we to the gods; they kill us for their sport."

The third example of serendipity, in Istanbul in 1951, led, after some intricate idea-tracking, to the strong suspicion that Shakespeare was thinking of a scandalous episode in the life of one of Queen Elizabeth's courtiers when he wrote his version of the old *Othello* story.

While filming the magnificent Bosporus, the strait or current that races from the Black Sea through the Sea of Marmara and the Hellespont into the Mediterranean, I paused to read the following in a travel guide: "In his *Metamorphoses*, Ovid reminds us that the *Bos* (ox) *porus* (ford) was given its name when the mythological Io, transformed into a heifer by Zeus after he raped her, swam the then-unnamed strait while fleeing the stinging gadfly set upon her by Zeus's madly jealous wife Hera. . . . After swimming the Ionian Sea, Io finally reached Egypt, where she became the goddess Isis." (Zeus saved her life by promising Hera to give up his rapine adventures. But he did not keep his promise.)

As I read this mythological tale, it reminded me at once of Edward de Vere, 17th Earl of Oxford, whom Queen Elizabeth fondly called "my Turk" because, like all well-read Europeans, she knew the Ovidian story of the Turkish "Bosporus" or "ox-ford."

Here are some of the major connections between the Earl of Oxford and the fictional Othello: like Shakespeare's victim-murderer, Oxford went to Venice to offer his military services in an impending war with Turkey. When a truce was declared, Oxford planned a trip to Constantinople (Istanbul), but canceled it when an Othello-like drama arose in his own life. He hurriedly returned to England to perform in the drama in which he was the Othello and his wife a Desdemona falsely accused of adultery by the treacherous Iago-friend, Lord Henry Howard.

3

Arthur Golding's translation of Ovid's
Metamorphoses, which is the most beautiful book
in the language (my opinion and I suspect it was
Shakespeare's).
—Ezra Pound, *A,B,C of Reading*

With this Elizabethan background in mind, I reasoned: If, as Pound and others have said, Shakespeare was strongly influenced by the *Metamorphoses*, then a search of *Othello* might reveal a mention of the Bosporus. Shakespeare loved such references.

At first, even with the help of a concordance, I did not find it, but a quick scanning of the drama revealed an unmistakable reference to the Turkish strait. The interested reader will find it in the third act's climactic scene: Just a moment after he has finally goaded Othello into swearing he will murder innocent Desdemona, Iago senses that his victim needs to be pushed past the point of no return. He says cunningly, "Patience, I say; perhaps your mind may change." This last needle-prick causes Othello to respond with an elaborate, nearly incomprehensible geographical metaphor which, when translated into simpler words, links the jealousy-maddened Moor to the Bosporus-Oxford. He rages:

> Never, Iago. Like to the Pontic Sea,
> Whose icy current and compulsive course
> Ne'er feels retiring ebb, but keeps due on
> To the Propontic and the Hellespont,
> Even so my bloody thoughts, with violent pace,
> Shall ne'er look back, ne'er ebb to humble love,
> Till that a capable and wide revenge
> Swallow them up.

Yes, in this baroque geographical metaphor, Othello likens his irreversible murderous intention to the Bosporus Strait, which flows "compulsively" from the Pontic Sea [Black Sea] through the Propontic [Sea of Marmara] and the Hellespont into the Mediterranean.

In Rome, in 1950, I had the good fortune to be present when the veteran actor-scholar Felix Aylmer, then filming *Quo Vadis?*, talked about

Othello. When I asked him what the "Pontic-Propontic" speech meant to him, he explained it and then said, "Nowadays the lines are obscure, but the educated Elizabethans understood the geographical allusions and their metaphorical meanings in the tragedy."

Some months later I met Orson Welles on a flight from Rome to Zurich and asked him the same question. He agreed with Aylmer and said, "The modern actor knows that the audience won't understand the 'Pontic-Schmontic' verbiage, so he uses it as ranting and raving double-talk to convey Othello's temporary madness."

As we walked up the ramp into the Zurich air terminal, I said, "After what you said about the Swiss in *The Third Man*— '. . . all they ever created was the cuckoo clock'—aren't you afraid to set foot in Switzerland?"

He laughed. "After the film was released here, twenty-nine Swiss sent me cuckoo clocks with the same message: 'You are wrong about us Swiss, Mr. Welles. We didn't even create the cuckoo clock. It was invented by an Austrian.' "

When we entered the building, Orson Welles said, "If you hear of anyone cuckoo enough to buy twenty-nine clocks . . ."

4

My travel notes continue: "Stopped off in Zurich for three hours that seemed like three hundred, waiting for the noon plane to Vienna. Though I'd not slept for nearly forty hours, I paced back and forth through the huge transient-passenger hall. Each time I approached the Duty-Free Shop, the same unnerving thing happened: a tiny, well-dressed woman in her eighties ran up to me and tensely whispered something to me, something that seemed tremendously important and alarming. Though I've worked and traveled in twenty-five countries, I couldn't recognize a single word she said. Finnish? Bulgarian? Croatian? Each time, as she waited apprehensively for my answer, I forced a smile, patted her on the shoulder reassuringly, and pointed jerkily to the pretty young woman at the nearby Information desk.

"This repeated encounter, like a scene from an Ingmar Bergman or Hitchcock film, finally unhinged me, and I thought: 'Is this woman insane? Or is she trying to warn everyone through me of an imminent disaster known only to her? That a bomb is about to explode in the passenger hall . . . or that the plane to Vienna is doomed?' Her manner and facial expression reminded me of the gaunt wild-eyed old woman who may still haunt the Athens-Piraeus waterfront, waiting, waiting, waiting for her son who went off to war in 1942. . . . When I gave her money, she let it fall from her hands, and walked away. . . .

"On my last walk past the Duty-Free Shop (I couldn't stay away), I was relieved but also strangely disturbed to find that the old woman had disappeared. Yes, this was like the Hitchcock movie, with Dame May Whitty as the mysterious Miss Froy, the lady who vanished, kidnapped because she carried a memorized message that could 'decide the fate of the Western world.' . . . 'Duty-Free' . . . there's a subtle Kafkian play on words here. I returned to the airport coffeehouse (I always eat several breakfasts when upset) and hauled out my bulky notebook to review my newly discovered 'Sigmund Freud Reenactment Syndrome.' "

5

> Strange to say, I really did once play the part of
> Brutus. I once acted in the scene between Brutus
> and Caesar from Schiller . . .
> —Freud, *The Interpretation of Dreams*

> SYNDROME, n., a group of related things, events,
> or actions, etc. From the Greek *syn* (together,
> and *drome* (to run).
> —*Random House Dictionary*

The hypothetical "Sigmund Freud Reenactment Syndrome or personal myth," discovered and developed by means of clues found in Freud's writings, letters and recorded conversations, may be defined roughly as his lifelong mode of accommodation to certain of his personal problems, dilemmas, and crises both large and small. I have found that when Sigmund Freud experienced an emotional "high" or "low," he habitually, compulsively, reacted by identifying consciously or unconsciously—

usually the latter—with a figure from mythology, legend, history, or some fictional work. Also, in some instances, having done so, *he went one giant step further and actually reenacted scenes, incidents, sometimes entire episodes from the lives of these real or fictional exemplars.*

The best-known example of this alleged "Reenactment Syndrome or personal myth" was, as Freud himself confessed, his prolonged identification with and "acting out" of Hannibal's relationship to the ancient walled city of Rome. (Because Hannibal *did not* enter Rome, Freud *could not.*) In another example, perhaps the most remarkable, I have found that, detail for detail, Freud seems to have reenacted or restaged an entire episode from Henrik Ibsen's *Hedda Gabler*—with himself in the title role. Yes, as Hedda Gabler!

Here are the most important of Freud's "syndromic identifications and/or reenactments or restagings" discovered thus far:

A. *Mythological*

1. *Hercules,* as cleaner of the manure-filled Augean stables.
2. *Antaeus,* murderer-wrestler whose strength came from Mother Earth.
3. *Theseus,* labyrinth-solver, slayer of the Minotaur.
4. *Oedipus,* early victim of the Complex.
5. *Odysseus,* naked before Nausicaa and her maidens.
6. *Medusa,* who killed with a stare.
7. *Hagen,* treacherous slayer of his friend Siegfried.
8. *Hercules,* again, as an early "psychiatric" patient.
9. *Melusina,* heroine of medieval fairy tale; protopsychiatrist.
10. *Lucifer,* alias the Devil, Satan.
11. *Artemis,* as defender of her suppliants against Aphrodite's attacks.

B. *Religious*

12. *Moses,* as crypto-Egyptian nobleman; as leader of the Hebrew Exodus; as the Jehovah-directed smasher of pagan sexual gods.

13. *Joseph,* as son of Jacob; as perpetrator of grim practical jokes against his brothers; as early dream-interpreter.
14. *Jacob,* as Joseph's father and as exiled Hebrew.
15. *Jonah,* God's punitive instrument against the walled city of Nineveh.
16. *Joshua,* God-directed conqueror of the walled city of Jericho.

C. *Historical*

17. *Ramses II,* as he sits before the Abu Simbel Temple.
18. *Amenhotep III,* posthumously attacked by his son Ikhnaton.
19. *Julius Caesar,* as invader of Britain.
20. *Napoleon,* at a theater in Erfurt, Germany.
21. *William Shakespeare,* as author of *Sonnets 80–92.*

D. *Fictional*

22. *Redcloak,* a character in Goethe's version of the fairy tale *The New Melusina,* in *Wilhelm Meister's Wanderings.*
23. *David Copperfield,* as husband of the child-like Dora.
24. *Torwald Helmer,* Nora's husband in *A Doll's House.*
25. *Johannes Rosmer,* in Ibsen's *Rosmersholm.*
26. *Mephistopheles,* in Goethe's *Faust.*
27. *Gulliver,* as volunteer fireman who put out the fire in the Lilliputian queen's palace by pissing on it.
28. *Gargantua,* another gigantic "micturator." He avenged himself against the Parisians by inundating them with urine.
29. *King Lear.*
30. *Hedda Gabler,* Machiavellian woman.

Though this seems like a long list, it is, I believe, only the tip of the Freudian iceberg. I would guess that many more examples of the alleged "Syndrome" will be found in Freud's private journals, diaries, and letters when they are published. I base this guess upon my accumulated observations of his lifelong compulsive habits. And the obvious fact that he lived a very long time.

I wish to say now as emphatically as I can that this hypothetical "Sigmund Freud Reenactment Syndrome or personal myth," or my observations based on it in the pages that follow, *do not* attack, contradict, replace, or minimize Dr. Sigmund Freud's theories or interpretations.

But I do believe that my literary detective and informal psychoanalytical methods have uncovered a hitherto-unknown *modus operandi* or pattern used by Sigmund Freud for the "acting out" of some of his all-too-human "complexes" and life situations.

6

> I was putting myself in the place of the exalted personages of those . . . times.
> —Freud, *The Interpretation of Dreams*

One startling example of Freud's compulsive restagings from ancient mythology may be seen in his profoundly autobiographical *Interpretation of Dreams*, which he once referred to with ironic self-revealment as "my Egyptian dream-book."*

While explaining one of his techniques for prying loose dream-secrets from stubbornly resisting patients, Freud says: "If the first account of a dream is too hard to follow, I ask him to repeat it. In doing so he rarely uses the same words, but the parts of the dream which he describes in different terms are by that fact revealed to me as the weak spots in the dream's disguise."

The "Viennese play-actor" Freud (this not-unfriendly allusion will be explained later) then takes syndromic leave of clinical psychoanalysis to "become" for a moment one of the most treacherous of mythological

---

*In a letter to Wilhelm Fliess in 1899. The reference to the "Egyptian dream-book" has at least two possible meanings. The first: he was referring self-mockingly to the cheap occult dream books sold in Vienna; the other meaning: it may have been one of his many references to one of his major identification-figures—Joseph of Egypt, dream-interpreter.

figures. He says, ". . . (the words revealing the 'weak spots' in the dream's disguise) *serve my purpose just as Hagen's was served by the embroidered mark on Siegfried's cloak.*" An editorial footnote explains: "There was one spot on Siegfried's body where he could be wounded. By a trick, Hagen persuaded Kriemhild, who alone knew where that spot was, to embroider a small cross on Siegfried's cloak at the vital spot. It was there that Hagen stabbed him." (It is interesting to note in passing that Freud's figure of speech presents patients as those whom Freud *penetrated.*)

Psychoanalytically trained observers may make what they will of the following: Siegfried's father was *Sigmund.* If, by his own admission, *Sigmund* Freud likened himself to Hagen, treacherous slayer of Siegfried, then who, if anyone, was Freud's "Siegfried"? Was it a particular patient? *Any* patient? Or was he thinking of someone close to him?

7

On December 18, 1912, about a month after Freud fainted in Munich during his historic quarrel with Jung, Jung wrote Freud a letter obviously calculated to end their relationship. Now, as I think about that letter, two of its words, italicized below, seem especially significant: ". . . stop playing the father to your sons and instead of aiming continually at their [my] *weak spots,* take a good look at your own for a change."

Jung's use of the words "weak spots" in this context seems to echo Freud's use of the same words in his self-description as Siegfried's slayer: ". . . the *weak spots* in the dream's disguise . . . serve my purpose just as Hagen's was served by the embroidered mark on Siegfried's cloak."

If Jung, who profoundly psychoanalyzed the Siegfried Saga in his 1912 *Psychology of the Unconscious,** did remember Freud's earlier self-identification with Hagen (how could he miss?), it seems to me that the embattled Jung may have seen himself in great peril at the hands of a Hagen-Freud, a disguise-penetrating seer who knew his weaknesses, and . . .

---

*See pages 30, 279, 358–64, 385–89.

If so, this may help explain Jung's post-Freudian "Siegfried" dream (see later) in which, as he says, he killed the "Siegfried" component within himself.

8

The first step toward the recognition of the hitherto-unknown (even to Freud) "Syndrome" was made when I remembered that Freud once confessed to reenacting physically a major episode from the life of the Carthaginian Hannibal, Rome's greatest enemy.*

In the course of his fascinating analyses of four dreams he had had about Rome, written before he finally overcame his resistances and visited the city, Freud skillfully leads his reader through a maze of childhood memories; they in turn remind him of Hannibal, who then reminds him of a most unpleasant incident told him by his father.

> It was on my last journey to Italy, which, among other places, took me past Lake Trasimeno (where Hannibal defeated a Roman army), that finally—after having seen the Tiber and sadly turned back when I was only fifty miles from Rome—I discovered the way in which my longing for the eternal city had been reinforced by impressions from my youth. I was in the act of making a plan to by-pass Rome next year and travel to Naples, when a sentence occurred to me which I must have read in one of our classical authors: "Which of the two, it may be debated, walked up and down in his study with the greater impatience after he formed his plan of going to Rome—Winkelmann . . . or Hannibal, the Commander-in-Chief?"

Freud knows the answer, of course: "I had actually been following in Hannibal's footsteps. Like him, I had been fated not to see Rome; and he too had moved into the Campagna when everyone expected him in Rome. But *Hannibal, whom I had come to resemble* [italics mine] in these respects, had been the favorite hero of my later schoolboy days. Like so many boys of that age, I had sympathized in the Punic Wars not with the Romans but with the Carthaginians. And when in the higher classes I

---

*In his *Interpretation of Dreams*.

began to understand for the first time what it meant to belong to an alien race, and anti-Semitic feelings among the other boys warned me that I must take a definite position, the figure of the Semitic general rose higher in my esteem. To my youthful mind Hannibal and Rome symbolized the conflict between the tenacity of Jewry and the Catholic church [of Vienna]. And the increasing importance of the effects of the anti-Semitic movement upon our emotional life helped to fix the thoughts and feelings of those days. Thus the wish to go to Rome had become in my dream-life a cloak and symbol for a number of other passionate wishes. Their realization was to be pursued with all the perseverance and single-mindedness of the Carthaginian, though their fulfillment seemed at the moment just as little favoured by destiny as was Hannibal's lifelong wish to enter Rome."

Freud then gets to the inner core of his analysis:

At that point I was brought up against the event in my life whose power was still being shown in all these emotions and dreams. I may have been ten or twelve years old, when my father began to take me with him on his walks and reveal to me in his talk his views upon the world we live in. Thus it was, on one such occasion, that he told me a story to show me how much better things were now than they had been in his days. "When I was a young man," he said, "I went for a walk one Saturday in the streets of your birthplace; I was well dressed, and had a new fur cap on my head. A Christian came up to me and with a single blow knocked off my hat into the mud and shouted: 'Jew! get off the pavement!' " "And what did you do?" I asked. "I went off the roadway and picked up my cap," was his quiet reply. This struck me as unheroic conduct on the part of the big, strong man who was holding the little boy by the hand. I contrasted this situation with another which fitted my feelings better: the scene in which Hannibal's father, Hamilcar Barca, made his boy swear before the household altar to take vengeance against the Romans. Ever since that time Hannibal had a place in my fantasies.

To this Freud adds and explains another of his identification figures: "I believe I can trace my enthusiasm for the Carthaginian general a step further back into my childhood; so that once more it would have been only a question of a transference on an already formed emotional relation to a new object. One of the first books that I got hold of when I learned to read was Thiers's *History of the Consulate and Empire*. I can still remember sticking labels on the flat backs of my wooden soldiers with the names of

Napoleon's marshals written on them. At that time my declared favorite was already Masséna (or to give the name in its Jewish form, Manasseh). (No doubt this preference was also partly to be explained by the fact that my birthday fell on the same day as his, exactly a hundred years later.)"

With his customary thoroughness Freud takes us to the deepest layer of his dream and analysis: "It may even be that the development of this martial idea is traceable still further back into my childhood: to the times when, at the age of three, I was in close relationship, sometimes friendly but sometimes warlike, with a boy a year older than myself, and to wishes which that relation must have stirred up in the weaker of us.

"The deeper one carries the analysis of a dream, the more often one comes upon the track of experiences in childhood which often have played a part among the sources of that dream's latent content."

9

> This Hercules was I . . . I was the superman.
> —Freud, *The Interpretation of Dreams*

Perhaps the most astonishing and amusing example of Freud's propensity for identification with mythical characters may be seen in his "Open-Air Closet (Toilet)" dream. Freud teasingly prefaces his account of this scatological beauty: "It is a short dream, which will fill every reader with disgust."

A hill, on which there was something like an open-air closet: a very long seat with a large hole at the end of it. Its back edge was thickly covered with small heaps of faeces of all sizes and degrees of freshness. There were bushes behind the seat. I micturated on the seat; a long stream of urine washed away everything clean; the lumps of faeces came away easily and fell into the opening. It was as though at the end there was some left.

He then asks and answers his rhetorical question: "Why did I feel no disgust during this dream? Because, as the analysis showed, the most agreeable and satisfying thoughts contributed to bringing the dream about. What occurred to me at once were the Augean stables cleansed by

Hercules. This Hercules was I. The 'hill' and 'bushes' came from Aussee where my children were stopping at the time. I had discovered the infantile aetiology (causes) of the neuroses and had thus saved my children from falling ill. The seat (except, of course, for the hole) was an exact copy of a piece of furniture given to me as a present by a grateful patient. It thus reminded me how much my patients honored me. Indeed, even the museum of human excrement could be given an interpretation to rejoice my heart. However much I might be disgusted in reality, in the dream it was a reminiscence of the fair land of Italy where, as we all know, the W.C.'s (toilets) are furnished in precisely this way."

He continues: "The stream of urine which washed everything clean was an unmistakable sign of greatness. It was the way that Gulliver extinguished the great fire in Lilliput—though incidentally this brought him into disfavour with its tiny queen. But Gargantua, too, Rabelais's superman, avenged himself in the same way on the Parisians by sitting astride on Notre Dame and turning his stream of urine upon the city."

Freud now explains several sources of the dream: "It was only on the previous evening before going to sleep that I had been turning over Garnier's illustrations to Rabelais. And, strangely enough, here is another piece of evidence that I was the superman. The platform of Notre Dame was my favorite resort (when I was a student) in Paris; every free afternoon I used to clamber about there between the monsters and the devil. The fact that all the faeces disappeared so quickly under the stream recalled the motto: '*Afflavit et dissipati sunt*,' which I intended one day to put at the head of a chapter upon the therapy of hysteria.

"And now," says Freud, "for the true exciting cause of the dream. It had been a hot summer afternoon, and during the evening I had delivered my lecture on the connection between hysteria and the perversions, and everything I had had to say displeased me intensely and seemed to me completely devoid of any value. I was tired and felt no trace of enjoyment in my difficult work; I longed to be away from all this grubbing in human dirt and to be able to join my children and afterwards visit the beauties of Italy. In this mood I went from the lecture room to a café, where I had a modest snack in the open air, since I had no appetite for food. One of my audience, however, went with me, and he begged leave to sit by me while I drank my coffee and choked over my crescent roll. He began to flatter me:

telling me how much he had learnt from me, how he looked at everything with fresh eyes, how I had cleansed the *Augean stables* of errors and prejudices in my theories of the neuroses. He told me, in short, that I was a very great man. My mood fitted ill with this paean of praise; I fought against my feeling of disgust, went home early to escape from him, and before going to sleep turned over the pages of Rabelais."

In one part of this analysis Freud refers to this dream identifying him with the three gigantic pissers (Hercules, believe it or not, cleansed the stables of all that shit with the waters of the River Peneus) as an expression of "both delusions of grandeur and megalomania."

Yes, many of Freud's "syndromic identifications" would also merit the words "delusions of grandeur and megalomania" had he not become as renowned as many of the great heroes and antiheroes he identified with.

10

"Afflavit et dissipati sunt"

Freud's use of the above Latin motto ("He [God] blew and they were scattered") may reveal another of his highly romantic restagings and "megalomaniac" identifications, this time as the Hebrew Jehovah performing a last-minute rescue of Queen Elizabeth's England when the Spanish Armada threatened.

In a footnote to his "Count Thun" dream, in which the Latin motto is repeated, Freud writes: "('He blew and they were scattered') footnote added 1925. An unsolicited biographer, Dr. Fritz Wittels (1924), has charged me with having omitted the name of Jehovah from the above motto. . . . The English medallion bears the deity's name in Hebrew lettering on a cloud in the background. It is so placed that it can be taken as being part either of the design or of the inscription. (The idea of using the words as a motto at the head of a chapter on therapy is mentioned in a letter to Fliess of January 3, 1897, editor.)"

Here again we witness the ease with which Freud leaves his clinical mode of thought and expression to perform syndromically. What starts out as a technical dream analysis of himself using his urinary stream to wash away accumulated shit (neuroses) ends with Freud likening the psyche to the British Isles being invaded by the mighty Spanish Armada (neuroses). And what saves Queen Elizabeth's defenseless domain (psyche)? The mighty therapeutic breath of Sigmund Freud, surrogate Jehovah!

This all checks out nicely: Freudian ideas transformed into words "blown" out of his mouth during psychoanalytical dialogues were therapeutic. Freud's words are, by his own set of associations, Gulliverian. Incidentally, Freud's association of "God's saving wind" may have been just as scatological as Gulliver's use of his stream of urine to put out the fire in the queen's palace. In English and several other languages, "wind" is synonymous with "fart."

11

> . . . my thirst for grandeur.

> I am really not a man of science, not an observer, not an experimenter, and not a thinker. I am nothing but by temperament a *conquistador* . . . with the curiosity, the boldness, and the tenacity that belong to that type of being.
> —Freud, in a letter to Wilhelm Fliess

While browsing through the Ernest Jones biography with the Hedda Gabler–Freud, Hannibal, Hercules, and other "reenactments" in mind, I found a boyhood incident that told this syndrome-spotter that as a ten-year-old child Freud may also have unconsciously reenacted a major episode in the life of Alexander the Great.

"The only difference between father and son," says Jones, "seems to have been the occasion when Sigmund, then seventeen, indulged his propensity for buying books to such an extent that he was unable to pay for them. Sigmund's father was not at all the strict paternal type then so common, and he used to consult his children over various decisions to be made. These discussions took place in what was called the 'Family Circle.'

"An example was the choice of a name for the younger brother [born in 1866 when Sigmund was ten]. It was Sigmund's vote for the name Alexander that was accepted, his selection being based on Alexander the Great's generosity and military prowess. To support his choice, Sigmund recited (from Plutarch) the whole story of the Macedonian's triumphs."

At first Jones's anecdote about the precocious *boychick*, seemingly exempt from the universal Oedipus complex, charmed me. But then, as one taught by Freud and Sherlock Holmes to accept nothing at face value, I read Plutarch and other classical biographies and found information which little Sigmund had read and obviously withheld from the Freud "Family Circle." It was the "undying rumor" repeated by Plutarch and others and never disproved, that Alexander masterminded or took part in the murder of his father Philip II because Philip was considering several others as his successor.

Plutarch tells Freud and us that when Philip divorced Alexander's mother Olympias and married Cleopatra (she predates Caesar's Cleo by four centuries), he commanded Alexander to attend the wedding feast. As anyone who knows *Hamlet* might guess, some monstrous Oedipal feelings were aroused. But the emotional volcano pent up in the son did not erupt until the alcoholic celebration became quite rowdy and the bride's uncle Attalus proposed the toast that the son born to his niece be named Philip's successor. At this Alexander exploded. Hurling his wine-cup at Attalus's head, he roared: "You villain, am I a bastard then?" King Philip, enraged by this breach of hospitality, leaped up with drawn sword and lunged at his son. "But fortunately," says Plutarch," his overhasty rage or the wine he'd drunk made him stumble and fall to the floor, where he lay in a semi-stupor." (The adult Freud might have added: "Or he really did not wish to kill his son.")*

Alexander then made things worse. Pointing derisively at the fallen king, he sneered: "This man, who makes military preparations to pass from Europe into Asia, is overturned when he passes from one seat to another." (As reported by Plutarch, Alexander's words seem to express his alleged patricidal intentions. His phrase "is overturned" may be interpreted to mean that he had already decided to overturn and supplant his father; and the words "when he passes from one seat to another" have, in

*Forty-three years later, Freud repeated this scene with Carl Jung in Bremen, Germany, during a celebratory wine-drinking meal. A quarrel with his "adopted son" Jung ended with Freud falling to the floor in a faint. As will be seen, there may have been a causal connection between the two "falls to the floor," one described as a "semi-stupor," the other as a "fainting fit." Clue: Both related to succession to a "throne."

English translation, two meanings, the less perverse of which implies his bitter resentment at his father's leaving his mother to copulate with Cleopatra.

Various interpretations may be drawn from young Sigmund's choice of the name Alexander for his newborn sibling rival. One, taught us by Freud, might be: Though Sigmund consciously loved his father and his baby brother, his unconscious mind, directed by his Oedipal feelings, yielded a fantasy in which his brother was cast as an "Alexander" who would do his father-slaying for him. Thus killing two Freudian birds with one Oedipustone.

12

> *Replay:* Strange to say, I really did once play the part of Brutus . . . in the scene between Brutus and Caesar.
> —Freud, *The Interpretation of Dreams*

Another unconscious/conscious reenactment: Freud begins his masterful dissection of his convoluted *"Non Vixit"* dream with images of himself as a male crypto-Medusa who "annihilates" his friend and rival "P." with a deadly "look." He then strips away layer after layer of hidden meaning to uncover and reveal his lifelong identification with and syndromic performance as Brutus, the protégé and "Oedipal" slayer of Julius Caesar. (The pre-Freudian authority for my use of the word "Oedipal" is Suetonius; he tells us that when Caesar saw Brutus among his assassins, he cried: *"Et tu, mi fili, Brute?"* [You, too, Brutus, my son?])

After explaining how the look-annihilated "P." became dream-merged with a statue on a Viennese royal monument bearing the words *"non vixit"* (he is not alive), Freud then writes the words which, when analyzed, enable him to see that his dream was in part his restaging of the ancient Caesarian tragedy, with himself in the antiheroic role of Brutus.

Freud explains his analytical breakthrough: "It then struck me as noticeable that in the scene of the dream there was a convergence of a hostile and affectionate current of feeling towards my friend P., the former being on the surface and the other concealed, but both of them being represented in the single phrase *non vixit*. As he deserved well of science, I built him a (dream) memorial; but as he was guilty of an evil wish (towards me), which was expressed at the end of the dream, I annihilated him."

He then interrupts himself: "I noticed that this last sentence has a quite special cadence, and that I must have had some model in my mind. Where was an antithesis of this sort to be found, a juxtaposition like this of two opposite reactions towards a single person, both claiming to be completely justified and yet not incompatible?"

He excitedly answers his own question: "Only in one passage in literature—but a passage which makes a profound impression on the reader—in Brutus's speech of self-justification in Shakespeare's *Julius Caesar* (iii. 2), 'As Caesar loved me, I weep for him; as he was fortunate, I rejoice at it; as he was valiant, I honour him; but as he was ambitious, I slew him.' Were not the formal structure of these sentences and their antithetical meaning precisely the same as in the dream-thought I had uncovered? Thus I had been playing the part of Brutus in my dream."

Then, characteristically, Freud carries his analysis back to his childhood: "Strange to say, *I really did once play the part of Brutus*. I once acted in the scene between Brutus and Caesar from Schiller [*The Robbers*] before an audience of children. I was fourteen years old at the time and was acting with a nephew who was a year my senior. He had come to us on a visit from England; and he, too, was a revenant [ghost], for it was the playmate of my earliest years who returned in him. Until the end of my third year we had been inseparable. We had loved each other and fought with each other; and this childhood relationship, as I already hinted above, had a determining influence on my subsequent relations with contemporaries."

Elsewhere Freud expands upon his lifelong continuation of his ambivalent relationship to his nephew John Freud; he does so in terms which help explain his relations with the close friends who later became his bitter enemies: Wilhelm Fliess, Carl Jung, Otto Rank, and others: "My emotional life has always insisted that I should have an intimate friend and a hated enemy. I have always been able to provide myself with both, and it has not infrequently happened that the ideal situation of childhood has been so completely reproduced that friend and enemy have come together in a single individual."

13

In his "Aetiology of Hysteria," a lecture published in 1896, the identity-shifting Freud, assuming the role of a romantic intellectual explorer like Heinrich Schliemann, discoverer of ancient Troy, uses an elaborate archeological metaphor to describe his psychoanalytical method: "Imagine that an explorer comes in his travels to a region of which little is known, and there his interest is aroused by ruins showing remains of walls, fragments of pillars and of tablets with obliterated and illegible inscriptions. He may content himself with inspecting what lies on the surface and with questioning the people who live nearby, perhaps semi-barbaric natives, about what tradition tells of the history and meaning of these monumental remains, and taking notes on their statements—and then go his way. But he may proceed differently:

> He may have come equipped with picks, shovels, and spades and may impress the inhabitants into his service and arm them with these tools, make an onslaught on the ruins, clear away the rubbish, and, starting with the visible remains, may bring to light what is buried. If his work is crowned with success, the discoveries explain themselves: the ruined walls are part of the ramparts of a palace or a treasure-house; from the ruined pillars a temple can be constructed; the many inscriptions, which by good luck may be bilingual, reveal an alphabet and a language, and when deciphered and translated may yield undreamed of information about the events of the past, to commemorate which these monuments were built. *Saxa loquuntur!**

In his biography of Freud, Ernest Jones tells of a summer vacation Freud spent with his brother Alexander in Greece: ". . . they sailed for Brindisi, a twenty-four-hour trip. Among the passengers was Professor Dorpfeld, the assistant of the famous archeologist, Schliemann. Freud gazed with awe at the man who helped to discover ancient Troy, but was too shy to approach him." (August 1904.)

---

*I am indebted to Stanley Edgar Hyman's *The Tangled Bank* for this example. I refer the reader to Hyman's long and brilliant study of Freud as a "dramatistic writer," who always placed himself at stage center in all his lectures and many of his writings.

14

. . . his history is, however, so interesting and constructive, that it tempts one to venture on a digression.
—Thomas Macaulay, *Collected Essays*

The shortest distance between any two intellectual points is through a maze.

Freud's remarkably casual self-description as a Siegfried-slaying Hagen incites a labyrinthine digressive soliloquy:* "This reminds me of the run of sadistic dreams and visions Jung experienced after his final break with Freud, especially the Wagnerian dream in which he also murdered 'Siegfried.' As I recall the dream, he doesn't accept the treacherous name 'Hagen.' . . . Jung never thought of himself in less than heroic terms . . . but he *was* Hagen . . . who else could he be? It's common knowledge that Jung converted Freud's discoveries, revolutionary theories, phraseology, and technical methods to his own use, but in this 'Hagen-Siegfried' thing, Jung seems to have imitated Freud even in his dreams!"

In the "Confrontation with the Unconscious" chapter of his *Memories, Dreams, Reflections,* Jung offers the following preface to the visions and dreams which I believe were caused by his violent break with Freud: "After the parting of the ways with Freud [non-Jungians call it a 'defection'] a period of uncertainty began for me. It would be no exaggeration to call it a state of disorientation. I felt totally suspended in mid-air, for I had not yet found a footing."

A bit later he adds: "Toward the autumn of 1913 [this was about nine months after the second public quarrel during which Freud fainted], the pressure which I felt in *me* seemed to be moving outward, as though there was something in the air. It was as though the sense of oppression no longer sprang from a psychic situation, but from concrete reality. This feeling grew more and more intense.

---

*I'm sure most readers will have no difficulty picking up the narrative thread when this digressive section dealing with Jung's visions and dreams is concluded.

"In October, while I was on a journey, I was suddenly seized by an overpowering vision: I saw a monstrous flood covering the northern and low-lying lands between the North Sea and the Alps. When it came to Switzerland I saw that the mountaintops grew higher and higher to protect our country. I realized that a frightful catastrophe was in progress. I saw the yellow waves, the floating rubble of civilization, and the drowned bodies of uncounted thousands. Then the whole sea turned to blood. The last vision lasted about one hour. I was perplexed and nauseated, and ashamed of my weakness."

As I read this I reacted: "There seems to be a significant act of omission or censorship or psychological blindness here. Jung says that in this obvious 'Biblical Deluge' vision he saw from his Mt. Ararat–like perch that only Northern and Western Europe was covered by the ocean-turned-to-blood. But to attain that level the deluge would have had to be worldwide and cover all the southern and eastern countries touching Switzerland— including *Austria*. If this reasoning is valid, then Jung's dream may be interpreted as his devious, unconscious death wish aimed at Freud and all his colleagues in the 'low countries.' The aftermath of such a self-serving holocaust would leave Jung, God's favorite, in sole possession of all the psychoanalytical marbles. Yet, Jung seems oblivious to this possible interpretation."

While reading these bloody visions which seemed so obviously related to Jung's recent "tearing away" from Freud, I came upon words which seem to refer to that dominant episode of his professional and personal life: "I asked myself whether these visions pointed to a revolution, but could not imagine anything of the sort. The idea of a (world) war did not occur to me at all."

After these "Deluge" dreams, which recall Noah and the myth of the virtuous Deucalion and Pyrrha, only survivors of Zeus's genocidal flood, Jung continued with more misanthropic fantasies derived from Greek mythology. Now he had a "thrice-repeated dream" in which destructive cold arrived, a dream obviously derived from the well-known Prometheus myth. When, disgusted with the unredeemable human race he had created, Zeus decided to deep-freeze us, Prometheus saved us with stolen Olympian fire.

In the last of these repeated dreams we see signs of Jung's messianic aspirations: "In the third dream, frightful cold had again descended from out of the cosmos. This dream had an unexpected ending. There stood a leaf-bearing tree (my tree of life, I thought) whose leaves had been transformed by the effects of the frost into sweet grapes full of healing juices. I plucked the grapes and gave them to a large waiting crowd." Jesus!

Jung's knowledge of the Deucalion-Pyrrha myth at the time of his "rebirth for me but death for everyone else especially Freud and his followers dream" is verified, I find, in his *Psychology of the Unconscious*, written during the emotional storm attending his break with Freud. In that book, Jung wrote: "The idea of anal birth" (common to primitives and children) "recalls the motif of throwing something behind. A well-known example of this is *the story of Deucalion and Pyrrha* [italics mine], the sole survivors of the flood, who were told by the oracle to throw behind them the bones of the Great Mother. They thereupon threw stones behind them from which mankind sprang."

15

... my book *The Psychology of the Unconscious* (1912). While I was working on this book, I had dreams which presaged my forthcoming break with Freud.

It was during Advent of the year 1913 . . . that I had the following dreams. . . .
—Carl Jung, *Memories, Dreams, Reflections*

ADVENT, from the Latin *adventus*, sc. *redemptoris* ("the coming of the Saviour"), the holy season of the Christian church, the period of preparation for the celebration of the nativity or Christmas.
—*Encyclopaedia Britannica*

Now Jung offers two more "fantasies" staged by his unconscious mind during the year following his violent break with his "father" Freud. The first is a "rebirth" vision in which he sees himself as a blond-haired corpse lying in a subterranean pool of bloody water. This womb-of-death image is replaced by a "red newborn sun" (son?) rising out of the symbolic obstetrical mess. Like his previous visions, this also ends with a vast outpouring of "nauseating" blood. (Since Jung is careful to say that this sanguinary vision and the one that follows occurred "during Advent of the year 1913," may this not be interpreted as Jung's desperate unconscious wish to be reborn as a Christian after ten years as the Jewish Freud's "crown prince, son and successor"?)

Then, "six days later" (December 18, 1913), the exact anniversary of his nasty letter to Freud (December 18, 1912) which ended their relationship, Jung dreamed that he murdered the divine Siegfried. I call this Jung's "Siegfreudream" because of my conviction that in it he really murdered Sigmund Freud.

The dream: ". . . I had the following dream. I was with an unknown, brown-skinned man, a savage,* in a lonely, rocky mountain landscape. It was before dawn; the eastern sky was already bright, and the stars fading. Then I heard Siegfried's horn sounding over the mountains and I knew that we had to kill him. We were armed with rifles and lay in wait for him on a narrow path over the rocks.

"Then Siegfried appeared high up on the crest of the mountain, in the first ray of the rising sun. On a chariot made of the bones of the dead he drove at furious speed down the precipitous slope. When he turned a corner, we shot at him, and he plunged down, struck dead."

Jung's Wagnerian dream continues:

> Filled with disgust and remorse for having destroyed something so great and beautiful, I turned to flee, impelled by the fear that the murder might be discovered. But a tremendous downfall of rain began, and I knew that it would wipe out all traces of the dead. I had escaped the danger of discovery; life would go on, but an unbearable feeling of regret remained.
>
> When I awoke from the dream, I turned it over in my mind, but was unable to understand it. I tried therefore to fall asleep again, but a voice within me said, "You *must* understand the dream and must do so at once!" The inner urgency mounted until the terrible moment when the voice said, "If you do not understand the dream, you must shoot yourself!" In the drawer of my night table lay a loaded revolver, and I became frightened. Then I began pondering once again, and suddenly the meaning of the dream dawned on me. Siegfried,

---

*His "shadow."

I thought, represents what the Germans want to achieve, heroically to impose their will, have their own way. "Where there is a will, there is a way!" I had wanted to do the same. The dream showed that the attitude embodied by Siegfried, the hero, no longer suited me. Therefore it had to be killed.

I do not accept Jung's interpretation, and at least one other interpretation may be of equal or greater significance. It is based on the well-known fact that the mythical *Siegfried was the son of Sigmund* and inheritor of his magic sword of power. When this is added to the already mentioned fact that Freud publicly and privately called Jung "my crown prince, son and successor," it becomes obvious that Jung's slaying of Siegfried is classically Oedipal in nature. He killed the part of himself that would succeed and "become" Sigmund Freud. Yes, one large fraction of the dream-murdered "Siegfried" was Sigmund (Sigm.) or Sig. Freud.

Some residual unexplained questions remain: I wonder, reader, if you are asking, as I am, Now why would Jung, resident of peaceful Switzerland, keep a loaded revolver in the drawer of the night table next to his bed? Had he been threatened by a psychotic patient? Did the emotional upheaval accompanying his break with Freud incite Hamletic suicidal feelings? Did he harbor unconscious homicidal intentions toward someone he knew intimately? Was there a "Freudian" sexual interpretation? Or was that (phallic) symbolic revolver kept in the symbolic drawer for symbolic use against someone he feared he might meet in one of his bloody nightmares?

My loaded questions about the erotic significance of Jung's "loaded revolver" are inspired by Jung's own comments about the sexual symbolism of firearms. In his *Symbols of Transformation*, the 1956 revision of his *Psychology of the Unconscious*, published shortly before his break with Freud, Jung wrote: "It is true that many dream-images have a sexual aspect or express erotic conflicts. This is particularly clear in the motive of *assault*. Burglars, thieves, murderers, and sexual maniacs figure prominently in the erotic dreams of women. It is a theme with countless variations. The instrument of murder may be a lance, a sword, a dagger, a *revolver*, a *rifle*, a cannon . . . or it may be someone hidden *under a bed.*" [Italics mine.]

Come to think of it, Jung's acceptance of the Freudian sexual symbolism as late as 1956, when he was eighty-one, permits another loaded question: Was Jung's dream-murder of "Siegfreud" with the penetrating bullet fired from the admittedly "sexual" rifle also the expression of latent homosexuality?

16

A supplementary, corroborative interpretation: Certain elements of Jung's "I killed the Siegfried or 'Siegfreud' part of myself" dream seems to be a reenactment of the clearly Oedipal myth of Phaëthon, natural son of the sungod Helios.*

As Edith Hamilton tells it in her *Mythology:* When Phaëthon reached manhood he confronted Helios: "My mother Clymene says you are my father. Are you my father?" Helios admitted that he was, and as a proof of his love (or unconscious hostility) he offered to gratify any wish his hitherto-ignored son might have. Instantly, acting out of his unconscious desire to replace his father as his mother's lover, the Oedipal jungster asked to drive his father's chariot (mother symbol) across the sky for one day. Trapped by his sudden fatherly impulse (or, again, wishing to kill his unwanted, incestuous son), Helios gave Phaëthon the "keys" of his heavenly car.

At sunrise Phaëthon *mounted* the chariot (!) and began his ride, but he could not of course control the tremendous horses. Soon, after a wild ride in which the sun almost destroyed the heavens and set ablaze all the forests of the earth, Zeus, father of gods, intervened to stop the forbidden symbolic (incestuous) drama.

Edith Hamilton says: "Jove [Zeus] seized his thunderbolt and hurled it at the rash, repentant [and terrified] driver. It struck him dead, shattered the chariot, and made the maddened horses rush down to the sea. Phaëthon all on fire fell from the car through the air to the earth. The mysterious river Eridanus, which no mortal eyes have ever seen, received him and put out the flames and cooled the body." (And concealed it from human gaze.)

---

*Jung's familiarity with the mythical Helios is shown in *Symbols of Transformation*, the first version of which *(Psychology of the Unconscious)* was published shortly before Jung had his dream partly based on the Phaëthon-Helios myth. Besides a picture of Helios, there are five extended comments about the Greek sungod. And of course Jung was a great master of the world's mythologies.

I find strong similarities between Jung's dream and the Phaëthon myth: both center on the melodramatic image of a heroic, mythical charioteer who is "struck dead" while driving his horses at high speed. In both myth and dream the driver falls out of his chariot. Both killings take place at the same time: sunrise. Unlike the Siegfried legend, in which he is killed with a silent spear, Jung's dream-Siegfried and -Phaëthon are killed with extremely loud weapons: a rifle and a thunderbolt. The bodies of Jung's Siegfried and Phaëthon are washed away or concealed after their deaths by a large quantity of water.

If Jung unconsciously killed the Siegfried (Siegfreud) part of himself, then, considered in the light of the "psychic fragmentation" thinking common to Freud and Jung, Jung is both Phaëthon and Zeus. As Phaëthon, Jung seeks to replace his father Helios (Freud) as the source of fertility and illumination on earth; as Zeus, he punishes Phaëthon-Jung for his hubristic and Oedipal offenses.

17

During the writing of the foregoing about Jung's dream of slaying a mythological charioteer who proves (to my satisfaction) to be a transformation of himself as Freud's son, a cluster of ideas and images haunted me: ". . . all this reminds me," I thought, "of another son of Sigmund who also rode in a chariot with a Siegfried-like mythical character . . . in the context of a battle to the death fought with primitive weapons . . ."

Then I remembered: All these elements are in a single dream analysis in Freud's chapter on "Dreams as Wish-Fulfillment" in his masterwork *The Interpretation of Dreams*. This dream, in the book that converted Jung to psychoanalysis, the book that was his bible during his long apprenticeship to Freud, and which he practically memorized—this dream was repeated in Jung's "Siegfreudream."

Freud wrote: "*My eldest son*, then eight years old, already had dreams of his phantasies come true: he *dreamt he was riding in a chariot with Achilles and that Diomedes was the charioteer.* As may be guessed, he had been excited the day before by a book on the legends of Greece which had been given to his oldest sister."

It is obvious, isn't it, that this dream anticipates the major elements of

Jung's later "Siegfreudream"? Observe the similarities: Like Siegfried, son of Sigmund, Sigmund Freud's son "rode" in a dream-chariot. Both dreams are anachronistic, since they feature a modern person who is present in an ancient mythological scene. Like the mythical Siegfried, the Achilles who rides with Freud's son has a vulnerable spot (heel) that proves fatal to him. And the image of a "son" riding in a chariot recalls Jung's preoccupation with the mythical Phaëthon.

Yes, all of the elements in Freud's son's dream are duplicated in Jung's imitative dream. One of the many interpretations suggested by this set of similarities is this: by killing the mythical Siegfried, son of Sigmund, Jung was, by dream-substitution, also disposing unconsciously of his rival, Freud's oldest son and heir. This interpretation is verified by the documented fact that Freud pushed aside his son to make Jung the inheritor of his intellectual estate. In a letter (April 16, 1909) I will refer to later several times, Freud wrote: "It is strange that on the very same evening when I formally adopted you as my eldest son and anointed you—*in partibus infidelium*—as my successor and crown prince, you should have divested me of my paternal dignity."*

It would seem—and this is only a guess—that Jung was highly ambivalent about his separation from Freud; though he was glad to be free of the king–crown-prince relationship, the loss of the psychoanalytical throne made him profoundly unhappy. (Later, he adjusted to this loss brilliantly.)

18

During my continuing search for proof or disproof of my interpretations of Jung's "anti-Freud" dreams, I read the writings of those closest to the two great antagonists at the time of their breakup and found that Jung's Oedipal Siegfried-Phaëthon dream could have been inspired by a monograph published in *Imago* about a year earlier (1912).

In that essay, about the Pharaoh Amenhotep IV (Ikhnaton), Karl Abraham reasoned that though Ikhnaton, founder of monotheism, be-

---

*Freud is referring to the "poltergeist" phenomena (noises) that occurred in his study while he was talking about occultism with Jung. In his memoirs, Jung claimed it was his supernatural powers that caused the "reports."

lieved that his erasure of his father Amenhotep III's name from all public records and monuments was an entirely altruistic act, he was *really* motivated by a violent unconscious hatred of his father.*

Abraham ended his monograph with words which recapitulate the elements and motivations of Jung's "Siegfreudream":

> From Greek mythology we have heard the story of the youth Phaëthon, the son of Helios, who made so bold as to drive the chariot of the sun across the sky in his father's absence.
>
> He lost control of his steed and plunged down through the sky, forfeiting his life. The fate of the son can be taken as a parable. Striving to attain the sun's height, he also let fall the reins which his father had held tight with strong hand. His fate was that of many idealists; living in a world of dreams, they come to grief in a world of reality.†

This same essay was the subject of the bitter quarrel (Munich, 1912) between Jung, who defended Ikhnaton's actions, and Freud, who identified with the dead Pharaoh Amenhotep III, Ikhnaton's father. The quarrel ended when Freud suddenly fell to the floor in a dead faint. A few months later the Freud-Jung "father-son" relationship was terminated.

I wonder: Did the gentle, noble, obedient Karl Abraham write this learned essay as an impersonal intellectual exercise, seeking to apply Freud's ideas to an ancient historical episode? Or was it part of his unconscious campaign against Jung, whom he had long since diagnosed as another potential Ikhnatonic slayer of Freud, who had made him his heir apparent?

As I see it: Like all the members of Freud's inner circle, Jung read Abraham's monograph likening Ikhnaton to Phaëthon and stored it in his memory. Then, a year later, he—that is, the Oedipal killer within him—transformed and utilized this information when he played the mythical roles in his "Siegfreudream."

19

Recalling the well-known analytical axiom that repressed love-hate feelings actively seek and find indirect outlets; and thinking that Jung's

---

*More about this later.

†His version of the story is different from Edith Hamilton's.

self-identification with the Siegfried-slaying Hagen *must* have surfaced in writings published during his great emotional crisis of 1912–13, I read Jung's *Psychology of the Unconscious* (1912)—and found much more than I had anticipated.

In this book, published some months before Freud's fainting spell in Munich (during the bitter argument with Jung), and shortly before the exchange of letters that ended the deteriorating relationship, I came upon several pages in which Jung, or "Hagen," equates Hagen's treachery with that of Loki, sneaky slayer of the noble Baldur; with Brutus, assassin of his loving and trusting "father" Julius Caesar; with Judas Iscariot; and with "Abbe Oegger," a character in Anatole France's novel *The Garden of Epicurus*.

As may be seen below, these Jungian guilt-by-association comparisons are indirectly self-incriminating. Though Jung does not consciously say, "*I* am a Loki, a Brutus, a Judas, an Abbe Oegger (ogre)," the feeling of kinship with these historic betrayers was, I suspect, guiltily present in the back of his mind when he wrote about them in the book that warned Freud he was becoming his arch-rival.

Here is Jung's synopsis and discussion of "Anatole France's story of the pious Abbe Oegger"; it is, I believe, a hidden paradigm of his own inner guilt and torment.

> This priest was something of a dreamer, and much given to speculative musings, particularly in regard to the fate of Judas; whether he was really condemned to everlasting punishment, as the teaching of the church declares, or whether God pardoned him after all. Oegger took up the very understandable position that God, in his supreme wisdom, had chosen Judas as an instrument for the completion of Christ's work of redemption. This necessary redemption, without whose help humanity would never have had a share in salvation, could not possibly be damned by the all-good God. In order to put an end to his doubts, Oegger betook himself one night to the church and implored God to give him a sign that Judas was saved. Thereupon he felt a heavenly touch on his shoulder. The next day he went to the archbishop and told him that he was resolved to go out into the world to preach the gospel of God's unending mercy.

Now Jung, who had dreamed he was Hagen, slayer of Siegfried, makes a most interesting set of comparisons:

Here we have a well-developed fantasy-system dealing with the ticklish and eternally unresolved question of whether the legendary figure of Judas was damned or not. The Judas legend is itself a typical motif, namely that of the mischievous betrayal of the hero. One is reminded of Siegfried and Hagen, Baldur and Loki: Siegfried and Baldur were both murdered by a perfidious traitor from among their closest associates. This myth is moving and tragic, because the noble hero is not felled in a fair fight, but through treachery. At the same time it is an event that was repeated many times in history, for instance in the case of Brutus and Caesar. Though the myth is extremely old, it is still a subject for repetition, as it expresses the simple fact that envy does not let mankind sleep in peace. . . . Thus the lives and deeds of the culture-heroes and founders of religions are the purest condensations of typical mythological motifs, behind which the individual figures entirely disappear.

Jung then returns to his theme with the remarks I find especially, if obliquely, self-revealing:

But why should our pious Abbe worry about the old Judas legend? We are told that he went out into the world to preach the gospel of God's unending mercy. Not long afterwards he left the Catholic Church and became a Swedenborgian. Now we understand his Judas fantasy: *he* was the Judas who betrayed his Lord. Therefore he had first of all to assure himself of God's mercy in order to play the role of Judas undisturbed. . . .
The case of the Abbe Oegger shows that his doubts and his hopes are only apparently concerned with the historical person of Judas, but in reality revolve round his own personality, which was seeking a way to freedom through the solution of the Judas problem. . . . For him Judas was the symbol of his own unconscious tendency, and he made use of this symbol in order to reflect his own situation—its direct realization would have been too painful for him.

Finally, as if referring unconsciously (?) to his own father-son relationship to Freud, he adds: "Jacob Burckhardt seems to have glimpsed the truth when he said that every Greek of the classical period carries in himself a little bit of Oedipus, and every German a little bit of Faust."

20

> SALOME, the name of one of the women present at
> the Crucifixion of Jesus and at the sepulchre. . . .
> She is probably the "damsel" (whose name is not
> given) mentioned in connection with the
> beheading-death of John the Baptist.
> —*Encyclopaedia Britannica*

The "Freud-related" death-visions continue: "In the next fantasy," says Jung, "I found myself at the edge of a cosmic abyss. It was like a voyage to the moon, or a descent into empty space. First came the image of a crater, and I had the feeling that I was in the land of the dead. The atmosphere was that of the other world. Near the steep slope of a rock I caught sight of an old man with a beard and a beautiful young girl. I summoned up my courage and approached them. The old man explained he was Elijah, and that gave me a shock. But the girl staggered me even more, for she called herself Salome! She was blind. What a strange couple: Salome and Elijah. . . . They had a black serpent living with them which displayed an unmistakable fondness for me. I stuck close to Elijah because he seemed to be the most reasonable of the three, and to have a clear intelligence. Of Salome I was distinctly suspicious. Elijah and I had a long conversation, which, however, I did not understand.

"Naturally," says Jung, "I tried to find a plausible explanation for the appearance of Biblical figures in my fantasy by reminding myself that my father was a clergyman. But that really explained nothing at all. For what did the old man signify? What did Salome signify? Why were they together? . . . Elijah is the figure of the wise old prophet and represents the factors of intelligence and knowledge; Salome, the erotic element. One might say that the two figures were personifications of Logos and Eros."

I do not know all that the "old man" and his "erotic" companion meant to Jung, but I, and others familiar with Freud's life, can guess that they were Freud and an extraordinary person who joined his circle shortly before Jung dreamed of "Salome."

In his Freud biography Ernest Jones wrote:

> There were often some intellectual women, usually a patient or a student, in Freud's life whose company he especially enjoyed. At this time (1914) it

was Lou Andreas-Salome, who had studied with him before the war (1912–14). She was a woman with a great remarkable flair for great men, and she counted a large number among her friends, from Turgenieff, Tolstoy and Strindberg, to Rodin, Rainer Maria Rilke and Schnitzler. It was said of her that she attached herself to the greatest men of the nineteenth and twentieth centuries: Nietzsche and Freud respectively. Freud greatly admired her lofty and serene character as something above his own, and she had a full appreciation of Freud's achievements.

Nietzsche, who wanted to marry her (the affair was blighted by his jealous mother and sister), said of her: "I have never known a more gifted or understanding creature." In his introduction to her *Freud Journal*, Stanley Leavy says: "Nietzsche attributed to her the immense enhancement of his productive powers in the year he associated with her." Jung knew "Salome." He met her first at the Weimar Psychoanalytical Congress in 1911 and many times after that, usually in "Freud's company," but possibly they were alone together as in the dream.

Did you, reader, "do a double-take," as I did, when you read Jung's unblinking remark about the "unmistakable fondness" displayed toward him by Elijah's serpent? One doesn't expect a man of Jung's great sophistication to say such things! Though here, as elsewhere, Jung assigns many profound "non-Freudian" meanings to dream or fantasy snakes, he also grants them what he calls a "monotonous or banal" erotic significance.

In the paragraph immediately following the above-quoted comments about the sexual symbolism of "revolvers" and "rifles," he adds "serpents" to the list of things, objects and fauna which symbolize the penis as a weapon of sexual assault: ". . . again the danger may be represented by wild animals, for instance a horse that throws the dreamer on the ground and kicks her in the stomach with his hind legs; by lions, tigers, elephants with threatening trunk; and finally *by snakes in endless variety.* Sometimes the snake creeps into her mouth; sometimes it bites the breast like Cleopatra's legendary asp. Sometimes it appears in the role of the paradisal serpent, or in the variations of Franz Stuck, whose snake-pictures bear the significant titles like 'Vice,' 'Sin,' 'Lust.' The mixture of anxiety and lust is perfectly expressed in the sultry atmosphere of these pictures, and far more crudely than in Mörike's piquant little poem:

Girl's First Love Song

What's in the net? I feel
Frightened and shaken!
Is it a sweet-slipping eel
Or a snake that I've taken?

Love's a blind fisherman,
Love cannot see;
Whisper the child, then,
What would love of me?

It leaps in my hands! This
Anguish unguessed.
With cunning and kisses
It creeps to my breast.

It bites me, O wonder!
Worms under my skin.
My heart bursts asunder,
I tremble within.

Where go and hide me?
The shuddersome thing
Rages inside me,
Then sinks in a ring.

What poison can this be?
O that spasm again!
It burrows in ecstasy
Till I am slain."

21

Did Freud, in a book extremely well known to Jung, ever refer to
Salome in the context of God's desire to wipe out the human race? The
answer: Yes, he did. In his fascinating analysis of his "Count Thun"
dream, in *The Interpretation of Dreams,* Freud referred to a play in which
the Devil rapes Salome. The play was *Das Liebeskonzil (Love's Council).* In

this play, God is portrayed as a sickly, doddering old crank who, like Zeus in the Deucalion and Philemon myths copied in Jung's dreams and visions, decides to exterminate the human race. When dissuaded by Christ and Mary, this vengeful God asks the Devil to afflict man- and womankind with a disease directly related to our "abominable sexual sins." Christ and Mary approve the plan!

Happy to oblige, the Devil rapes Salome, his prisoner in Hell, because "she could love only John the Baptist's severed head." Moments later Salome gives birth to a fully grown, irresistibly beautiful woman who personifies syphilis. This femme fatale proceeds at once to infect the entire human race, beginning with the Pope. What a nauseating plot! (If any masochistic reader wishes to know more about this lulu, which I nominate as one of the ten worst plays ever written, he may read the play—or the synopsis, my source—in Dr. Alexander Grinstein's *On Sigmund Freud's Dreams.*)

22

Proof that Carl Jung dream-envisioned Freud as Elijah, the greatest of the Hebrew prophets, who cast out "false gods" like Baal, may be seen in the eulogy he wrote in his memoirs long after Freud's death.

Freud's greatest achievement probably consisted in taking neurotic patients seriously and entering into their peculiar individual psychology. He had the courage to let the case material speak for itself, and in this way to penetrate into the real psychology of the patients. He saw with the patient's eyes, so to speak, and so reached a deeper understanding of mental illness than had hitherto been possible. In this respect he was free of bias, courageous, and succeeded in overcoming a host of prejudices. *Like an Old Testament prophet, he undertook to overthrow false gods* [italics mine], to rip away the veils from a mass of dishonesties and hypocrisies, mercilessly exposing the rottenness of the contemporary psyche.

The rest of this magnanimous tribute also merits attention:

[Freud] did not falter in the face of the unpopularity such an enterprise entailed. The impetus which he gave to our civilization sprang from his discovery of an avenue to the unconscious. By evaluating dreams as the most important source of information concerning the unconscious processes, he gave back to mankind a tool that had seemed irretrievably lost. He demonstrated empirically the presence of the unconscious psyche which had hitherto existed only as a philosophical postulate, in particular in the philosophies of C. G. Carus and Eduard von Hartmann.

It may well be said that the contemporary cultural consciousness has not yet absorbed into the general philosophy the idea of the unconscious and all it means, despite the fact that modern man has been confronted with this idea for more than half a century.

23

Philemon

"Soon after this Elijah fantasy," continues Jung, "another figure rose out of the unconscious. He developed out of the Elijah figure; I called him Philemon. Philemon was a pagan and brought with him an Egypto-Hellenic atmosphere with a Gnostic coloration." (By 1912, Freud had already acquired many of the Egyptian and Hellenistic icons and artifacts which Jung saw during his numerous visits to Freud's home and office.)

"His [Philemon's] figure first appeared to me in the following dream:

There was a blue sky . . . suddenly there appeared from the right a winged being sailing across the sky. I saw an old man with the winged horns of a bull. He held a bunch of keys, one of which he clutched as if he were about to open a lock. He had the wings of a kingfisher with its characteristic colors. Since I did not understand this dream-image, I painted it to impress it on my memory . . ."

Referring again to a dream-mentor created to replace his lost teacher or "guru" Freud, Jung explains: "It was Philemon who taught me psychic objectivity, the reality of the psyche; psychologically, Philemon represented superior insight. He was a mysterious figure to me. At times he seemed quite real, as if he were a living personality. I went walking up and down the garden with him, and to me he was what the Indians call a guru, who would untangle for me the involuntary creatures of my imagination.

This task was undertaken for me by the figure of Philemon, whom in this respect I had to recognize as my psychogogue."

Repeating Jung's questions about Elijah and Salome—"What did the old man signify? What did Salome signify?"—I asked myself, "What did Philemon *really* signify to Jung? What did he look like?" I turned the pages of Jung's memoirs, found the "painting" he had made of Philemon—and saw that it was an unmistakable portrait of Sigmund Freud. Others to whom I showed the image and asked, "Who does this look like?" all answered at once—"Sigmund Freud."

24

The "Philemon" dream is directly related to Jung's previous genocidal "Deluge" dreams through the name "Philemon." Ovid, source of the nearly identical Deucalion-Pyrrha myth, tells us that Philemon and Baucis were an impoverished old Phrygian couple who gladly gave food and shelter to the disguised Jupiter and Mercury when all their richer neighbors rudely turned them away. Jupiter drowned all the inhospitable Phrygians. He then rewarded Philemon and Baucis by appointing them custodians of the magnificent temple he built to replace their "miserable hovel." Here again we see one part of Jung's unconscious mind as a savagely misanthropic "playwright" who adapted ancient myths to satisfy his deepest emotional needs.

If, for the sake of idea exploration, we accept the "Elijah-and-Philemon-as-Freud" supposition, we may then grope for further interpretations, one of which would go something like this: Jung tried to kill the Freud component within himself by dreaming of Freud as a dead customs official, as the murdered Siegfried, and as the unnamed citizen of lands destroyed by pre–Judeo-Christian gods. But then, realizing existentially that he could not entirely eradicate Freud without also destroying himself intellectually (so much of his psyche and thought was built on Freud as foundation), he was forced to compromise.

His ingenious unconscious mind then staged some additional dramas in which Freud was resurrected in a more acceptable or usable form. First, he was the Jewish prophet Elijah to whom he "stuck close" and with whom he had friendly, fruitful conversations (like those he had actually had with Freud). Then, as Jung says, Elijah became transformed into the non-Jewish Philemon, "who brought with him an Egypto-Hellenic atmosphere with a Gnostic [early Christian] coloration." Like Elijah, Philemon was a friendly guru who taught Jung "psychic objectivity, the reality of the psyche" (just as Freud had done formerly). Though Jung's drawing shows clearly that Philemon is really Freud, all Jewish traces have been eliminated, for over his head floats a Christian saint's halo.

25

Jung probably derived his specific dream-image, and the name of the haloed Philemon, from the early Christian Philemon to whom St. Paul wrote begging him to forgive his runaway slave Onesimus, who had, according to the *Britannica*, stolen from him. St. Paul, citing the reformed Onesimus's Christian work, asked Philemon to restore him to his household "Not now as a servant, but above a servant, a brother beloved, especially to me, but how much more unto thee, both in the flesh, and in the Lord."

If Jung saw his dream-Philemon as a Christianized transformation of the Jewish prophet Elijah (Freud), then may we ask, Did Jung, by means of these substitutions, equate himself with the "reborn" thief Onesimus, the reborn Christian sponsored by one of Jesus's disciples? Something to think about.

26

My feelings of intellectual aloneness and uncertainty (am I the only one who has spotted the alleged "Reenactment Syndrome"? Is all this just an eccentric reading of the great man's personality and work? Is there some mischievous "resistance" toward Freud at work here?) were somewhat relieved when I found that two other admirers had come quite close to the same discoveries.

The first, my star witness, is Hilda Doolittle (H.D.), whom Norman Holland has called the finest American poetess since Emily Dickinson. In her *Tribute to Freud*, based on her profound analytical colloquies with Freud, she relates that, after some months of acute observation of this "Supreme Being" and of his collection of art objects associated with ancient myth, religion, and history, she came to see him as a replacement figure (avatar) for many magical figures of the remote past. (Miss Doolittle, a keen reader of Freud, also took her cue from Freud's confessed identifications with Hannibal and others.)

One of these replacement figures, says Doolittle, was "Janus, the old Roman guardian of gates and doors, patron of the month of January, with all its 'beginnings.' " Then, comparing Freud and his consulting room with the all-seeing Janus, she adds: "Janus faced both ways, as doors opened and shut. Here in this [consulting room] we had exits and entrances. . . . We have only begun our 'studies,' the old Professor [Freud] and I."

Next, Freud is seen by H.D. in the role of the ancient Greek healer:

It was Askelapios, who was called the *blameless physician*. He was the son of the sun, Phebos Apollo . . . and this half-man, half-god (Fate decreed) went a little too far when he raised the dead. He was blasted by the thunderbolt of an avenging deity, but Apollo, over-riding his father's anger, placed Askelapios among the stars . . .

Our Professor stood this side of the portal. He did not pretend to bring back the dead who had already crossed the threshold. But he did raise from dead hearts and stricken minds and maladjusted bodies a host of living children. . . .

This old Janus, this beloved lighthouse keeper, shut the door on transcendental speculation, or at least transferred this occult or hidden symbolism to the occult or hidden regions of personal reactions, dreams, thought "transferences" of the individual human mind. . . . As to what happened, after this life was over . . . we as individuals had profited so little by the illuminating teachings of the Master who gave his name to the present era, that it was well for a Prophet (like Freud), in the old tradition of Israel, to arise, to slam the door on visions of the future, of the afterlife . . .

H.D. then recognizes Freud in the role of ". . . the Roman centurion before the gate of Pompeii who did not move from his station since he received no order to do so, and who stood for future generations to wonder at, embalmed in hardened lava, preserved in the very fire and ashes that had destroyed him."

Her metaphorical gears now shift to another mythical duo: "Eros and Death, those were the chief subjects—in fact, the only subjects—of the Professor's eternal preoccupation. They are still gripped, struggling in the dead-lock. Hercules struggled with Death and is still struggling. But Freud himself proclaimed 'the Herculean power of Eros, and we know that it was written from beginning that Love is stronger than Death.' "

Now Hilda Doolittle recognizes Freud as Hercules:

> He would clean the Augean stables, he would tame the Nemean lion, he would capture the Erymanthian boar, he would clear the Stymphalian birds from the marshes of the unconscious mind.* These things must be done. He indicated certain ways in which they might be done. Until we have completed our twelve labors, he seemed to reiterate, we (mankind) have no right to rest on cloud-cushion fantasies and dreams of an afterlife.

Finally, as climax to this burst of recognition of Freud's mythical identifications, H.D. equates "The Professor" with none other than Jesus Christ: "There was another Jew who said, *The kingdom of heaven is within you*. He said: *Unless you become as little children, you shall not enter the kingdom of heaven.*"

A second star witness, who also comes quite close to a recognition of the "Freud Reenactment Syndrome," is Jack J. Spector, author of the illuminating *The Aesthetics of Freud:* "If there is one thread that connects the complicated turns and changes of Freud's theories, it is his continuous preoccupation with himself; briefly, Freud is the hero of his own work. He makes himself the central character of the Oedipus myth; he identifies with the problems of Leonardo and the genius of Goethe, and responds with romantic intensity to Michelangelo's 'Moses.' "

---

*H.D. probably read Freud's comparison of himself with Hercules in his *Interpretation of Dreams*.

27

Another writer who has observed one of Freud's "identifications," but not as a part of a highly repetitive, compulsive pattern, is Dr. Alexander Grinstein. In his fascinating amplification of Freud's interpretation of his "*Non Vixit*" dream, this psychoanalyst has written: "Freud speaks of Shakespeare's Prince Hal (Henry IV, Part 2) who 'could not even at his father's sick bed resist the temptation of trying on the crown.' In the context in which this is mentioned *Freud seems to identify himself with Prince Hal and his ambition to replace his father and become king. . . .*"* [Italics mine.]

To this syndrome-watcher this is just another example of Freud's lifelong habit of identification with royal or ruling figures like Ramses, Alexander, Cromwell, Napoleon, Caesar, Lear, Joseph, and the great Moses.

28

During my study of this modern man who compulsively identified with mythical and historical figures, a half-remembered passage in Herman Melville's allegorical novel *Mardi* nagged at me. Finally, wondering if the haunting words played any part in my Freudian delvings, I found the passage and saw that they had indeed influenced me. In words that remind one of Hilda Doolittle's comparisons of Freud with Janus, Hercules, and even Christ, Melville asks, "Do you believe that you lived three thousand years ago? That you were at the taking of Tyre, were overwhelmed at Gomorrah? No? But for me, I was at the subsiding of the Deluge . . . with the Israelites I fainted in the wilderness; was at court when Solomon outdid the judges before him. I, it was, who suppressed the lost works of Manteo, on the Egyptian mythology, as containing mysteries not to be revealed to posterity. . . . I originated the conspiracy against the purple murderer Domitian; I who in the senate moved that the great and good Aurelian be

---

*On Sigmund Freud's Dreams. (Detroit, Wayne State University Press, 1968.) An intellectual feast.

Emperor. I instigated the abdication of Diocletian, and Charles the Fifth; I touched Isabella's heart that she listened to Columbus. I am he, that from the King's minions hid the charter in the old oak at Hartford. . . . I am the leader of the Mohawk Masks, who in the old Commonwealth harbour, threw overboard the East India Company's Souchong;* I am the veiled Persian Prophet; I am the man in the iron mask; I Junius."

Melville, a great reader and borrower, may have taken the above-quoted first-person litany from the sixth-century Welsh bard Taliesin, who wrote in his *Red Book of Hergest:*†

. . . call me Taliesin.
I was with the Lord in the highest sphere.
On the fall of Lucifer into the depths of Hell.
I have borne a banner before Alexander.

I was in Canaan when Absalom was slain.

I was at the place of the Crucifixion of the merciful Son of God.
I have been the chief director of the work of the Tower of Nimrod [Babel].

I have been in Asia with Noah at the Ark.
I have witnessed the destruction of Sodom and Gomorrah.

I have been with my Lord in the Manger of the Ass.
I strengthened Moses through the water of the Jordan.

I have been teacher to all intelligences.
I am able to instruct the whole universe.

29

The idea of Freud, inhabitant of Vienna for nearly eighty years, as a compulsive "actor" or "reenactor" was implanted in my mind, I believe,

---

*In a sense Melville *was* there. His grandfather Major Thomas Melville was one of the "Mohawk Masks" who dumped the English Souchong tea into Boston harbor forty-six years before Melville was born.

†From Robert Graves, *The White Goddess,* 1947.

by something I read long ago in Hanns Sachs's memoir: *Freud, Master and Friend*. Sachs, a member of Freud's inner circle, wrote: "All Vienna was stagestruck. The plays, the actors and their merits or shortcomings on the stage and off were the topics of general interest and an inexhaustible subject for passionate debates, as much as if not more so than stars of the movies, the gridiron, and the diamond in this country. At parties the talk about the theater and the performers took first place, with politics and social problems far in the rear.

"The theater craze went much further than that. It did not stay in the playhouse, but overflowed richly into life. I could observe it best when I returned to Vienna after a stay abroad, which made comparisons easy and opened my eyes to the peculiar ways of my home town. I saw that every incident was used as an opportunity for play-acting; its real content was hardly more than the pretense for a bit of comedy or tragedy—preferably the first. The policeman who warned the driver, the housewife who bargained for her cabbages, the tram-conductor and the woman with the bundle, the prosecutor and the defendant, all took their part, as it came to them, with gusto and acted it more than they lived it, not with pathos and high-declamation, as you see it in Latin countries, but rather going in for character impersonation and witty repartee.

"The famous Viennese politeness and amiability were a part of this game. It was not downright intentional lying, but to believe that any real result would come of a smoothly played scene would have been as naïve as to expect that an actor would continue in the character after the fall of the final curtain. Not only the shopkeeper in his store, but even the high dignitary in his office assured the visitor (the lower officials played their parts too, but in a quite different key) that he was quite overwhelmed by so much kindness and condescension, but when the scene had been acted, it was all over and nothing came of it. On the other hand, two friends who had quarreled violently became friendly again, like a pair of actors who had insulted each other in a dramatic scene."

Hanns Sachs then adds his considered opinion that Freud never played the Viennese theatrical game: "It is obvious that Freud's personality, his way of life as well as living, represents the diametrical opposite of everything that has been described here as typical of Vienna. In the place of insincerity, superficial amiability, and the wish to gloss over unpleasant facts, he put insistence on merciless truth, the severities of unrelenting inquiry, and the courage to disturb the sleep of the world."

Though I do not dispute this accurate portrait of Freud as one who refused to play the Viennese "theater game" in the style of his fellow citizens, my accumulated observations tell me that like all the others he was also an "actor." He was, as Sachs and many others have told us, a brilliant performer-lecturer. Moreover, as the rest of this book will reveal, Freud responded to the many great and small crises in his life by assuming "roles" not only from the theater (Goethe, Shakespeare, Schiller, and others) but from history, mythology, and fictional works as well.

But Sigmund Freud was far more than a "stagestruck Viennese" performer. Though he seems to have played that game, though he did so to fulfill his inner need to achieve greatness through mimesis, he always subordinated his compulsive play-acting to his monumental work as an empirical scientist and healer.

PART TWO | # Freud's Vienna

ABREACTION, the process of working off a pent-up emotion by reliving it again in feeling or action.
—Ernest Jones, *Papers in Psychoanalysis*

1

I sensed that my questing voyage (pilgrimage?) to "Freud's Vienna" was off to a promising start when I learned that, with so many hotels to choose from, Swissair had booked me into one on the Ring, the boulevard girdling Vienna's ancient Inner City; my maps told me that the accidentally chosen Hotel de France was only five short blocks from the house where Freud created psychoanalysis, and an easy walk to most of the places I wanted to see.

The Hotel de France was also perfectly situated for another planned exploration: From the Jones biography I'd learned that Freud began his furious daily marches around Vienna's inner core directly in front of my hotel.* Now acutely aware of Freud as a tireless reenactor of scenes from legend, history, and fiction, I wanted to verify my guess that his daily constitutional masked yet another of the hypothetical "reenactments."

(And of course I prepared myself for disappointment: "Probably nothing shall come of all this, but at least I will see a part of the Vienna Freud passionately hated—and loved.")

Freud expressed his powerful ambivalence toward the city he lived in for seventy-seven years in two letters written nearly four decades apart. In the first, sent to Wilhelm Fliess, his only "outside" intellectual friend during his agonizing period of ostracism (Austracism?)—from 1895 to 1902—Freud vented his frustration and anger. He also, true to form,

---

*Ernest Jones tells us that Freud began his daily circumambulations of Vienna on the segment of the Ring called the Schottenring, the site of the northern gate of the old city walls torn down in 1859–60, when Freud was an infant. The Hotel de France is at Schottenring 3.

identified with a mythical figure (in this case in a contrary or negative way) while emotionally disturbed:

> I hate Vienna with a positively personal hatred, and, just contrary to the giant Antaeus, I draw fresh strength whenever I remove my feet from the city which is my home.

As everyone knows (who knows), the North African Antaeus, son of the sea god Poseidon, was the murderer-wrestler who remained invincible as long as he could touch his mother Gaea, the earth. (Hercules learned his secret, lifted him off the ground, and strangled him.) Antaeus forced all strangers who ("Freudianly") entered his "mother country" to grapple with him—in what an analyst might explain as an unconscious homoerotic replay of the violent sexual embraces Antaeus may have witnessed in his parents' bedroom.

After killing the "father substitutes" (strangers), he used their skulls to build a temple honoring his father. Surely Freud or Jones or Rank or Abraham could have written a deliciously ironic essay about this compulsive Oedipal wrestler who acquired thousands of severed heads in such a manner for the death-temple he *erected for his father.*

2

Taught by Freud to look for everyman's Oedipal drives, I next examined the related Hercules myth and discovered that, like Antaeus, the original Superman also spent most of his time compulsively "acting out" his own variant of the basic complex: Hercules seems to have been the victim of the massive rejection inflicted by his father Zeus—who did nothing to prevent his wife Hera (mother figure to all Greeks) from savagely persecuting his son.

When the madly jealous Hera learned that Zeus had raped and impregnated the mortal Alcmene (while disguised as her husband Amphitryon), she unjustly vented all her rage on their innocent son Hercules. First she sent two snakes to kill or devour him in his crib, but the newborn superchild easily strangled them.

Then, about a quarter of a century later, the unrelenting goddess cast a spell of unconsciousness upon Hercules and directed him to kill his beloved wife and children. When revived and told what he had done during his mental blackout, Hercules thought only of suicide. But Theseus and Amphitryon restrained him and brought him to the judge and proto-psychiatrist Eurytheus, King of Mycenae.

Eurytheus, anticipating the legal "McNaghten Rule" by more than four millennia, declared that Hercules could not be held accountable for acts committed while he was deranged. The pre-psychoanalytical king then persuaded Hercules to purge his terrible guilt feelings through a program of perilous deeds benefiting mankind—the celebrated "twelve labors."

3

To Freud, Vienna was an imprisoning "mother earth" who weakened him, from whom he longed to escape. The "weakened" image in Freud's "Antaeus" letter will be seen again, dramatically, during my later probe of an hysterical seizure Freud suffered shortly after his secret betrothal to Miss Martha Bernays.

4

The second letter: Writing from his London home-in-exile in 1938, Freud revealed the other half of his ambivalence toward Vienna. "The feeling of triumph at being freed [from the Nazi terror] is strongly mixed with sadness, for we loved the prison from which we have just been released."

Thirteen years after his "Antaeus" letter, Freud complained again: "Vienna has done everything possible to deny her [note his use of the feminine pronoun] share in the origin [birth] of psychoanalysis. Nowhere else is the hostile indifference of the learned and cultured circles so clearly evident to the psychoanalyst."

He adds: "Perhaps I am somewhat to blame for this by my policy of avoiding widespread publicity. If I had caused psychoanalysis to occupy the medical societies of Vienna with noisy sessions, with an unloading of all passions, wherein all reproaches and invectives carried on the tongue or in the mind would have been expressed, then perhaps the ban against psychoanalysis might, by now, have been removed, and its standing might no longer have been that of a stranger in its native city."

Freud's pained expression of rejection and anger recalls Hanns Sachs's perceptive remarks about reality-evading Vienna as a stagestruck town where *everyone* was an actor, where serious problems could be dealt with only when transformed into commedia dell'arte skits. Freud verifies Sachs's witty observation by ending his complaint with lines from Schiller's *Wallenstein:*

But this the Viennese will not forgive me;
That I deprived them of a spectacle.

Amusingly, characteristically, paradoxically, Freud uses a scene from a drama to say that his own private drama forbids him to stage spectacles that will make him better liked by his fellow Viennese.

5

After a midafternoon arrival in Vienna on December first, a dismally overcast, cold, rainy, windy day (Northern Europe in the wintertime), I checked into the hotel and rested a bit. Then, fortified by an inch of hotel-bar schnapps, I walked bravely out into the beastly weather, turned right at the nearest corner and, as anticipated, saw two landmarks associated with Sigmund Freud.

The nearer, directly to the west, was a building fronting on the Ring. This was a part of the University where Freud studied, worked, and lectured for more than thirty years: ". . . the Institute in which I spent the happiest hours of my student life, free from other desires." Then, syndromically assuming the role and words of Mephistopheles, who, disguised as Faust, is deceiving a young student, our chronic reenactor Freud writes:

Thus at the breasts of Wisdom clinging,
Thou'lt find every day a greater rapture bringing.

Here at this University in 1882, shortly after his secret betrothal (he was too poor to announce it), Freud, twenty-six, asked Professor Ernst Brücke, whom he dreamed of succeeding one day, for the top assistant's job. Brücke turned him down. Though sympathetic, Brücke reminded the young doctor of the two capable men with seniority and advised him to abandon pure science, then a rich man's game, and enter private practice. (If Brücke had sponsored Freud's high scientific ambitions, there would have been no Freudian psychotherapy. I agree with others, however, that Freud, whose *Totem and Taboo* was hailed as a "literary masterpiece" by Thomas Mann and who won the Goethe Prize for Literature, would have "discovered his America" and expressed his psychoanalytical ideas in fiction or drama, as Schnitzler and Chekhov, both physicians, did. But, on the other hand, as we kids in Cleveland used to say: "IF is a big stiff!")

Freud reluctantly accepted Brücke's chilling practical advice and remained his friend and admirer; but eighteen years later, in his *Interpretation of Dreams*, Freud, merciless self-exposer, confessed that he had, in one of his dreams, completely "annihilated with a look" a dream-disguised Brücke, dream-merged with one of the men who was given the job he wanted desperately. (We will return to this revengeful *"Non Vixit"* dream later: it is a prime example of Freud's unceasing need to restage certain scenes from mythology with himself in a leading role.)

Another remembered Freud-University association: Here, in 1913, Freud's son Martin, a member of the Jewish defense corps Kadimah, was knifed while battling with the anti-Catholic, anti-Semitic, anti-Italian, anti-Slav "fraternity men" who terrorized the school.

Then, as I continued to stare at the fog- and time-enshrouded University, I recalled the Wienerschnitzlerian drama that ended happily for Freud. For many years the University establishment, enraged by his "unacceptable," "obscene," "disgusting," even "insane" pronouncements about the role of sexuality in human behavior, denied Freud the professorial status he badly wanted. Finally a grateful patient, the Baroness von Ferstel, who knew how things were managed in Vienna, persuaded an art minister to trade the long-overdue professorship for a painting owned by her aunt.

Elated, Freud wrote to his intimate friend Wilhelm Fliess: "I have obviously become reputable again, and my shyest admirers now greet me from a distance in the street. . . . The public enthusiasms keep coming in. . . ." Then, always the self-dramatist, he added: "[It] is as if the role of sexuality had suddenly been recognized by his Majesty [Franz Josef], the interpretation of dreams by our Council of Ministers, and the necessity of the psychoanalytical therapy carried by a two-thirds majority in our Parliament."

6

The early resistance to Freud's Oedipus complex discovery is illustrated in a section of the book he wrote during the First World War: "Here is an incident which occurred in the present war. One of the staunch adherents of psychoanalysis was stationed on the German front in Poland; he attracted the attention of his colleagues by the fact that he occasionally effected an unexpected influence upon a patient. On being questioned, he admitted that he worked with psychoanalytical methods and with readiness agreed to impart his knowledge to his colleagues. So every night the medical men of the corps, his colleagues and his superiors, met to be initiated into the mysteries of psychoanalysis. For a time all went well, but when he introduced his audience to the Oedipus complex a superior officer arose and announced that he did not believe this, that it was the behavior of a cad for the lecturer to relate such things to brave men, fathers of families, who were fighting for their country, and he forbade the continuation of the lectures. This was the end: the analyst got himself transferred to another part of the front."*

Another example of resistance to Freud's sexual discoveries may be seen in a letter written to Freud by Dr. Karl Abraham, the first German psychoanalyst. Referring to a certain Dr. Ziehen, who ridiculed Freud's (and Abraham's) ideas at Berlin medical meetings, Abraham wrote:

---

*A General Introduction to Psychoanalysis, 1920.

. . . a little satire from Ziehen's clinic: a demonstration of a case of obsessional neurosis. The patient suffers from the obsessional idea that he must put his hands under women's skirts in the street. Ziehen to the audience: "Gentlemen, we must carefully investigate whether we are dealing with a compulsive idea with sexual content. I shall ask the patient whether he also feels this impulse with older women." The patient, in answer to the question: "Alas, Professor, even with my own mother and sister." To which Ziehen says, "You see, gentlemen, there is nothing sexual here." To his assistant: "Note in the case history—patient suffers from a non-sexual but senseless obsessional idea." (November 2, 1911.)*

7

When, as planned, I walked north on the Währinger Strasse (mentioned by Freud in one of his dream dissections), the dominant neighborhood landmark loomed higher and higher: it was the twin-spired Votive Church built to thank God for saving the bewhiskered Franz Josef from assassination. My notes told me that "the little park before the church was the outer boundary for the Freud children"; that "Martin's nanny often took him into the church to 'rest her feet' (and ease her soul). She didn't know it, but she was reenacting scenes in the infancy of Martin's father; for when Sigmund was two years old and living in Freiberg, now part of Czechoslovakia, *his* old nanny, a second mother, also took him to Catholic masses; and, says Jones, 'she implanted in him ideas of Heaven and Hell, and probably also those of salvation and resurrection. After returning from Church the boy used to preach a sermon at home and propound God's doings.'

"Later the sudden disappearance of this pathetic woman—she was sent to prison for ten months for stealing money and *toys*—panicked and traumatized the two-year-old Sigmund: the unconsciously retained emotions, ideas associated with this female Jean Valjean surfaced in bad dreams struggled with by the grown-up Freud during his epochal self-analysis."

An afterthought: I am reminded here of Freud's study of Leonardo, the

*The Psychoanalytic Dialogue—Letters of Sigmund Freud and Karl Abraham. (New York, Basic Books, 1966.)

infant bastard whose father cruelly snatched him from his mother in Vinci and took him to be raised by his wife in Florence. Freud, who according to Jones "identified" strongly with Leonardo, reads this brutal act as the single psychic injury which determined Leonardo's abnormal sexual life and gave him the "double mother" image seen in his paintings and drawings.

Like Leonardo, Freud also had "two mothers," the surrogate (nanny) who was socially ruined and cast aside, the other accepted. Like Leonardo, little Sigmund was separated permanently from his "mother" in Freiberg and raised in far-off Vienna. Of course all this may be purely coincidental, but one guesses that these facts provided the background for Freud's empathetic explorations of Leonardo's life, personality and paintings.

As I continued my walk past the Votive Church, I opened my notebook and read: "The Jones biography and maps of Freud's neighborhood show that Freud passed the Votivkirche each time he walked to and from his lectures at the University. Hanns Sachs, one of the first to attend them, says that for many years the average attendance was 'five or six.' Sometimes only three. But by 1912 there were as many as fifty. (Later, be sure to take a good look at the interior and exterior of the church, usually referred to as 'False-Gothic.')"

8

A second afterthought: Moses, the dominant identification figure of Freud's later years and the subject of his controversial *Moses and Monotheism*—in which he insisted that Moses was not a Hebrew but an Egyptian Prince—also had two mothers.

When the Pharaoh ordered the drowning of all sons born to the Hebrew minority, the unnamed mother of one child (later given the Egyptian name Moses) placed him in an "ark of bulrushes" and "hid him among the flags at the river's brink." She then stationed her daughter Miriam "to wit what had been done to him."

When the Pharaoh's daughter found the infant and decided to raise it as her own, Miriam approached the Princess and said, "Shall I go and call a nurse of the Hebrew women, that she may nurse the child for thee?" The compassionate Egyptian agreed, and Moses was given to his own mother Jochebed until he was weaned. He was then permanently separated from her and raised by the Pharaoh's daughter.

This generally overlooked detail in the life of Freud's great prototype may have been the emotional key to his profound identification with Moses. The equation for this inner dramatization is a simple one: "Moses had 'two mothers.' I, Sigmund Freud, also had 'two mothers.' Therefore, according to the curious illogic of the unconscious mind, I am Moses."

(Some weeks after writing this, I read Hilda Doolittle's *Tribute to Freud* and learned that Freud was acutely aware of this part of the Moses legend. Miss Doolittle (H.D.) says, "The Professor [her name for Freud] asked me if I were the child Miriam who in the Doré picture stood, half-hidden in the river reeds, watching over the newborn child who was to become leader of a captive people and founder of a new religion.")

9

After coolly ignoring three streets because of their *ungemütlich* refusal to tell me anything about Freud, I came to the Türkinstrasse, a street name that recalled Austria's greatest disaster before the partial destruction of Vienna's Inner City during the Second World War.

"In 1683," said my notebook, "200,000 Turks and insurgent Hungarians invaded the Austro-Hungarian Empire. The army ravaged all the outlying towns and villages and surrounded the walls of Vienna on July 14 (later Bastille Day) to begin the siege that ended in September when John Sobieski's army drove them off. The Turks encamped in the rural area then surrounding the city: there were thousands of tents in the area where Freud's house now stands.

"While bivouacked on the northern height (the Kahlenberg) one of Sobieski's officers wrote: 'What a scene was revealed to our eyes from the crown of the hill! The great space around the Vienna walls was thickly covered by tents—even the island of Leopoldstadt [the Jewish district where Freud lived until he was thirty] was hidden by them. The frightful thunder of the Turkish siege-cannon, and the answering fire from the walls of the town, filled the air. Smoke and flames enveloped the city to such an extent that only the tops of the church towers were visible in between.' "*

10

My good friend Henry Koerner, Vienna-born painter of profound and witty allegories, told me recently: "Yes, the Turks were encamped in what you call 'Freud's neighborhood.' The Turkish Army engineers began to dig there a deep tunnel towards the walls where the Schottenring now is. They were going to bring in hundreds of barrels of gunpowder to blow up the walls.

"But Sobieski's army chased away the Turks before they reached the walls." Henry then cocked his good eye at me, smiled, and said mischievously: "I think maybe that tunnel went right under the spot where Freud's house was later built."

We then both laughed at the further suggestion that Freud, a modern "Turk" who besieged Vienna for half a century, might have found and secretly extended the old Turkish tunnel, and brought in his psychonuclear sexplosives. Later I sent Harry a copy of one of Freud's own dreams in which a Viennese "stranger" tried to prevent him from trying on a Gogolian overcoat decorated with *Turkish designs*. With it I enclosed Freud's comment to a patient (Hilda Doolittle) after an especially productive session: "Today we have tunneled very deep." (The suggestion of the psyche as a besieged Vienna behind whose walls neuroses cower pleases me.) Freud's dream:

I put on an overcoat. But the first one I tried on was too long for me. . . . A second one I tried had a long strip with a Turkish design let into it. A stranger with a long face and a short pointed beard came up and tried to prevent me from putting it on, saying it was his. I showed him that it was embroidered all over with a Turkish pattern. He asked: "What have the Turkish (designs, stripes, etc.) to do with you?" But then we became quite friendly with each other.

---

*Henry Dwight Sedgewick, *Vienna*. (New York, Bobbs-Merrill, 1939.)

In his explanation of this dream, Freud says that the "stranger" with the "long face and a short pointed beard" with whom he became "quite friendly" may have been based on a local merchant named Popović who sold fabrics to Mrs. Freud. The name "Popović" reminds Freud of *"Popo,"* the German term of endearment for a person's rear end. (I include this as a small "reader's dividend" for collector-consumers of Freudian delisextessen.)

11

An afterword: Some months after writing the above, I read Dr. Alexander Grinstein's brilliant explication *On Sigmund Freud's Dreams* and found that he had dealt with the same dream. In the course of his study Grinstein quotes an adjacent part of Freud's analysis as his prelude to an eye-opening interpretation. The segment is:

> He was called Popović, an equivocal name (*"Popo"*=buttocks or bottom) on which the humorous writer Stettheimer has already made a suggestive comment: "He told me his name and blushingly pressed my hand."

Of this amusing dream-snippet, Grinstein, a psychoanalyst, says: "The homosexual implications of this association may also be seen in the last sentence of the manifest content of the dream, *'But then we became quite friendly with each other.'* As the homosexual allusion follows immediately after the remark about the stranger who interfered with Freud's putting on the overcoat, it would appear that Freud was using a homosexual type of defense against the inhibiting parental figure.* This allusion, however, is also censored, for he again avoids any further discussion of the sexual theme and continues on in a general vein."

> [Freud]: Once again I found myself misusing a name, as I had done with Pelagie, Knodl, Brücke and Fleischl. It could hardly be denied that playing around with names [in dreams] like this was a kind of childish naughtiness.

---

*This is one of Dr. Grinstein's several matter-of-fact references to Freud's unconscious "homosexuality" as revealed in his dreams.

But if I indulged in it, it was as an act of retribution, for my own name had been the victim of feeble witticisms like those on countless occasions.

Freud is probably referring here to the lascivious play on words associating his name to the Viennese word for a prostitute: "*Freudenmäd-chen*" or "*joy-girl*" (*Freude*=joy; *mädchen*=girl). This wordplay with its suggestion of sexual crossover will be mentioned later.

12

Many of the buildings in Freud's neighborhood—banks, apartment houses, insurance companies, official-looking structures—display mythical sculptures like those I'd photographed many times in Berlin, Munich, and Frankfurt. I found here a similar abundance of topless caryatids with breasts like cannonballs, and an equal number of grotesque fig-leafed atlantes (singular, atlas), all valiantly but foolishly propping up useless architectural protrusions. All around them, over doorways and windows, the typical nineteenth-century apotropaic or evil-averting severed heads of ferocious Germanic and Roman warriors, gargoyles, ancient gods and goddesses—all displayed as status symbols; and, as Otto Rank and other scholars tell us, as visual repellents of thieves, subversives, hostile spirits, jealous neighbors, and would-be sexual intruders, especially those with unconsciously incestuous desires.

Though all these carved heads have been rendered impotent by weak design and over-familiarity, they sent strong messages to at least one man who walked past them on his way to Freud's house.

13

Continuing along the Währinger Strasse, I came to the Hotel Regina, where Freud reserved rooms for his visitors and more affluent foreign patients. Jung stayed there during his frequent meetings with Freud; the poet Hilda Doolittle (H.D.) lived at the Regina for months while being treated for the hallucinations she had suffered in Greece. The Hotel Regina is mentioned in a dramatic passage in her beautiful *Tribute to Freud*.

But now, while looking at this not unusual building, my thoughts were riveted on a young man who stayed there seventy years ago and played a solitary little scene in his room—a scene from what could be one of Freud's most revealing self-dramatizations.

The man? Dr. Karl Abraham, age thirty. The "solitary little scene"? A recent convert to psychoanalysis, Abraham came to Vienna for his first discussions with Freud. After five days of meetings and social gatherings, he attended the Wednesday night seminar held in Freud's waiting room. Late that night, after saying his farewells, he returned to his hotel room, where he was surprised to find that *Freud had secretly placed in his briefcase "two small Egyptian objects from his collection."**

Opening my notebook again, I reread the letter written by Abraham three days after his return home:

> Berlin
> 21.12.1907
>
> Dear Professor Freud:
>
> When I got back to my hotel on Wednesday night, I found a little box in my briefcase. The contents and the accompanying words gave me much pleasure. This charming gift is the climax of a most enjoyable visit. Let me thank you for all the instruction and stimulation I received. I very much hope that the followers of your science increase in numbers. . . . The days that I was privileged to spend in your company and that of your family were most beneficial to me. To be surrounded by so much kindness and so much culture is a rare joy, and I came away with the feeling of being deeply indebted to you. Maybe I shall succeed in paying some of this debt by my theoretical contributions.

My notes continue: "This all sounds very friendly, and indeed it was. Until his untimely death eighteen years later, Karl Abraham was not only one of Freud's most brilliant and trusted disciple-colleagues, but a warm

---

*A footnote in *The Letters of Sigmund Freud and Karl Abraham*. (New York, Basic Books, 1965.)

friend as well. His death was a grave loss to Freud and to the cause of psychotherapy."

14

I deduce that, on the conscious level, Freud gave his new disciple the Egyptian figurines, probably found in a nobleman's or Pharaoh's tomb, after he learned that Abraham shared his passion for ancient art, archeology, and history. Later, we will see that it was Abraham's essay about Pharaoh Ikhnaton's "Oedipal" behavior that triggered Freud's faint-inducing argument with Jung at Munich's Park Hotel in November 1912.

But my discovery that, when in crisis, Freud often unconsciously replayed scenes from ancient exemplars leads me to suspect that his "charming act" of hiding two Egyptian art objects in Abraham's briefcase on the eve of his departure for Germany might be his reenactment of the Biblical story of Joseph and his jealous brothers. (Many readers have guessed it at once.)

I have two separate but complementary reasons for thinking so. The first is based on a detailed comparison of the "briefcase" incident with the well-known Biblical story, the other on my knowledge of the circumstances surrounding Freud's relationship to Abraham at the time of his first visit to Vienna. Both sets of reasons are centered on the theme of *intense sibling rivalry*.

Here, for aid in evaluating the first of the comparisons, is a brief summary of the Old Testament story: When the centenarian Jacob, grandson of Abraham,* unwisely showed his greater love for Joseph (because he was the "son of his old age") and gave him the "coat of many colors," his jealous sons decided to kill Joseph.

One day, while tending the flocks, they seized him, ripped off the offending coat, and threw him naked into a deep pit. The coat was then dipped in kid's blood and shown to Jacob as a proof that Joseph had been devoured by an "evil beast." "And Jacob rent his clothes and mourned his son many days."

---

*Jacob was the name of Freud's father; in a letter to Jung, Freud linked Karl Abraham to the old Testament's "eponymous Abraham."

But Jehovah, who had prearranged this sibling drama as a part of his long-range plans for Joseph, the later Moses, and the creation of the nation Israel, directed the brothers to sell Joseph to Ishmaelite traders on their way to Egypt. There he was resold to Potiphar, the Pharaoh's chief eunuch and steward.

After being imprisoned for allegedly attempting to rape horny Mrs. Potiphar (the archetypal bum sex rap), Joseph, still God's unwitting instrument, interpreted the Pharaoh's "great plenty and famine" dream and advised him to store up surplus grain against the "seven years of famine." For this single analysis, Joseph, greatest pre-Freudian dream interpreter, was rewarded rather generously: the Pharaoh made him "the ruler of all the land of Egypt," with full power to implement the fourteen-year plan.

After the foreseen drought arrived to devastate the entire Middle East, a great many starving people from the neighboring countries, including Israel, came to Egypt, hoping to buy food.

When Joseph's ten brothers, sent by Jacob, appeared before him, he recognized them at once, ". . . though they knew him not." After learning that his father Jacob was still alive, Joseph decided to forgive his brothers, but not before having a bit of sadistic fun with them.

First, through an interpreter, he roughly accused them of being spies. That shook them up. Then, after jailing them, he relented, sold them all the grain their little asses could carry, and sent them home. He then ordered his steward to return their money and to put it into the mouths of their sacks, where they would soon find it.

During the long trip home, the grain sacks were opened and the money found. The brothers, fearing entrapment, or worse, possibly even death, were paralyzed with fear. But when no police arrived, they continued on their way.

Later, during their second trip for food, Joseph repeated his cruel charade, but this time he added a new wrinkle: he surreptitiously hid his valuable silver divining cup (*Egyptian work of art*) in his brother Benjamin's luggage. The familiar story ends with Joseph revealing himself, forgiving the rotten brothers, and asking them to bring Jacob, now 136, back from Israel—all of them to live under his protection in Egypt.

15

You, reader, may now be thinking: "If, for the sake of 'idea exploration'—and that is the name of your intellectual game—we grant the resemblance between Joseph's hiding a valuable Egyptian work of art in his brother's luggage before his departure for the neighboring country of Israel, and Freud's hiding Egyptian works of art in Abraham's luggage before he departed for neighboring Germany—what then? What was Freud's unconscious or conscious motive for reenacting the ancient incident?"

If you are indeed responding in this manner, my tentative answer is this: Though Freud was delighted with his brilliant new recruit and expected great things from him, Abraham presented some serious problems. Before setting up his psychoanalytical practice in Berlin, he had worked with Jung at the Burghölzli Sanatorium in Zurich; there had been a clash of personalities (which Freud chose to regard as mere sibling rivalry), and both men had already expressed their mutual dislike in letters to Freud.

Jung thought Abraham "unoriginal" and competitive; Abraham, a keen observer of men, warned Freud not only that Jung was an occultist, but that he would in time turn against Freud and his theories.

Freud, professionally and perhaps emotionally enamored of Jung, whom he was soon to call "my crown prince, son and successor," sided with Jung; then, thinking of the larger issues involved, he wrote a tactful but firm disciplinary letter to Abraham:

> Please be tolerant and do not forget that it is really easier for you than it is for Jung to follow my ideas, for in the first place you are completely independent and then you are closer to my intellectual constitution because of racial kinship, while he as a Christian and a pastor's son finds his way to me only against great inner resistance. His association with us is the more valuable for that. I nearly said that it was only by his appearance on the scene that psychoanalysis escaped the danger of becoming a Jewish national affair. I hope you will do what I ask, and send my cordial greetings.

Three years later, once again using the syndromic royal metaphor, Freud wrote to his confidant Dr. Ludwig Binswanger: *"When the empire I founded is orphaned, no one but Jung must inherit the whole thing. As you see, my politics incessantly pursue this aim, and my behavior towards Stekel and Adler fits into the same scheme.*" [Italics mine.]

16

A tentative summary: Karl Abraham arrived in Vienna for his first meeting and showed a keen interest in and advanced knowledge of Freud's collection, especially its dominant Egyptian objects. When, at the first meeting, Freud learned that what he called "sibling rivalry" had developed between Abraham and Jung, he decided consciously or unconsciously (or both) to issue a friendly, subtle "Joseph in Egypt" warning (the hidden objects) as a reminder of the consequences of brotherly antagonism. When Abraham's prophecies came true six years later, Freud reluctantly admitted that Abraham had been right about Jung and himself all along.

Later we shall see how Karl Abraham, taking a lesson in tactics from Freud, retaliated most ingeniously against Freud's persistent refusal to heed his personal and professional warnings against Carl Jung.

17

It seems that Freud, son of Jacob, did sometimes identify consciously with the main actors in the story of Joseph and his brethren. In his analysis of his dramatic "*Non Vixit*" dream, he wrote: "It will be noted that the name Josef plays a great part in my dreams. . . . *My own ego finds it easy to hide behind people of that name,* since Joseph was the name of the man famous in the Bible as an interpreter of dreams."* [Italics mine.]

And, in 1938, while he was on his way to exile in England, the eighty-two-year-old man wrote to his son Ernst: "I sometimes compare myself with the old Jacob, who, when he was a very old man, was taken to

---

The Interpretation of Dreams.

Egypt by his children, as Thomas Mann is to describe in his next novel."*
(Another reenactment.) "Let us hope that it won't be followed by another
Exodus from Egypt [England]. It is high time that Ahasuerus came to rest
somewhere."

In this single letter we see that Freud has clearly identified with the
Biblical Jacob and Joseph and with the Wandering Jew Ahasuerus. He has
also evoked the image of his great exemplar Moses, who, hundreds of years
after Joseph brought the Jews to Egypt, led them back to Israel. It is a little
jackpot of "restagings."

18

BAGGAGE, portable luggage.
BAGGAGE, a worthless, good-for-nothing woman;
a woman of disreputable or immoral life,
a strumpet; used playfully or familiarly of any
woman.
—*Oxford Unabridged Dictionary*

"Boxes, cases, chests . . . represent the uterus."
—Freud, *The Interpretation of Dreams*

What would Freud have said or thought if any male patient had told
him he'd surreptitiously placed two hard objects in another man's briefcase? I ask this rhetorical question because Freud relates two dreams of
one of his patients in which he openly categorizes luggage as female sexual
symbols, and the hiding of objects in luggage as an act of phallic intrusion.
Also, in the second of these dreams, Freud discovers himself as an
authority figure who, like Joseph's steward, manually searches a man's
baggage for hidden phallic objects. The last not only is an almost perfect
paradigm of Freudian psychoanalysis but strengthens the notion that
Freud unconsciously or consciously reenacted the "Joseph in Egypt"
episode.

The first of these revealing dreams and interpretations reads:

---

*Joseph and His Brethren, 1933–43.

He was starting on a journey: his luggage was taken to the station in a carriage, a number of trunks piled on it, and among them two big black ones, like boxes of samples. He said to someone, consolingly, "Well, they're going with me as far as the station."

Freud comments: "He [the patient] did in fact travel with a great deal of baggage; but he also brought a great many stories [about his conquests] of women into the treatment. The two black trunks corresponded to two dark women who were at that time playing the main part of his life. One of them wanted to follow him to Vienna; but, on my advice, he had telegraphed to put her off."

The second one, I believe, links Freud, as analyst and man, to the symbolic details in both the "Joseph in Egypt" and Freud-Abraham incidents:

A scene in the customs house: Another traveller opened his box and, coolly smoking a cigarette, said: "There's nothing in it." The customs officer seemed to believe him, but felt inside it, and found something quite particularly prohibited. The traveller said in a resigned voice: "There's nothing to be done about it."

"He himself," interprets Freud, "was the 'traveller.' I was the customs officer. As a rule he was very straightforward in making admissions, but he intended to keep silent to me about a new connection he had formed with a lady, because he rightly suspected she was not unknown to me. He displaced the distressing situation of being detected on to a stranger, so that he himself would not appear in the dream."

The dream recorded by Freud set some memory-wheels in motion: I vaguely remember reading another dream exactly like this one . . . in which Freud is also an "Austrian customs officer" whose search through a man's luggage is equated with a psychoanalyst's search for the forbidden thoughts the dream-traveler is trying to hide from him . . . (long pause) I have it! It's in Jung's memoirs, in the chapter about his long discipleship with Freud and then the final break. Yes, on reflection, Jung's dream contains exactly the same situation, the same images and psychoanalytical elements as the dream recorded by Freud. To me, nearly convinced that

Jung's "I killed Siegfried" dream was an unconscious steal from Freud's self-identification with Siegfried's killer, Jung's "customs official" dream is another example of his desire to supplant Freud through magical mimicry. Here is Jung's dream:

   While I was working on this book [*The Psychology of the Unconscious,* 1912], I had dreams which presaged the forthcoming break with Freud. One of the most significant had its scene in a mountainous region on the Swiss-Austrian border. It was toward evening, and I saw an elderly man in the uniform of an Imperial Austrian customs official. He walked past, somewhat stooped, without paying any attention to me. His expression was peevish, rather melancholic and vexed. There were other persons present, and someone informed me that the old man was not really there, but was the ghost of a customs official who had died years ago. "He is one of those who still couldn't die properly." That was the first part of the dream. [The second part of the dream deals with a knight in armor.]

"I set about analyzing this dream," says Jung. "In connection with 'customs' I at once thought of the word 'censorship.' In connection with 'border' I thought of the border between consciousness and unconsciousness on the one hand, and between Freud's views and mine on the other. The extremely rigorous customs examination at the border seemed to me an allusion to analysis. At a border, suitcases are opened and examined for contraband. In the course of this examination, unconscious assumptions are discovered. As for the old customs official, his work had obviously brought him so little that was pleasurable and satisfactory that he took a sour view of the world. I could not fail to see the analogy with Freud.

"At that time Freud had lost much of his authority for me. But he still meant to me a superior personality, upon whom I projected the father, and at the time of the dream this projection was still far from eliminated. . . . Under the impress of Freud's personality I had, as far as possible, cast aside my own judgments and repressed my criticisms. That was the prerequisite for collaborating with him. I told myself, 'Freud is far wiser and more experienced than you. For the present you must simply listen to what he says and learn from him.' And then, to my surprise, I found myself dreaming of him as a peevish official of the Imperial Austrian monarchy, as a defunct and still-walking ghost of a customs inspector. Could this be the death wish which Freud insinuated I felt toward him? I could find no part of myself that normally might have had such a wish, for I wanted at all costs to work with Freud, and, in a frankly egotistic manner, to partake of his wealth of experience. His friendship meant a great deal to me. I had no reason for wishing him dead. But it was possible that the dream could be regarded as a corrective, as a compensation or antidote for my conscious high opinion and admiration. Therefore the dream recommended a more critical attitude toward Freud. I was distinctly shocked by it, though the final sentence of the dream seemed to me an allusion to Freud's potential immortality."

Amusingly, Jung prefaces this and other dreams filled with death wishes for Freud with remarks which he then contradicts completely: "I was never able to agree with Freud that the dream is a 'façade' behind which its meaning lies hidden—a meaning already known but maliciously, so to speak, withheld from consciousness."

19

My Freud-taught curiosity aroused by the possible sexual implications of Joseph's act of hiding his magical divining cup in his brother Benjamin's seedbag (*grain* is *seed;* or, in Freudian terms, *sperm*), I delved a bit and found that ancient Jewish scholars had referred to Joseph as a bisexual with a "fix" on his brother Benjamin.

In their *Hebrew Myths*, derived mainly from the principal rabbinical commentaries, the cabalistic *Zôhar* and the *Midrash*, Robert Graves and Raphael Potai describe Joseph as a youth "who daubed his eyes with *kohl* [powdered antimony], dressed his locks like a woman, and walked mincingly." In his *Erotica Judaica*, Allen Edwardes adds, "A *saris*, or 'gelding,' was Potiphar, Pharaonic chief eunuch in the pre-Mosaic period, who purchased Joseph for 'sinful purposes' *(Zôhar)* or for 'purposes of sodomy' *(Midrash)*."

Again relying on the gravely sober rabbinical commentaries, Edwardes underscores Joseph's reputed bisexuality (he married and had children) with the comment, "[Upon their arrival in Egypt] Joseph's brothers are said to have visited the harlots' quarters on the assumption that so handsome (and effeminate) a boy would have been sold to a sodomitic brothel."

Also, speaking of Joseph's possible erotic feelings toward Benjamin, in whose sack he hid the incriminating goblet, Edwardes says, "The *Midrash Rabbâh* is quite decisive in telling how Judah accused Joseph of wanting to commit incestuous pederasty with kid-brother Benjamin: 'You are even like Pharaoh.' (Genesis 44:18); i.e., 'As Pharaoh lusts for males, so do you.' "

With all these kosher rabbinical comments about Joseph in mind, we return to our starting point to ask: Was Freud's furtive act of hiding the Egyptian objects in Abraham's case a generous, Freudianly innocent act? Or was it tinged with his psychoanalytical knowledge, augmented by his possible knowledge of Joseph's multivalent traits as revealed by the *Zôhar* and the *Midrash?*

The pursuit of these questions led me to David Bakan's *Sigmund Freud and the Jewish Mystical Tradition* and the following: "Both of Freud's parents came from Galicia, a region saturated with Chassidism, a late and socially widespread form of Jewish mysticism. Freud says explicitly, in a letter to Roback, that his father came from a Chassidic milieu. And from a paper by W. Aron we learn that Tysmenitz, the birthplace of Freud's father, was filled with Chassidic lore and learning. Aron also reports a conversation between Freud and Chaim Bloch in which they discussed Kabbala, Chassidism, and Judaism in general. Aron remarks, 'What it was that moved Freud to interest himself in Kabbala and Chassidism is not hard to understand. He must have felt himself to be spiritually at home in these worlds.' "

Yes, Sigmund Freud did have access to the rabbinical works that dealt with the story of his Biblical exemplar Joseph, but only he could have told us whether he knew what the *Zôhar* and *Midrash* said about Joseph, perpetrator of unconsciously homoerotic charades.

(Now, as we read the "Joseph" and "Potiphar" references in the rabbinical *Zôhar* and *Midrash,* an entirely new light is thrown on the story of Potiphar's wife: she was the love-and-sex-starved wife of a eunuch. And Joseph may have spurned her for reasons never taught us in Sunday school.)

20

My own ego finds it easy to hide behind people
[named Josef], since Joseph was the name of the
man famous in the Bible as an interpreter of
dreams.
—Freud, *The Interpretation of Dreams*

A Supplementary Self-Dramatization

Freud's hiding of the Egyptian objects in his disciple's case may have
been inspired in part by another Jacobean episode: When Jacob, wishing
to escape his father-in-law Laban's authority, eloped with Laban's daughter Rachel, she involved him in a situation almost identical with that of
Joseph and his brothers.

Without telling Jacob, Rachel stole her father's household gods and
hid them in her luggage. After a long forced march, Laban overtook them,
accused Jacob of the theft, and searched his packs. But he didn't find
them, because crafty Rachel had them hidden under her seat on a camel.*
(The Egyptian objects Freud "planted" on Abraham came from his collection of ancient religious icons and artifacts, his own "household gods.")

Have you noticed how intertwined these clustered Biblical names are?
They all come from the same small family groups: Freud was the son of a
Jacob; the Biblical Joseph was also the son of Jacob and the great-
grandson of Abraham. At different times during his life, Freud consciously
identified with Joseph and Jacob.

Also, by surreptitiously hiding several of his "household gods" in
Abraham's case, Freud seems to have crossed the sexual line to identify
with Rachel. Did he do so consciously? Unconsciously? Your guess is as
good as mine.

All this may seem confusing to some, but, as Freud taught us, the
labyrinthine unconscious mind possesses its own thoroughly consistent
form of illogical logic: it invests every action with a number of seemingly
contradictory, even crazy-seeming, motivations.

---

*A medieval rabbinical commentator wrote: "Probably Laban did not ask her to move
from her seat when she told him she was menstruating painfully."

21

. . . back to the Hotel Regina

In her *Tribute to Freud* (1956), Hilda Doolittle wrote: "Already in Vienna, the shadows were lengthening or the tide was rising. The signs of the grim coming events, however, manifested in a curious fashion. There were, for instance, occasional coquettish, confetti-like showers from the air, gilded paper swastikas and narrow strips of paper like the ones we pulled out of Christmas bon-bons. . . .

"I stooped to scrape up a handful of these confetti-like tokens as I was leaving the Hotel Regina one morning. They were printed on those familiar little oblongs of thin paper that fell out of the paper cap when it was unfolded at the party; we called them mottoes. These [Viennese] mottoes were short and bright and to the point. One read in clear primer-book German, 'Hitler gives bread.' 'Hitler gives work.' And so on.

"Was I the only person in Vienna who had stooped to scrape up a handful of these tokens? It seemed so. One of the hotel porters emerged with a long-handled brush-broom. As I saw him begin methodically sweeping the papers off the pavement, I dropped my handful in the gutter."

As she walked to her appointment with Freud, Hilda Doolittle saw more "signs of grim coming events":

> There were other swastikas. They were chalk ones now. I followed them down the Berggasse as if they had been chalked on the pavement for my benefit. . . . They led to Professor Freud's door. . . . No one brushed these swastikas out. It is not easy to scrub death-head chalk marks from the pavement.

22

This real-life incident experienced by Hilda Doolittle in front of the Hotel Regina in 1933 bears an uncanny resemblance to a personal dream published by Freud in his masterwork *The Interpretation of Dreams*, printed in 1900. The recorded dream reads in part:

I was riding a grey horse, timidly and awkwardly at first . . . (then) I began to find myself sitting more firmly and comfortably on my intelligent horse. . . . After riding some distance up the street . . . I tried to dismount in front of a chapel. . . . My hotel was in the same street; I might have let my horse go to it on its own, but I preferred to lead it there. It was as though I should have felt ashamed to arrive on horseback.

Freud then relates the part of his dream that seems so similar to Hilda Doolittle's real-life experience: "A *hotel* 'boots' [*porter* who shines shoes] was standing *in front of the hotel*; he showed me *a note* of mine he had *found*, and laughed at me over it. In the note was *written*, doubly underlined: '*No food*' and then another remark (indistinct) such as '*No work*,' together with a vague idea that I was in a strange town in which I was doing no work." [Italics mine.]

In his customarily lucid and convincing interpretation of this dream (I recommend it to every reader), Freud suggests that "his timid and awkward" riding of the "intelligent horse" might be a reenactment of the Jewish joke about a fellow Jew named Itzig who rides a horse in imitation of the enviable upper-class Gentiles. When a friend sees this ridiculous figure bouncing along, he shouts: "Itzig! Where are you riding to?" Itzig answers breathlessly: "Don't ask me! Ask the horse!"

This self-denigrating comparison mirrors Freud's great struggle to find work and food for himself and his family during his early days as a doctor in anti-Semitic Vienna. Clearly, in this dream interpretation Freud saw himself as a ridiculous Jew aping the Viennese Gentiles who rode, as the saying goes, "high and mighty."

When placed side by side, the elements in Freud's dream and Doolittle's actual experience prove to be almost identical:

Freud's dream: He is a traveler.
Doolittle's incident: She is a traveler.

Freud: He is staying at a hotel.
Doolittle: She is staying at a hotel.

Freud: "I was doing no work."
Doolittle: As Freud's patient she was also not working. Doolittle was doing little.

Freud: He reads the note (paper) found by a hotel porter.

Doolittle: She reads messages on pieces of paper swept up by the hotel porter.

Freud: The message on the found paper mentions the *scarcity of food and work*—*"No food"* and *"No work."*

Doolittle: The messages on the found papers she picked up refer to the shortage of food and work among the Vienna poor in almost identical words: "Hitler gives *bread*" *(food)* and "Hitler gives *work.*"

Freud: The hotel porter is the only other person in his dream.

Doolittle: The hotel porter is the only person mentioned.

Freud: The feeling of embarrassment is mentioned: He is "ashamed" to be seen riding the horse up to the front of the hotel.

Doolittle: When she realizes that the hotel porter has seen her pick up the propaganda papers, she, embarrassed, throws them into the gutter.

Freud: His dream ends with a little scene played at the front of the hotel where he's staying.

Doolittle: Her little scene is played in front of the hotel where she is staying.

Freud: He found the dream interesting and meaningful enough to include in his book, much of which is about himself, Sigmund Freud.

Doolittle: She found this incident meaningful enough to include in her *Tribute to Freud.*

A few days later the poetess left her room and found the hotel lobby and the streets completely deserted. When she arrived at Freud's office, the frightened-looking maid Paula ushered her into the waiting room, where she stared at a large print of Henry Fuseli's "Nightmare." She waited. "Finally, Freud opened the door and said, 'But why did you come today? No one has come here today, no one. What is it like outside? Why did you come out?'

"I said: "It's very quiet. There doesn't seem to be anyone about in the streets. . . . But otherwise it's the same as usual.' He said, 'But why did you come?' It seemed to puzzle him; he did not understand what brought me."

23

Snapping shut my notebook, I turned away from the Hotel Regina to look down the street Freud lived on: the *Berggasse* or *mountain lane*. As I did so I mused: "Berggasse, once a rural path . . . a steep, sloping lane, but hardly 'mountainous.' Still, it's hilly enough to qualify as the possible arena of Jung's 'Hagen-Siegfried' dream. In his account of that Freudicidal nightmare Jung refers to his place of ambush as 'a narrow path' at the 'crest of a mountain,' and as a 'precipitous slope.' These dream-exaggerated images match perfectly those associated with Vienna's (Freud's) *Berggasse* or *mountain lane*. Yes, Jung may have unconsciously selected the narrow street Freud lived on as the stage-setting of his Wagnerian 'Siegfreudream.' Jung may even have stood here at this corner, looking down the street, before he began his first walk to begin his ill-fated friendship with the man who would soon call him 'my crown prince, son and successor.' Them's fightin' words in Oedipal circles!"

Three days later, while repeating Freud's famous high-speed walks around old Vienna—at low speed—looking for places, objects, statues mentioned in his dream analyses, I came to the Vienna Parliament and was arrested by the sight of magnificent bronze statues of charioteers reining in their wild horses. As I stared at them I realized that Freud was confronted by these statuary groups every time he walked here; I then remembered the words I'd copied from Friedrich Heer's essay, "Freud, the Viennese Jew": "Outside the Vienna Parliament stood statues of charioteers. They were supposed to represent man's ability to control his urges."* Then, as if referring to Freud the *psych*otherapist, Heer said: "According to the Platonic parable, the soul [psyche] is a chariot from which the mind must direct the horses or passions."

Later, in a café, I reread these words in my notebook, and added: "Yes, Heer's words are a precise description of Freud and psychoanalysis.

---

*Freud: The Man, His World, His Influence, edited by Jonathan Miller. (Boston, Little, Brown, 1972.)

Freud, syndromist, seems to have assumed the role of that mythic charioteer, probably the sun god Helios. Jones says that Freud always invited his visiting disciples to join him on this daily walk round the Ring or to the museum which housed the superb Egyptian collection. I see it clearly: When Freud and Jung first walked past the Parliament, they stopped in front of the charioteers and Freud explained their symbolism to his new friend and future enemy. The name 'Phaëthon,' tragic son of Helios who tried to take his father's place in the sun-chariot, was mentioned—or carefully *not* mentioned. Later, when Jung awakened from his 'Siegfried-Siegfreud-Phaëthon' dream, he failed to recognize Freud's role as the dream's victim; he failed also to realize that he may have staged the dream *in Vienna*, merging two dramatic images associated with Freud: the street he lived on, the *Berggasse*, and the Vienna Parliament's spectacular *charioteers*. Distance of the latter from Freud's house? About a half mile."

My first response to "Freud's street" continued: "Like the rest of Vienna's 9th District, the Berggasse is lined with gray look-alike buildings, some with stores on the ground floor. The Viennese who've written about Freud usually call this street 'déclassé,' 'shabby,' even 'grimy,' but it doesn't look too bad to me; certainly more attractive and far cleaner than comparable streets near the centers of most American cities. Were the Viennese thinking of more elegant or prestigious neighborhoods? But Freud must have liked it here or he wouldn't have remained for forty-seven years, even when he could well afford a swankier neighborhood or his own house in a fashionable suburb.

"Did he stay here to be near the University, the art museums he loved and visited constantly? Did he want to be near the Ring he marched on every day until old age and illness stopped him? Perhaps, like Jonah, who camped outside the walls of Nineveh, angrily, stubbornly waiting for God to destroy the city and its sinners, Freud waited here, just outside the now-vanished walls of Vienna (an almost perfect anagram of Nineveh!) in the same manner and for somewhat the same reasons. But perhaps other less fanciful reasons for his staying here will appear.

"As I walked down the even-numbered side of the narrow street (for a better, earlier sighting of number 19 on the other side), I found myself looking also with faint apprehension, irrationally, for the 'swastika chalk marks' seen by Hilda Doolittle forty-two years earlier. They had, of course, vanished. In their place I suddenly 'saw' something else:

It is the summer of 1947. I am on assignment in Germany, stationed in Berlin, sent here to photograph and interview the Jewish survivors of the German concentration camps now living in Displaced Persons Camps; to record the American Occupation of this defeated country, and document the aftermath of war: the vast ruins of Berlin, Frankfurt, Cologne, Stuttgart—and the last of the Nuremberg criminal trials. Now my U.S. Army driver and I are on the way to the Austrian border, photographing as we go all the autobahn bridges dynamited by the Nazi SS storm troopers when they retreated from General Patton's tanks. The autobahn is so deserted that we have seen only one other vehicle in the last two hours.

Each time we come to one of the fallen bridges, I climb down the steep banks of the valley to make low wide-angle shots of the vast concrete wreckage, an awesome sight. At the bottom of each valley I see in the mud and grass hundreds of black-and-red swastika armbands, jackets, caps, torn-off uniform buttons with the SS insignia. They were thrown here in panic by the fleeing storm troopers who had tortured, mutilated, murdered American prisoners: they knew what would happen to them if they were captured and identified.

At first I greedily scoop up handfuls of these swastikas, buttons, and stuff them into my camera cases. But later (like Hilda Doolittle) I throw the accursed things away . . . out the car window, scattering them in the wind. . . . But somewhere among my files are negatives of the rotting and rusting swastika armbands and other Nazi garbage as I saw them lying in the mud and grass under the fallen bridges."

24

"A minute or two later I came to the middle of 'Freud's block,' and my Mission Control countdown . . . 39 . . . 37 . . . 35 . . . 33 . . . 31 . . . 29 . . . 27 . . . came to an abrupt halt when some bare-breasted mermaids caught my eye: This must be the Export Academy where Freud's younger brother, Alexander Freud (name suggested by the ten-year-old Sigmund after his hero Alexander the Great, one of the earliest of his self-dramatizations), transportation expert, taught. These naked mermaids or sirens— sandstone?—were put here, one imagines, to lure young men into careers in lands reached by sea in those days, the 1890s. Freud's son Martin heeded their siren call and studied here, he says, before entering the nearby university.

"But these aren't ordinary mermaids. They are, probably, repeated images of the tragic Melusina, the fairy-tale nymph, as she was seen when she was startled by the sudden intrusion of her vow-breaking husband (he forcibly entered her bathroom to discover that she was really a mermaid, half-human, with a tail of a fish or serpent). Is it an optical illusion, or are these Melusinas staring right at Freud's second-floor apartment? As *I* should be doing now?"

25

I turned from the Melusina carvings to give undivided attention to Freud's house, and was very disappointed. Except for a ground-floor marble plaque, number 19 was no different from the ordinary buildings to which it was attached. Though this had been obvious a block away, still, on closer examination one hoped to see something different, something worthy of so great a man. Yes, the Viennese who'd used the word "déclassé" were right. Did it look this uninspiring when Freud moved here in 1891?

As I continued to direct my pilgrim's gaze at the house, I observed and wrote: "Like all the others: five storeys high. Exactly like thousands of similar apartment houses in France and Germany—debased copies of classical buildings in Renaissance Florence and Rome. Over some windows are blank escutcheons which seem to say: 'No Hapsburg coats of arms or noble crests permitted here; only middle-class nobodies within.' Scattered nondescript floral carvings . . . a long row of dentals at roof level . . .

"Though it is getting dark now, I can make out two heads of Roman ladies over the jutting windows on the fourth floor. But, looking closer . . . the wavy lines around their faces are snakes . . . the eyes closed in death. These must be Medusas or Gorgons on Freud's house. Amusing! Amazing! Mind-boggling! 'That was no lady! That was Medusa!' Yes, this is Gorgo-Medusa as she must have looked after Perseus beheaded her in her sleep, and as she looked when Athena attached her bloody head to her breastplate to warn off all offenders.

"Did Freud, tireless negotiator for forty years of such mythic symbols in dreams, fantasies, and parapractic happenings, ever react to these evil-repelling resident Medusas? Surely, during his half-century here, Freud must have seen or sensed—or resisted and repressed—these images many thousands of times whenever he approached his house. Henry Miller once remarked that a work of art stares right back at the viewer, but Freud goes one long step further and tells us that all images stare piercingly at you even when you try to ignore them."

(Later, in the Freud Museum now installed in the professional half of his apartment, I saw displayed a Gorgoneion plaque of the sixth century B.C. This Medusa head, bought and profoundly studied by Freud, once hung in his inner sanctum in plain view of the doctor and his encouched patients.)

26

While browsing through Freud's case histories in search of dreams in which the seen-unseen commonplace street imagery might have played a part in the therapeutic process, I found two examples.

In the first, Freud reports: "One of my patients dreamt in the course of a fairly lengthy dream that he ordered a '*Kontuszowska*' while he was in a café. After telling me this, he asked me what a *Kontuszowska* was, as he had never heard of the name. I was able to tell him that it was a Polish liqueur, and that he could not have invented the name, since it was long familiar to me on billboards. At first he could not believe me, but a few days later, after making his dream come true in a café, he noticed the name on a billboard which (he said) he must have gone past at least twice a day for several months."

In the second example, more germane to Freud's possible responses to his own street and house imagery, he recalls some *carved façade figures, seen only once,* that became buried in his unconscious mind and haunted his dreams for twelve years:

During later years, when I was already deeply absorbed in the study of dreams, the frequent recurrence in my dreams of a particular unusual-looking place became a positive nuisance to me. In a specific spatial relationship to myself, on my left-hand side, I saw a dark space out of which glimmered a number of grotesque *sandstone figures*. A faint recollection, which I was unwilling to credit, told me that it was the entrance to a beer-cellar. But I failed to discover either the meaning of the dream-picture or its origins.

Then, Freud resolves the little psychic mystery: "In 1907 I happened to be in Padua, which, to my regret, I had not been able to visit since 1895. My first visit to the town had been a disappointment, as I had not been able to see Giotto's frescoes at the Madonna dell'Arena. I had been turned back half-way along the street leading there, on being told that the chapel was closed on that particular day. On the second visit twelve years later . . . in the street leading to the chapel, on the left-hand side as I walked along . . . I came upon the place I had seen so often in my dreams, with the *sandstone figures* [italics mine] that formed a part of it. It was in fact the entrance to the garden of a restaurant."

27

Two other well-known Viennese works of art became the *foci* of Freud's dreams. In one, to be discussed later in its proper context, Freud's dreamachinery transformed him into a mythological character he saw in a mural painted by Moritz von Schwind. In the other dream, a royal statue he passed during his daily walks around Vienna's Innerstadt provided the enigmatic words he spoke before he dream-exorcized the ghost of his friend "P."

A part of the latter dream reads:

My friend Fl. [Fliess] had come to Vienna unobtrusively in July. I met him on the street in conversation with my (deceased) friend P., and went with them to some place where they sat . . . at a small table. . . . As P. failed to understand him, Fl. turned to me and asked me how much I had told P. about his affairs. Whereupon, overcome by strange emotions, I tried to explain to Fl. that P.

(could not understand anything at all, of course, because he) was not alive. But what I actually said—and I myself noticed the mistake—was "*non vixit.*" I then gave P. a piercing look. Under my gaze he turned pale; his form grew indistinct and his eyes a sickly blue—and finally he melted away. I was highly delighted at this. . . .*

In his fascinating analysis of this neo-Gothic dream, Freud discloses the meaning of the mysterious Latin words: "It was a long time, however, before I succeeded in tracing the origin of the '*non vixit*' with which I passed judgment in the dream. But at last it occurred to me that these two words possessed their high degree of clarity in the dream not as words heard or spoken but as *words seen.* I then knew at once where they came from. On the pedestal of the Kaiser Josef Memorial in the Hofburg [Imperial Palace] in Vienna the following impressive words are inscribed:

Saluti patriae vixit non diu sed totus.
(For the well-being of his country he lived not long but wholly.)"

In a later edition of his dream-interpretation book, Freud added a footnote correcting his transcription of the words carved on the royal statue: "The actual wording of the inscription is:

Saluti publicae vixit non sed totus

The reason for my mistake in putting '*patriae*' for '*publicae*' has probably been rightly guessed by Wittels."

His acknowledgment of his unconscious mistake reveals his tacit agreement with Wittels's suggestion that he was in his dream a female prostitute, or "*Freudmädchen*" ("joy-girl").

In the biographical study Freud refers to, Fritz Wittels explains Freud's "mistake":

For the sake of my readers whose latinity is not of the best I had better explain that "*publicae*" may signify "*puella publica,*" a prostitute. . . . One of

---

The Interpretation of Dreams.

the German words for prostitute is *"Freudmädchen,"* the equivalent of the French *"fille de joie,"* or the Chaucerian-English "gay-girl."*

The rest of Wittels's analysis of Freud's dream relates to his response to his father. But as I read the interpretation, in which he links the name of Kaiser *Josef* to the image of a "public prostitute," it reminded me of the rabbinical speculation about the Biblical *Joseph* as a "male prostitute" in ancient Egypt. If this is a valid association, it would help explain Freud's self-confessed "mistake" in confusing the words *publicae* and *patriae* on Kaiser Josef's monument. The psychic equation may run something like this: Kaiser Josef=Biblical Joseph=male prostitute=*puella publica*= *Freudenmädchen*=Freud.

28

Perhaps the most amusing example of Freud's acute awareness and symbolization or mythicizing of commonplace architectural "adornments" in Vienna may be seen in his son Martin's published memoirs: After an amusing account of his father's daily obsessive "marches" around Vienna's Inner City, Martin adds an anecdote which, in passing, offers the devil and his grandmother as fellow residents of Vienna:

> Father might sometimes tell a favorite joke during our walks [around the Ring], one of a number which we had heard dozens of times without ever failing to be delighted. A certain part of Vienna, namely the Franz Josef Quay, had, like all cities, its share of chimney pots and other jutting-up adornments. My father often explained this phenomenon by telling us the story of the [*kaffeeklatsch*] given by the devil's grandmother. It seems that this old lady was flying over Vienna with an enormous tray upon which she had put her very best coffee service, a large quantity of pots, jugs and cups and saucers of devilish design. Something happened, my father never explained just what, but I expect she entered an air-pocket; at any rate the great tray turned over and the coffee service was distributed on the roofs of Vienna, and each piece stuck. My father always enjoyed this joke as much as we did.

---

*Quoted by Dr. Alexander Grinstein in his *On Sigmund Freud's Dreams.*

Did Freud, after his kids grew older, ever explain to them the nifty classic sexual and scatological symbolism of his oft-repeated "joke" about Vienna's *chimney pots* and other *jutting adornments?* Did he elucidate the scato-erotic significance of the *fly-grandmother* whose *enormous tray* spilled down a great quantity of (full? empty?) spouted pots, jugs, creamers, sugar-jars? A flying woman who loses such an array of bisexual parts seems closely related to Freud's well-known, presently disputed female who is consumed by "penis envy." Her grandmother?

A Chassidic or Zen-like parable given to his disciples at a seminar held at his home suggests that Vienna's airborne devil-grandmother may have been Freud's own *bubbeh.* When, during a discussion of Moritz von Schwind's painting of "St. Jerome Being Plagued by the Devil," Freud's reverent pupils likened him to the saint, Freud exclaimed: "You don't know, then, that I'm the Devil!"

And in a letter to Otto Rank (1915), Freud, referring to his painful self-analysis, wrote: ". . . that murderous firebrand and ever-active devil in me (who has become visible) . . . . (I must) bury him so deeply even from myself that I could regard myself as a peace-loving man of science."

29

As it is related in Ovid's *Metamorphoses,* the Medusa myth reads like a Freudian case history of an innocent woman whose sexual trauma and unjust punishment by a "mother figure" turns her into a murderess who is then—with the intervention of the hateful "mother figure"—finally destroyed.

Ovid tells us that one day Athena entered her temple and found the sea god Poseidon raping the lovely maiden Medusa. Enraged at this desecration of her sacred abode, Athena vented all her anger upon the helpless mortal victim, transforming her into a hideous monster whose appearance or baleful stare would kill any man she met.* Medusa survived in this

---

*Athena seems here to be aping Hera's irrational and unjust retaliation of Hercules, the innocent child born of Zeus's rape of Alcmene.

dreadful form until the hero of a tangential drama killed her: When Perseus, son of Danaë (he was the "shower of gold" baby), learns that King Polydectes is about to marry his mother, he responds Hamlet-like and tries to (a) delay the wedding; (b) procure a suitable wedding present; (c) prove he is a man; and (d) commit suicide by offering to hunt down and kill Medusa and to bring back her head as proof and trophy.

When Polydectes, wishing perhaps to rid himself of the Oedipal young man, agrees to let him go on this suicidal mission, Perseus's half-sister Athena intervenes. In a scene reminding one of a James Bond picture, she briefs him and supplies him with the magical gadgets needed for the nasty job: the *cloak of invisibility,* the *winged sandals,* and, most important, the *mirror-shield* which will enable him to look at Medusa indirectly while lopping off her head. Later, her insensate vengeance against poor Medusa completed, Athena wears the awful rotting head on her body armor.

Now, Freud's household Gorgo-Medusas reminded me of the rare Etruscan coin I bought in London in 1956. Hand-stamped in the sixth century B.C., the silver piece displayed the earliest form of Gorgoneion, an insane expression on its androgynous face, wild snake-hair shooting out in all directions, boar's tusks for teeth, and a mocking, obscene, protruding tongue.

At first the silver coin intrigued me, but something about it must have aroused a subconscious fear, because I soon lost the valuable piece and forgot it completely. But then in 1971, fifteen years later, while repairing a jammed mechanical "jig-dancer" in my antique toy collection, I opened its base, and there, sticking out her tiny clitoris-tongue at me, was— Medusa! How did she get there? I cannot for the life of me remember putting her into that box.

Soon afterward, on an impulse probably connected with my latent fear of the object, I offered it to an English coin dealer; when he made me a good offer, I, superstitious fool, sold the exquisitely ugly talisman from the mysterious Etruscan past.

Now, standing before Freud's house, I thought: "And ever since then Medusa has reared her severed head during most of my idea explorations. First with Herman Melville, then with Arthur Conan Doyle and Oscar

Wilde. Now she has reappeared. Will she tell me anything at all about the Romantic side of Freud's personality?"

30

The exiled Medusa first returned to haunt me during a reading of *Moby Dick*. While enjoying Melville's descriptions of the many masks worn by Captain Ahab—King Ahab, Milton's Lucifer, and others—I was more than startled to find the author saying: "His whole, high, broad form seems to be made out of solid bronze and shaped in an unalterable mould, like Cellini's cast 'Perseus.' "

Later, after exploring the implications of this strange comparison, I wrote:*

> Captain Ahab is linked to Perseus in several ways. First, Perseus slew the sea monster who was about to devour Andromeda. But his most famous act was that depicted in Benvenuto Cellini's statue (to which Ahab is compared): the decapitation of Medusa.
>
> Medusa? The beautiful severed head, with its writhing phallic snakes for hair, is the bisexual Gorgon's head that stalks Melville's *Moby Dick* and *Pierre; or the Ambiguities*, as his symbol of unconscious homosexual guilt. She turns men to stone when they gaze at her, even in their dreams or fleeting fantasies.

"When Captain Ahab (with harpoon) takes on the identity of the bronze Perseus standing with knife in one hand and the blood-dripping Medusa head in the other, we may deduce that if Captain Ahab is Perseus, then the white whale may be Medusa. But, if so, where in *Moby Dick* is she to be found?

"Melville's Gorgo-Medusa is first seen in the tortured soliloquy of Starbuck, who clearly identifies her presence on the *Pequod:* 'The white whale is their [Ahab and his crew] demi-*gorgon*.' Then, following up this clear identification, we read further in the great book and find two extraordinary scenes peopled by 'stone men' resembling those later

---

The Come As You Are Masquerade Party. (Englewood Cliffs, New Jersey, Prentice-Hall, 1970.)

painted by René Magritte or the 'living statues' of Jean Cocteau's fairy-tale films. They are scenes which reveal that Ahab's men have been turned to stone because they have seen the Medusa-whale or because they *wish* to see her.

"In the first of these mythicized tableaux, Melville describes the men who stand perpetual watch on the masthead, looking out for the symbolic whale. They are compared first to the men who once stood atop the Tower of Babel (punished by God); second, to the sentinels atop the Pyramid, where, says Melville, the idea of the terrible Jehovah was born; and third, George Washington, Napoleon Bonaparte, and Lord Horatio Nelson, all three 'turned to stone' and standing on their respective granite pillar-mastheads in Baltimore, Paris, and London!

"But the obsessed sailorboys who look out for Medusa-whales are not the only men metamorphosed into statues. One hundred feet below the *Pequod*'s crow's nest, the rat-infested forecastle becomes, through the fairy-wand of Melvillean metaphor, an underground Gothic crypt in whose 'triangular oaken vaults' (hammocks) the sleeping men lie like stone effigies of 'kings and counsellors in chiselled muteness.' "

31

> . . . his terrible glaring eyes that held you at his mercy.
> —Black Gorgiano, in Sir Arthur Conan Doyle's *His Last Bow*

In his *Adventure of the Red Circle*—based, I find, on the Zeus-Danaë-Perseus-Athena-Medusa myth—Conan Doyle split the ancient story and its characters into jigsaw pieces and then ingeniously reassembled them into his own version. (In so doing he anticipated James Joyce and other writers who have based their modern allegories on mythological themes.)

In the *Red Circle*, Sherlock Holmes is first a "Perseus" who uses several devices and methods suggested by Mrs. Warren, a landlady who has asked him to investigate the mysterious man who has not been seen since renting her top floor. One "device" is a *dark room* in which Holmes remains *invisible* while spying on the reclusive man—who turns out to be an even more mysterious woman. This device resembles, does it not, the "cloak of invisibility" given by Athena to Perseus for his "Operation Medusa"?

The second device suggested by Mrs. Warren, the "Athena" of this story, is also familiar: a large *mirror in the dark room* which enables Sherlock to look *indirectly* at the hidden woman's Medusa-like "beautiful, horrified face." Perseus, as we have seen, used Athena's mirrorlike shield to look indirectly at the sleeping Gorgon while he was beheading her.

Doyle, recalling also that Danaë's father imprisoned her in a tower to prevent any man from taking her sexually, has Gennaro Lucca hide his wife in Mrs. Warren's top floor (tower) to prevent her from being raped by the villainous *Gorg*iano, a male Gorgo-Medusa with "terrible glaring eyes." Thinking again of the old story in which Zeus transformed himself into a beam of light to enter Danaë's prison-tower to impregnate her, Doyle has his own "Zeus-Holmes" signal "Mrs. Lucca-Danaë" with a beam of (phallic) candlelight.

Finally, Gennaro becomes the second "Perseus" in the modern myth when he slays the Gorgonian Gorgiano in the appropriate manner: by slashing his throat from ear to ear, almost severing his head.

32

Medusa's Third Home Visitation

In his comic masterpiece *The Importance of Being Earnest*, Oscar Wilde presents his Lady Bracknell as a funny Medusa whose annihilating looks and withering appraisals reduce Earnest Worthing to zero. After she brutally vetoes her daughter Gwendolen's marriage to the orphaned "parcel left in the cloak room of Victoria station," Earnest complains weakly: "I've never met a Gorgon. I really don't know what a Gorgon is, but surely Lady Bracknell is one. In any case, she is a monster without being a myth, which is rather unfair." Later, this titled Gorgon inflicts her "stony glare" on Miss Prism, the nursemaid who twenty-nine years earlier, "in a moment of abstraction," had left the infant Earnest in a "handbag."

But Lady Bracknell is not the only man-killing Medusa feared by

Wilde's alter-ego Earnest. After voicing his dread of his future mother-in-law, Earnest asks nervously: "You don't think there is any chance of Gwendolen becoming like her mother . . . do you, Algy?" And Algy, who is Wilde's voice of truth, answers ambisextrously: "All women become like their mothers. That is their tragedy. No man does. That's his." (Even as these clever lines revealing Oscar Wilde's homosexual fear of and contempt for women were being uttered at London's St. James Theatre, the author was already embroiled with Lord Alfred Douglas's father in the scandal that destroyed him.)

33

GORGON, mythological creature whose look turned men to stone.
—*Oxford Unabridged Dictionary*

"I annihilated P. with a look."
—Freud, *The Interpretation of Dreams*

Sensing that the insidious Medusa heads of Freud's residence must have found their way into Freud's dreams and work, and also into the psyches of those stared at by the Medusas when they came to Freud's home, I searched the literature and found (a) his sketch, "Medusa's Head"; (b) several of his own dreams; and (c) the "Medusa" meditations in Hilda Doolittle's *Tribute to Freud*.

Here is, first, "Medusa's Head," the brief sketch for an extensive work abandoned by Freud:*

We have not often attempted to interpret individual mythological themes, but an interpretation suggests itself easily in the case of the horrifying head of Medusa.

To decapitate=to castrate. The terror of the Medusa is thus a terror of castration that is linked to the sight of something. Numerous analyses have made us familiar with the occasion for this: it occurs when a boy, who has hitherto been unwilling to believe the threat of castration, catches sight of the female genitals, probably those of an adult, surrounded by hair, and essentially those of his mother.

The hair upon Medusa's head is frequently represented in works of art in

---

Collected Papers, vol. 5, page 105. (New York, Basic Books, 1959.)

the form of snakes, and these once again are derived from the castration complex. It is a remarkable fact that, however frightening they may be in themselves, they nevertheless serve actually as a mitigation of the horror. This is a confirmation of the technical rule to which the multiplication of penis symbols signifies castration.

The sight of Medusa's head makes the spectator stiff with terror, turns him to stone. Observe that we have here once again the same origin from the castration complex and the same transformation of affect! For becoming stiff means an erection. Thus in the original situation it offers consolation to the spectator: he is still in possession of a penis, and the stiffening reassures him of the fact.

This symbol of horror is worn upon her dress by the virgin goddess Athena. And rightly so, as thus she becomes a woman who is unapproachable and repels all sexual desires—since she displays the terrifying genitals of the Mother. Since the Greeks were in the main strongly homosexual, it was inevitable that we should find among them a representation of woman as one who frightens and repels because she is castrated.

If Medusa's head takes the place of a representation of the female genitals, or rather if it isolates their horrifying effects from the pleasure-giving ones, it may be recalled that displaying the genitals is familiar in other connections as an apotropaic act. What arouses horror in oneself will produce the same effect upon the enemy against whom one seeks to defend oneself. We read in Rabelais how the Devil took flight when the woman showed him her vulva.

The erect male organ has an apotropaic effect. But thanks to an entirely different mechanism, to display the penis (or any of its surrogates) is to say: "I am not afraid of you. I defy you. I have a penis." Here, then, is another way of intimidating the Evil Spirit.

In order to substantiate this interpretation, it would be necessary to investigate the origin of this isolated symbol of horror in Greek mythology as well as parallels to it in other mythologies.

34

The Medusa head . . . is worn upon her dress by the goddess Athena.
—Freud, "Medusa's Head"

Am I looking at the Gorgon's head, a suspect, an enemy to be dealt with? Or am I myself Perseus?
—H.D., *Tribute to Freud*

The second Medusa influence: Impressed at once by H.D.'s superior intellect, sensibility, and profound appreciation of art, Freud conducted much of her treatment by means of a running discussion of some of the art objects that filled his professional suite.

This unique therapeutic method was established during their first meeting when the poet, "a lover of Greek art," became so overcome by Freud's collection that she temporarily lost her power of speech. But, as she tells it, she retained her responsiveness and stood there thinking: "He is part and parcel of these treasures. I have come a long way. I have brought nothing with me. He has his family, the tradition of an unbroken family, reaching back through the old heart of the Roman Empire, further into the Holy Land."

After keenly observing this profound shock-response to his collection—and her equally profound resistance to him—Freud said "a little sadly," "You are the only person who has ever come into this room and looked at all the things in the room before looking at me."

From that dramatic moment, says H.D., Freud constantly elicited her responses to the surrounding works of art. Once, "the Professor" led her into his adjoining study to show her two shrewdly selected pieces from the many on his desk.

"Did he want to find out how I would react to these little statues, or how deeply I felt about the dynamic ideas implicit in spite of the ages and aeons of time that have flown over them? Or did he mean simply to imply he wanted to share his treasures with me, those intangible shapes before us that yet suggested the intangible superior treasures of his own mind? . . . If it was a sort of *game*, a sort of roundabout way of finding something that my guard or censor was anxious to keep from him—well, I would do my best to play this game, this guessing game or whatever it was."

The nature of this deadly serious "game" played between these two geniuses is intimated by the two objects shown to the poet: first, as a teaser, a benign-looking Vishnu figure surmounted by a circle of Medusan serpent heads. Then, following this mild Gorgonian suggestion, Freud placed in H.D.'s hands his "favorite" from among his collection of more than a thousand pieces. "It was a little bronze statue of Athena, helmeted. One hand was extended as if holding a staff or rod. 'She is perfect,' he said, '*only she has lost her spear.*'" [Italics hers.]

Knowing full well that the doctor was goading her therapeutically about her previously discussed "penis envy," H.D. did not say anything. "He knew that I loved Hellas. I stood looking at the Pallas Athena."

The answer to the question "Why did 'the Professor' show his patient the two antique figures?" was of course known only to him, though H.D., no fool, must have guessed later on. But here is my guess: She was shown the Vishnu figure as a "warmup" to the far more provocative figure of Athena. Though Freud directed her attention to the missing phallic "spear," he knew that she would not miss the statue's most salient feature, which, as he says in his essay, was "the Medusa head . . . the goddess Athena wore on her dress."*

Did H.D. consciously or unconsciously see the confronting Gorgonian suggestions? She doesn't say so, but, as one may see in her book, the private Medusa exhibit plus the hovering façade Medusas, and the Gorgoneion plaque hanging on a nearby wall, soon had their combined effect; finally, under Freud's masterful guidance, the dramatic collaboration between this extraordinary duo reached its climactic hour of truth.

One day, as H.D. lay in her "Madame Récamier" position on the celebrated couch, her terrifying Greek hallucinations began to reappear. But now they were mingled with fleeting counter-images of the prophylactic Medusa heads to which she had been environmentally and therapeutically exposed. Later, while still shaken by this phantasmagoria, the analysand-poet recorded her experience: "Am I looking at the Gorgon head, a suspect, an enemy to be dealt with? Or am I myself Perseus, the hero who is fighting for Truth and Wisdom?"

Recognizing that she had been led by Freud to the inmost core of her problem, she added: "But Perseus could find his way about with winged sandals and a cloak of invisibility. Moreover, he himself could wield the ugly weapon of the Gorgon's head, because Athena . . . had told him what to do. He was able to manipulate his weapon, this ugly severed head of the enemy of Wisdom and Beauty, by looking at it in the polished metal of his shield. Even he, the half-god or hero, would be turned to stone, frozen, if he regarded it too closely and without the shield to protect him, in its new quality as looking-glass or reflector, the ugly Head or Source of evil. So though I did not make this parallel at the time, still wondered. But even as I wondered, I kept the steady concentrated gaze at the wall before me."

*In his fascinating Greek Myths, Robert Graves repeats the ancient belief that ". . . [Athena's] shield or armor was the skin of Medusa the Gorgon, whom she flayed after Perseus decapitated her."

35

What overwhelmed me were the terrible blue
eyes he turned on me and by which I was reduced
to nothing.

"I annihilated P. with a look."
—Freud, *The Interpretation of Dreams*

In Freud's two-part *"Non Vixit"* dream, which may derive its dominant
image of "killing with a look" from the influence of Freud's ever-present
household Medusas, we see his own ocular destruction of a "revenant"
ghost merging with his memory of an annihilating look of contempt shot at
him by his *father figure* Professor Brücke—a look which he reciprocates in
full measure. A convoluted but crystal-clear dream of Oedipal revenge,
dream-distortedly revealed.

"I had a very clear dream," writes Freud. "I had gone to Brücke's
laboratory one night, and, in response to a gentle knock at the door, I
opened it to (the late) Professor Fleischl, who came in with a number of
strangers and, after exchanging some words, sat down at a table."

And, as mentioned previously, Freud then adds: "This was followed by
a second dream: My friend Fl. [Fliess] had come to Vienna unobtrusively
in July. I met him in the street in conversation with my [deceased] friend
P., and went with them to some place where they sat opposite each other as
though they were at a small table. . . . Fl. turned to me and asked me how
much I had told P. about his affairs. Whereupon, overcome by strange
emotions, I tried to explain to Fl. that P. (could not understand anything at
all, of course, because he) was not alive. But what I actually said—and I
myself noted the mistake—was *'non vixit.'* I then gave P. a piercing look.
Under my gaze . . . his form grew indistinct and his eyes a sickly
blue—and finally he melted away. I was highly delighted at this and
realized that Ernst Fleischl, too, had been nothing more than an appari-
tion, a 'revenant' [ghost]; and it seemed to me quite possible that people of
that kind only existed as long as one liked and could be got rid of if
someone else wished it."

36

"The central feature of the dream," says Freud, "was the scene in
which *I annihilated P. with a look*. His eyes changed to an uncanny blue

and he melted away. The scene was unquestionably copied from one I had actually experienced. . . . It came to Brücke's attention that I sometimes reached the student's laboratory (where I was a demonstrator) late. One morning he turned up punctually and awaited my arrival. His words were brief and to the point. But it was not they that mattered. *What overwhelmed me was the terrible blue eyes with which he looked at me and by which I was reduced to nothing*—just as P. was in the dream, where, to my relief, *the roles were reversed.*" [Italics mine.]

"*The roles were reversed.*" In his study *On Sigmund Freud's Dreams*, Dr. Alexander Grinstein stresses the Oedipal suggestions hidden in the "*Non Vixit*" dream: "Ernst Brücke as himself does not appear in the manifest content of Freud's dream. Instead there are two figures from the Physiological Institute (Brücke's department): Ernst Fleischl and P. (Joseph Paneth, 1857–1890). By a reversal of roles, Freud himself is now able to reduce someone to nothing by a piercing look. Brücke had reduced Freud to nothing with his 'terrible blue eyes,' but now the tables were turned. Freud's ambition is realized in this dream, for in this way he is able to attain his long-felt desire to replace Brücke. He is 'highly delighted' by the power he has attained in the dream of being able to identify with this aspect of Brücke's omnipotence. Brücke's position as a father figure is obvious."

To this I would add: Freud's wishful dream replacement of his father figure Brücke is shown in the dream's beginning, when, as he says, he occupied Brücke's laboratory in Brücke's absence and conferred with people as Brücke did.

37

> Approach the chamber, and destroy your sight with a new Gorgon. See and then speak for yourselves.
> —Macduff in *Macbeth*, after seeing the body of Duncan

A digression: Freud's switching sexes to become a death-dealing male Medusa in his "*Non Vixit*" dream made me wonder if his idol Shakespeare, whom he quotes so often, had ever created a male Medusa. A search of the plays reveals two such references: in *Antony and Cleopatra* and the one quoted above in *Macbeth*.

When a messenger from Rome tells Cleopatra that her great lover Antony is married to Octavia, she, feeling that she is "turning to stone" from grief, likens the messenger to a "Fury crowned with snakes." (Medusa was sometimes depicted on vases as a Fury-messenger of ill tidings.) Then, assuming the role of Perseus for a moment, Cleopatra draws a knife and wields it in a decapitating manner. The messenger, clutching his throat, runs for his life.

Later, minutes before she places the fatal snake to her breast, Cleopatra repeats the Medusa metaphor, ambivalently, saying of Antony:

> Though he be painted one way like a Gorgon,
> The other way's a Mars.

The above quotation from *Macbeth* also offers a male Medusa, since it refers to the sight of King Duncan murdered (like Medusa) in his sleep by Lady Macbeth. The "new Gorgon" image also suggests that the overzealous Lady Macbeth sawed off Duncan's head with her dagger. (If Duncan is Medusa, that makes Lady Macbeth Perseus—a mind-boggling confusion of the sexes.)

38

At seven in the evening of that first day in Vienna, the genial hotel manager answered my questions Socratically: "Do I know a café where the food is good and students from Freud's old University 'hang out'? Yes, I do. There are several, but the one I recommend is there across the Ring in the Schottengasse, where the old city gate was. There you will find a good Hungarian goulash and many students."

I thanked him and turned to look at picture postcards on a nearby revolving rack. There were colorful postcards of Johann Strauss, the "Waltz King"; Schönbrunn Castle; "the beautiful Danube"; the houses Mozart, Schubert, Beethoven, Schopenhauer, Goethe, and Napoleon had visited, worked, prospered, starved, lived, loved, and died in. There were cards galore of the prancing Spanish Riding School horses. But not one of Freud. Nor did I find any during my stay in the city. It seems that thirty-seven years after Freud had been driven into exile, the Viennese still hadn't forgiven him for his repeated invitations to face the reality of sexuality in human behavior: they had erased him from mass consciousness. (The postcard I sent to my sister Edna in East Lansing, Michigan, reads: "Having fine time despite $1.00 for cup of coffee. Wish you were here. Obverse of card shows Johann Strauss fiddling while Freud burned.")

Though the respectable Hotel de France offers no postcard images of the world-famous doctor who treated sexual abnormalities, it does have a display rack (opposite the elevators) filled with cards offering cafés, jewelry, antiques, perfumes—and whorehouses. One card, with a drawing of a naked woman wearing only high leather boots and a smile suggestive of sadomasochistic fun and games, says: *"Privat Strip-tease für Sie! Strip-tease en Privater Atmosphäre."* And, translated, *"Home visits for qualified clients."*

39

The recommended café was filled with noisy, happy young men and women crowded around tiny tables served by agile, bustling waiters. In time the waiter who had found a window seat for me came to take my order. He looked like Charlie Chaplin, wore the famous little mustache, smiled and mimed and jauntily carried his tray exactly like Chaplin in *The Waiter*—a funny and clever impersonation.

The delicious hot, peppery goulash was unlike any I'd ever tasted in Cleveland's now-vanished Hungarian restaurants or in the home of our neighbor from Budapest; after finishing the mysterious delicacy, I eagerly awaited my waiter's return. Recalling Hanns Sachs's remark that every Viennese waiter believed he was a famous actor merely *pretending* to be a waiter, I wanted to test this comedian in a little improvisation.

When he danced up to the table to take my dessert order, I beckoned him closer and whispered conspiratorially, "Charlie, has anyone ever told you that your 'Hungarian goulash' tastes exactly like Texas *chile con carne?* But *mit noodles* instead of *beans?*"

He leaped into the improvisation with lightning speed. Mimicking my tone and manner, he answered, "*Mit noodles* instead of *beans?*" Then, looking about to make sure we were not being overheard, he whispered, "Yes, many Texans have told me. But be careful, sir; we are surrounded by Hungarian spies. If they heard you, it could lead to interballistic goulash war between Hungary and Texas, and I hate to tell you who would win." Then, straightening up, he said loudly: "Yes, sir! *Apfel strudel und coffee!* Right away, sir! Thank you, sir!" And off he went at high speed, executing all his skittery one-legged turns in sharp right angles just like "The Little Tramp." As I enjoyed a coffee and strudel, I looked about at the students and wondered, "Could this be the café . . . it looks old enough . . . where in 1882 Freud, twenty-six, had his little quarrel with his fiancée's admirer, Fritz Wahle? The comic tiff that erupted into another of Freud's compulsive identifications with royalty . . . and maybe even with Jesus Christ?" As Jones tells it: One evening, in a student café just like this, Fritz, Sigmund, and a mutual friend, Ignaz Shönberg, were talking about Sigmund's engagement to Martha Bernays. Fritz, still sweet on Martha, though involved with another girl, suddenly threatened to kill Freud and then himself if "Sigmund did not make Martha happy." When Freud laughed at him, Fritz shouted hysterically that if he told Martha to stop seeing Sigmund, she would obey him at once.

"When," says Jones, "Freud still did not take him seriously, Fritz called for a pen and paper and wrote a letter to her on the spot. Freud insisted on reading it, and the blood rushed to his head. He then tore it to bits, at which Fritz left in mortification. Freud and Shönberg followed him and tried to bring him to his senses, but he only broke down in tears. This brought tears to the eyes of Freud, and a reconciliation followed."

But shortly afterward Freud wrote to Martha: "The man who brings tears to my eyes must do a great deal before I can forgive him. He is no longer my friend, and woe to him if he becomes my enemy. I am made of sterner stuff than he is, and when we match each other, he will find he is not my equal."

After this bit of operatic sabre-rattling, Sigmund added syndramatically: "I can be ruthless. *Guai a chi la tocca!*" Jones translates this as: " 'Woe to him who touches it (or her)!' The cry of the Kings of Lombardy upon assuming the crown."

40

The Iron Crown of Lombardy

Jones's translation and comment on the Italian words uttered grandiloquently by young Freud reminded me at once of my own previous mention of that obscure royal crown in an essay about Herman Melville and his *Moby Dick:** After gazing in awe at the many "masks" worn successively by the Protean Captain Ahab: the Medusa-slaying Perseus, the evil King Ahab, the noble St. George, Vishnu, Prometheus, and Lucifer-Satan, I wrote:

"But before you choose your favorites from among these masks, you may discover as the late Charles Olson did in his *Call Me Ishmael* that Ahab carries a 'crucifixion' in his face. Now his mask begins to resemble Christ as he soliloquizes: 'Is, then, the crown too heavy that I wear? this Iron Crown of Lombardy . . . 'Tis split, too, that I feel; the jagged edge galls me so, my brain seems to beat up against the solid metal . . .' " Olson explains: "It is the Iron Crown which Napoleon wore. Its 'jagged edge' formed from the nail of the Crucifixion galls him."

Did Sigmund Freud, who could recite the coronation "cry" so perfectly in Italian, share Melville's and Olson's esoteric knowledge of the tragic Christ and Napoleon symbolism of the Iron Crown and withhold it from his "little royal princess" Martha? Did he recall and recite the coronation oath because of his resonant feelings of emotional "crucifixion" and illusions of grandeur? Jones's detailed account of Freud's sufferings during his long, frustrating engagement tells this viewer that the young man's anguished recital of the coronation "cry" was made with a full sense of identification with the kings who once wore the Iron Crown of Lombardy.

41

On another, later occasion, Freud publicly "performed" as Napoleon Bonaparte for a moment. During a lecture, Jones tells us, Freud spotted

---

*The Come As You Are Masquerade Party. (Englewood Cliffs, New Jersey, Prentice-Hall, 1970.)

his four loyal disciples, Karl Abraham, Sandor Ferenczi, Hanns Sachs, and Jones, "seated together in the front row."

"Freud made a graceful bow," says Jones, "and murmured, *'Un parterre des rois.'* " (An orchestra or pit occupied by kings.) In a footnote, Jones explains: "An allusion to Napoleon's comment in the theatre at Erfurt (Germany)."*

The captive audience of four kings and thirty-four princes who were forced to pay homage to Napoleon at Erfurt, seated among the groundlings, could not have relished Napoleon's sadistic crack at their helplessness and humiliation. Jones seems to have missed—or ignored—the implications of Freud's identification of himself with Napoleon, and his sarcastic likening of his four disciples to the "four kings" at Erfurt.

In his *Napoleon*, Emil Ludwig offers a detail in Bonaparte's stay in Erfurt which may help explain why Freud made his syndromic remark about the attendant kings. Ludwig says that Napoleon, thinking perhaps of the ulterior-motivated Hamlet's staging of a play-within-a-play, ordered a production of Sophocles's *Oedipus Rex*, his favorite drama, in the Erfurt Theater. Though Jones doesn't tell us the subject of the lecture during which Napoleon was quoted so aptly, we guess that Freud had (a) mentioned his famous "Oedipus complex." He then spotted Jones, who (b) had written a study of the dominant Oedipal factors in Napoleon's life. This combination of ideas then reminded Freud of (c) Napoleon's staging of *Oedipus Rex* at Erfurt; this in turn recalled Napoleon's ambivalent remark to the "four kings" who sat together in the theater's *parterre*, just as Freud's disciples, his own "Oedipal sons," did.

42

And ye shall compass the city, all ye men of war, and go round the city once.
—Book of Joshua

. . . the Ringstrasse, on that circuit around which my father used to storm his way.
—Martin Freud, *Glory Reflected*

When I saw that the café habitués were settling down to an evening of chess, checkers, reading, and conversation, I opened my notebook and

---

*In his biography, *The Life and Work of Sigmund Freud*.

city map to review the next item on my agenda: "A walk, weather and obesity permitting, around the two-mile-long Ring in hot mental pursuit of Freud. Recently, while reading Martin Freud's memoirs, I, always on the lookout for vivid examples of his dad's restagings, was struck by Martin's description of Freud's daily walks around the Innerstadt: 'My father began work at eight every morning, and it was not uncommon for him to work through until perhaps three in the following morning, with breaks for luncheon and dinner, the former extended to include *a walk which nearly always took in the full circle of the Ringstrasse*, although he sometimes shortened it to collect, or deliver proofs to his publishers.'*

"Freud's son continues: 'However, it must not be imagined that the excursions took the form of leisurely promenades designed to enjoy the beauty of the Ringstrasse and its flowering trees in Springtime. *My father marched at a terrific speed*. The Italian Bersaglieri were celebrated for the speed of their marching; when, during my travels, I saw *these* highly decorative *soldiers tearing along*, it occurred to me that each of them marched like *Sigmund Freud*.' [Italics mine.]

"Ernest Jones, who accompanied Freud on many of his walks, adds to the picture of Freud as a tireless walker over Alpine trails and city streets who 'left breathless' most of the younger men who tried to keep up with his high-speed military pacing."

Now, as I sat in a café on the Schottengasse, just a few feet from the corner where Freud began his daily circumambulations, reading Martin Freud's words, I wrote: "We seem to have here what a psychoanalyst might call a 'compulsive ritual.' On the conscious level it was a physical regime self-prescribed by a man working in the most sedentary of professions, but who loved to walk. What interests me is the *persistence* of his walk over so many decades, the *unvarying route* counterclockwise *round and round the now-vanished walls of the city he hated and loved* . . . past the government and Imperial buildings and churches which reminded him as he raced along of their bitter antagonism to him as a Jew, iconoclast, and ruthless exposer of their inner emotional secrets. And then: the *military manner* observed by his son who is reminded of the high-speed *foot soldiers*, all of whom 'marched like Sigmund Freud.' Did the son sense the powerful

*From *Sigmund Freud, Man and Father*. (New York, Vanguard Press, 1958.) Published in England as *Glory Reflected*.

unconscious motivations directing his father's march around the city? He doesn't say so. Nor does the immensely self-aware Freud, though he may have done so in his private journals or in letters which, I'm told, have been locked away by Anna Freud until the year 2000. This amazingly persistent walk reminds me, as it will many readers, of the Israelite promenades around the ancient walled city of Jericho."

As everyone (who hasn't forgotten) knows, the walled city of Jericho was conquered, not by military assault or treachery from within, but by a noisy, magical parade choreographed by Jehovah: "And the Lord said unto Joshua, 'See, I have given unto thy hand Jericho. And the king thereof, and the mighty men of valour. *And ye shall compass the city,* all *ye men of war . . .* and *go round the city once.* This shalt thou do for six days . . . and the seventh day ye shall compass the city, and the [seven] priests shall blow with the trumpets . . . and all the people shall shout with a great shout, *and the walls of the city shall fall down flat.'* " [Italics mine.]

The Israelites followed Jehovah's scenario exactly. Each day they marched around the city in vocal silence and returned to their camp. On the seventh day the walls of Jericho, assailed by the sound of tramping feet and the mass shouting, "came a tumblin' down." "And *they utterly destroyed all that was in the city,* both man and woman, young and old, ox and sheep and ass, with the edge of the sword . . . and *they burnt the city with fire* and all that was therein; only the silver and the gold, and the vessels made of brass and iron, they put into the treasury of the house of the Lord." [Italics mine.]

Many of the details of Joshua's attack on Jericho were uncannily duplicated by Freud and, later, during the fall of Vienna in 1945. Like the besieging Joshua, Freud encamped just outside the "walls" of the Inner City; he also "encompassed the city . . . once a day." But with a difference: he usually walked alone, unaccompanied by shouting multitudes and a priestly trumpet septette.

The similarity between Freud and Joshua—and Moses, who appointed Joshua his successor—is heightened when we read a letter Freud wrote to *his* appointed "son and successor" Jung in 1909: "If I am Moses, then you are Joshua and take possession of the promised land of psychiatry, which I can only glimpse from afar." (Freud hands over his Joshua role to Jung.)

This last "reenacting" remark may also help explain why Freud walked on the *perimeter* of Vienna's inner core, why he could never bring himself to live within the "heart of the city," as many other Jews did. Theodor Herzl, founder of the Zionist movement (who was also called a "second Moses"), did not hesitate to live just a few blocks from the centrally located St. Stephen's Cathedral. But then Herzl did not confuse Austria with "The Holy Land," as Freud did. Nor did he unconsciously mistake Vienna for Jerusalem.

Like his great model Moses, Freud did not survive to see the invasion of his "Canaan" and the fall of his "Jericho-Vienna." Had he lived only six years beyond his death in 1939, he would have "seen" the fiery destruction in the Inner City. Like the God-punished Jericho, Vienna's Innerstadt was nearly fire-consumed by the heaven-sent incendiary bombs and shells that indiscriminately killed "man and woman, young and old," along with the modern equivalents of "sheep and ox and ass."

For all this I divide the credit or the responsibility equally among the Allied bombers, the Russian artillery, and Freud's 9,000 vengeful walks around the metaphorical walls girdling Vienna's ancient Innerstadt.

43

In the course of repeated readings of the Joshua-Jericho story, I noted that one part of it supported Freud's dictum that human actions contain a powerful sexual component. I refer to the story-within-the-story of Jericho's harlot Rahab, the female "Quisling" who gave aid and comfort to Joshua before he decided to lay sonic siege to the city.

As the brief synopsis below tells it, she had a strong motive for doing so: she wanted to save her own life and that of her family. I speculate also that she may have been motivated by an equally strong desire to wreak vengeance on the community that had forced her into a "life of shame."

Here, as I've told it in an entirely different context in another book,* is that story-within-a-story:

Joshua, directed by Jehovah to conquer Jericho, kill all its inhabitants, and level it to the ground, began his campaign of conquest by sending two spies to appraise Jericho's vulnerability. This God-directed action is a curious heterosexual replay of His earlier and similar action of sending two androgynous angelic spies into the sodomitic city of Sodom as his genocidal agents.

*Naked Is the Best Disguise. (New York, Bobbs-Merrill, 1974; Penguin Books, 1975.)

The two spies infiltrate Jericho with the help of the harlot Rahab, ferret out the weak spots in the city's defenses, and are about to leave, when Rahab stops them. She knows, she tells them, who they are, why they have come, how the Israelites killed all the people in the other cities they conquered, and begs them to spare her and her entire family.

When the grateful spies agree, the delighted and relieved Rahab asks them to swear they will keep their promise. Later, the promise was kept: when all the men, women, and children were slain, Rahab and her family were spared.

44

During a recent talk with Henry Koerner, who spends part of the year in his native Vienna, I verified another possible exemplar for Freud's symbolical walkabouts, one much closer to home than Joshua.

When I asked Henry: "Didn't you tell me, years ago, that as a child you saw the political demonstrations in Vienna?" he answered: "Yes, I saw them many times. Whenever there was a crisis—and we had them every week—thousands of shouting, chanting people would march. Sometimes with military bands or drum and bugles. It was thrilling! And then frightening."

"Where did they march?"

"On the Ring. Always on the Ring, the boulevard that goes around the old Innerstadt. In the 1880s and '90s it was first the Socialists who marched. Then later it was also the Communists and the Nazis. Toward the end, there was more and more bloody street fighting and murders."

"Henry, what you just told me verifies . . . adds to a remarkable coincidence I've discovered about Freud. As I told you, he left his Berggasse flat every day to besiege the invisible powers of the Inner City. But another revolutionist of a different kind also left the *same flat* years before to lead demonstrations around the same circuit. He was Viktor Adler, the head of the Austrian Socialist Party and a leader of the Second International. He lived in the same flat at 19 Berggasse before Freud moved into it in 1891."

45

The image of Freud as the conscious-unconscious attacker of a Vienna-like walled city (in fantasy) is verified in a letter he wrote to Carl

Jung four months after he staged his alleged "Joseph in Egypt charade" with Karl Abraham. The letter begins:

> I have a great favor to ask of you. It has not escaped me that a rift is in the making between you and Abraham. There are so few of us that we must stick together . . . and a rift for personal reasons is less becoming in us psychoanalysts than in anyone else. I regard him as a man of great worth and should not be obliged to give him up, though there can be no question of his replacing you in my eyes. Accordingly, I have this request to make of you: be helpful if he consults you about the publication of his dementia paper.

Now we come to the dramatic point: Agitated by this threat of serious dissension in the ranks, the compulsive "actor" Freud assumed another of his masks to perform in a Sophoclean tragedy. "We mustn't quarrel," he adds, "when we are besieging Troy. Do you remember the lines from *Philoctetes:* 'These arrows alone will take Troy'?"

The Sophoclean line refers to the prophecy that the walled city of Troy would not fall until Philoctetes, using the poisoned arrows given him by Hercules, joined the siege to kill Helen's abductor, Paris.

Freud as a "Philoctetes"? Only Freud could have told us if he meant to suggest that he was the "slayer" of Paris. Suspecting there might be a homoerotic overtone here (who, if anyone, was the "Paris" in this Trojan fantasy?), I searched the indexes of the books dealing with such images and found "poisoned arrows" in Marie Bonaparte's Freudian study of Poe's *A Tale of the Ragged Mountains.** In the course of her exposure of Poe's latent homosexuality as revealed in this and other stories, Princess Bonaparte says, ". . . the unconscious (phallic) symbolism of a poisoned, snake-like arrow . . ."

46

. . . mythology and poetical language enable us
to add "city," "citadel" and "fortress" as further
symbols of "woman."
—Freud, *Lectures on Psychoanalysis*

Captured cities are symbols of captured women.
—Marie Bonaparte, *The Life and Works of Edgar Allan
Poe*

The Life and Works of Edgar Allan Poe, A Psychoanalytical Interpretation. (London, Imago Publishing Co., Ltd., 1949.)

> Helen, the most beautiful woman in Greece, was
> induced by Paris, with the connivance of Aphro-
> dite, to flee with him to Troy.
> —*Encyclopaedia Britannica*

Freud's assumption of the role of Philoctetes, slayer of Paris, invites an amusing Freudian wordplay: In German, "arrows" are *"Pfeile"* (masculine); but in English, fluently written and spoken by Freud, "arrows" and "Eros" sound alike. Using the free-associational method, we see that Troy, besieged because Paris, aided by the love goddess, had seduced and stolen Helen, was conquered with the matching sexual counter-weapon: the poisoned phallic arrows of Eros.

When we take this Freudian psychopun a step further, we see that with his use of the Philoctetes quotation Freud is saying, in effect, "We psychoanalysts are besieging the fortified (walled) establishment with my secret Herculean weapon: the arrows of Eros, or sexual determinisim."

(This reminds me, as it may remind some readers, of Freud's previous self-identification with Hagen, slayer of Siegfried.)

47

Freud's unconscious desire to destroy Vienna's metaphorical walls by means of his magical circumambulations may have been thwarted by their inherent counter-magic. In his *Mythology of the Soul,* Jungian H. G. Baynes says: "The ring . . . is the 'charmed circle'; from immemorial time it has been employed to protect the sacred place, the shrine or the dwelling place from hostile spirits. The circular earthwork such as surrounds the sun-temple at Stonehenge, the *circumambulatio* (parade) performed to secure the Roman stronghold, the circle used in magical practice—all demonstrate the universal cogency of the limiting ring to the primordial mind."

Early prints and drawings of Vienna show quite clearly that its walls were surrounded by a wide band of earthwork: the Ring now encircling the Innerstadt was built upon the old earthworks.

48

The image of Vienna as a metaphorical "walled city," a popular one in Freud's time, is commented on in Friedrich Heer's essay "Freud, the Viennese Jew"*: "Freud's 'unconscious,' " he writes, "is as much a product of the Jewish spirit as it is of Vienna, of the old Austria. In 1910 Karl Kraus published an essay entitled 'The Chinese Wall.' This was a Viennese catchphrase at that time (also used in the following context: 'the Austrians are the Chinese of Europe'). Count Heinrich von Lützow, a diplomat in the Imperial Service as ambassador to Rome . . . often refers to this Viennese 'Chinese Wall' in his memoirs, *In the Diplomatic Service of the Imperial Monarchy*, published in Vienna in 1971. The Great Wall was, in 1911–14, as Lützow emphasizes, what divided Austrian 'society'—that is, those nobles eligible to be received at court (you had to be able to trace your family back through eleven ancestors on both your father's and your mother's side of the family)—from all the rest of the population, and particularly from the middle-class intelligentsia."

49

Again: the popular image of the once-ramparted Vienna as a metaphorical "Chinese Wall," excluding the rising middle class and Jewish intelligentsia, seems to have inspired Franz Kafka's parable "The Great Wall of China." Like Karl Kraus and Freud, Kafka (of Prague) was a Jewish citizen of the Austro-Hungarian Empire who looked to Vienna as his capital. Like Freud, Kafka was denied admittance to the metaphorical "walled castle" ruled by an invisible Christian "Lord."

After his detailed account of the building of the immense structure he calls "the foundation of another Tower of Babel," Kafka asks, "Against whom was the Great Wall built?" With his characteristic ambiguity he answers, "Against the people of the north." He then explains that no one has ever seen the dreaded northern invaders: they exist only in propaganda cartoons and slogans used to frighten unruly children.

---

*In *Freud: The Man, His World, His Influence,* edited by Jonathan Miller. (Boston, Little, Brown, 1972.)

Like all of Kafka's luminous parables, this one invited interpretations which often reveal more about the interpreter than about Kafka's fables. Here is my perhaps self-revealing guess: To Kafka, scion of a Jewish family resident in Austro-Hungary for some generations, the mysterious "northern invaders" were probably the masses of impoverished Jewish refugees from the northern countries of Poland and Russia. (An example, Freud's father, a Polish Jew from Galicia, came south to Vienna when Freud was about three years old.)

I deduce that Kafka's parable was motivated by his prophetic fear that the Jews fleeing the northern pogroms and persecutions would inevitably create an anti-Semitic backlash against all Austro-Hungarian Jews, including Kafka and his family.

50

The combined image of a "dream interpreter" who is with an army besieging a Vienna-like walled city has been noted earlier in this book. In his *Interpretation of Dreams* Freud wrote: that Alexander dreamt he saw a satyr *(satyros)* dancing in a shield. Aristander happened to be in attendance on the King during the Syrian campaign. By dividing the word for satyr into *sa* and *tyros,* meaning 'Tyre is thine,' he encouraged Alexander to press home the siege so that he became the master of the city.

The reader will recall my deduction that the ten-year-old Sigmund Freud identified with Alexander the Great. If so . . .

51

It was well said of a German book that *"es lässt sich nicht lesen"*—it does not permit itself to be read.
—Edgar Allan Poe, *The Man of the Crowd*

As I sat in the Vienna café thinking of the putative allegory of Freud's tireless marches, and of my own analytical pursuit, there suddenly flashed before me the images of two nearly perfect matching characters from fiction: one, like Freud, a man whose inner compulsions drove him persistently to walk the streets of a great European city; the other, like me, a man whose aroused curiosity led him to pursue and investigate the "compulsive" walker. They were the mysterious *stranger* and the unnamed *narrator* of Poe's enigmatical psychological tale *The Man of the Crowd.*

In this well-known Doppelgänger story, written shortly before Poe introduced C. Auguste Dupin, the first "private eye," Poe offers himself as a detective of the psyche who compulsively shadows a passing stranger who seems to possess a terrible secret.

The Man of the Crowd begins with the narrator (Poe) seated in a London café, "scrutinizing" the passing throng with a clairvoyantly sharp eye. Like the hyper-analytical Dupin or the later Sherlock Holmes (modeled by Doyle after Dupin and Poe), the narrator is able to guess accurately the profession of everyone who passes by: businessman, beggar, nobleman, gambler, pickpocket, or prostitute. "Suddenly there came into view a countenance (of an elderly man) which at once arrested and absorbed my whole attention on account of the absolute idiosyncrasy of its expression." Thinking excitedly: "How wild a history is written within that bosom!" he responds like a bloodhound that has just picked up a fugitive's scent. "There came a craving to know more about him." Hurriedly throwing on his coat and seizing his hat and cane, he races after the stranger.

He soon finds himself engaged in a desperate pursuit. Though elderly, *his quarry is a prodigiously fast walker.* Now consumed with curiosity and caught up in the excitement of the chase, the narrator cannot quit. And so this strange, grim race continues hour after hour, with neither man stopping to rest, eat, drink, or pee.

At first the pursuer cannot fathom the manner, direction, and goals of the weird pedestrian, a modern successor to *The Flying Dutchman* or *The Wandering Jew.*

But soon, the flight pattern is understood: an agonizingly guilty conscience or inner necessity makes it impossible for the old man to be alone, even for a minute. So he races about the metropolis from one crowded place to another. But in every crowd he paces feverishly back and forth. When each group disperses, he rushes off through broad boulevard and back street or alley to find another place where people congregate. Finally, after twenty-four hours, the narrator, "wearied unto death," quits the chase. Defeated, he watches the perpetual walker plunge on to find another gathering.

Later, when I reread Poe's moving story to find the exact quotations used above, there came a second startling flash of recognition: "Perhaps it was this Poe-etic story that alerted me to look for the 'wild history written within [Freud's] bosom,' his incessant walks around Vienna's encircling Ring. Am *I* reenacting Poe's *Man of the Crowd* in my own life? At the moment it seems so. But, far more important, *did Freud know this story* and did he reenact the . . . ?"

52

Just before leaving the café (the pendulum wall-clock read 10:30 P.M.), I idly turned the pages of my notebook and found yet another "scene" Freud played in a café in the same neighborhood. It is a scene related to my previous discussion of the dream of the "Open-Air Closet (Toilet)" which you will recall (how could you forget?) as the one in which Freud washed away heaps of poo-poo with his mighty stream of pee-pee. You will recall also that Freud clearly identified himself with (a) Hercules, hydraulic cleaner of the Augean stables; (b) Gulliver, who made himself *pissona non grata* by extinguishing the royal palace fire with his fire-hose penis; and (c) Gargantua, who avenged himself on his fellow Parisians by drowning them in a flood of urine.

In the course of this psycho-urinalysis, Freud says:

> And now the true exciting cause of this dream. It had been a hot summer afternoon: and during the evening I had delivered my lecture (at the University) on the connection between hysteria and the perversions, and everything I had to say displeased me intensely and seemed devoid of any value. I was tired and felt no trace of enjoyment in my difficult work; I longed to be away from all this grubbing about in human dirt and to be able to join my children and afterwards visit the beauties of Italy. In this mood I went from the lecture room to a café, where I had a modest snack in the open air, since I had no appetite for food. One of my audience, however, went with me, and he begged to sit with me while I drank my coffee and choked over my crescent roll. He began to flatter me: telling me how much he had learned from me, how he looked at everything now with fresh eyes, how I had cleansed the Augean

stables of errors and prejudices in my theory of the neuroses. He told me, in short, that I was a very great man. My mood fitted ill with this paean of praise; I fought against my feeling of disgust, went home early to escape him, and before going to sleep turned over the pages of Rabelais and read one of Conrad Ferdinand Meyer's short stories, *"Die Leiden eines Knaben"* ("A Boy's Sorrows").*

Freud then adds: "Such was the material out of which the dream emerged. Meyer's short story brought up in addition a recollection of scenes from my childhood. (See the last episode in my dream about Count Thun.)" Here Freud is referring to his naughty eight-year-old act: after witnessing (?) his parents copulating, he "answered a call to nature" in their bedroom. Was little Sigmund being revengeful, or was he, as his later self would explain, trying in his infantile confusion to imitate the witnessed or fantasized sexual act between his parents?

53

SIREN, a mermaid.
—*Webster's Dictionary*

Sirens, sweet murderers of men.
Sirens, murderers of men's reason.
—James Joyce, *Ulysses*

Next morning, as I set up my tripod-mounted camera with its telephoto lens to shoot closeups of Freud's Medusas, I stared again at the four sandstone mermaids or sirens on the Export Academy and reflected: "Why didn't I *really look* at them yesterday? Tunnel vision, I guess. Much too involved, transfixed by the sight of great Freud's house and then those totally unexpected Gorgon heads.

"I read about mermaids, sirens, Lorelei and Melusina only two weeks ago while tracking the imagery of Jung's dreams about Freud, and here I am gawking at their sisters on a building across the street from Freud's house in Vienna. A small mythic world! The sirens were the cannibalistic sea nymphs whose 'honeyed songs' lured sailors to their destruction.

*This is repeated for emphasis.

Ulysses, forewarned, stuffed wax into the ears of his crew and had himself tied tightly to the mast so that he could hear the siren crooners and know when they were in and out of audible range.

"Freud may have reenacted that scene from Homer's epic right here in Vienna. Ernest Jones wrote that Freud had a 'marked aversion to music'; once when he and Freud entered a musical café, Freud, in pain, 'clapped his hands over his ears *to drown out the sound.*' "

Later, upon checking Jones's exact words, I see he made a "Freudian mistake" that shows he too may have been thinking of the Homeric sirens. One cannot *"drown out"* sounds by clapping one's hands over the ears. That action only *muffles* or *shuts out*. Jones may have been thinking of Edith Hamilton's words about Orpheus's rescue of the Argonauts: *"He snatched up his lyre and played a tune so loud and ringing that it drowned out the fatal siren voices."*

54

Now, as I stared at the Viennese mermaids, the kinescope in my penny arcade of memory flicked a familiar scene: Hanging on the wall of my workroom, a gaudy yellow display card offering "Cocktail Picks" made in Hong Kong. Stapled to the card, a transparent little box containing fifty tiny ivory-plastic nude mermaids, all innocently awaiting the fatal cocktail party where they will serve and then be thoughtlessly thrown away. To use one of these expendable Melusinas, delicately but firmly grasp her pretty little breasts, torso, and *popo*. Then pierce the cocktail *hors d'oeuvres* with her sharp little tail. (I cherish this example of kitschy commercial surrealism and plan to keep it unused in my folk-art collection. "You won't ever have to leave your snug little plastic box, dear Melusinas. As long as I live you are safe with me.")

Another sirenic item in my collection is a colorful little advertising card from a Victorian child's scrapbook. In this "humorous" chromolithograph, a school of sirens like those on the Vienna Export Academy have lured a clipper ship to its destruction on a coral reef—to steal its cargo of *Ayer's Natural Hair Vigor,* "a preparation which Restores Gray Hair to Its

Natural Vitality & Colour." In the foreground are four sirens, mirrors in hand, happily applying the dye to their long, flowing locks. Once again the male chauvinist image-maker has "comically" presented mythicized females who callously destroy men and property to satisfy their selfish vanity. Or so it seems.

55

The Berggasse rumination continued: "These sexy Melusinas, probably turned to (irving) stone by the rival Gorgons across the way, may have sent hot psychic messages to Freud whenever he looked out the second-storey window or walked out that front door. Did he ever gallantly, or nervously, tip his hat to them, or—attention, Freudians!—did he ever wave his cane at them flirtatiously or threateningly?" (As I looked at these figures, I did not anticipate how much they would later reveal about a certain hysterical charade performed by Freud ninety-three years earlier.)

"Yes, each of these sandstone ladies is a Melusina, from the waist up a beautiful naked woman, but with a fish or serpent tail, as she was seen at the exact moment when her husband broke his vow and surprised her at her Saturday-night bath. In Freud's symbology, the tail, the fish, the serpent are phallic symbols. If Freud is right, as he almost always is, then it would seem that the captivating mermaids of folklore and fairy tale were really *hermaphrodites*, which may account for their terrific appeal to their mortal victims and to the polymorphously perverse audiences over many hundreds of years. After all, it takes two to tango or fantasize: a storyteller must resonate with a reader or spectator on the same psychic wavelength.

"I know Melusina pretty well . . . read about her recently in S. Baring-Gould's *Curious Myths of the Middle Ages* (1880s) while looking for background facts relating to my suspicion that Freud was the intended victim in several of Jung's dreams. First I read Baring-Gould's chapter on Tannhäuser, the knight-crusader who lived with Venus within the 'magic mountain' Venusberg; then, after reviewing all the erotic legends about doomed men who try to escape from supernatural femmes fatales, I reread the chapter on Melusina."

As Baring-Gould tells it, the original French version of the familiar *Melusina* genre, as transcribed by Jean d'Arras in 1387, begins with what we call nowadays an "Oedipal twist":

> Out of compassion for his kinsman, Emmerick, the Count of Poitou, adopted his youngest son Raymond, a beautiful and amiable youth, and made him his constant companion in hall and in the chase. One day the Count and his retinue hunted a boar in the forest of Colombiers, and, distancing his servants, Emmerick found himself alone in the woods with Raymond. Night came on, and the two huntsmen lost their way. They dismounted, and were warming themselves at a blaze, when suddenly the boar plunged out of the forest upon the Count. Raymond, snatching up his sword, struck at the beast, but the blow glanced off and slew the Count. A second blow laid the boar at his side. Raymond then perceived that his friend and master was dead. In despair he mounted his horse and fled, not knowing whither he went.

After racing hysterically through the deep forest, Raymond finally stopped at an open glade "illumined by the new moon," where he saw three exquisite maidens bathing at an artesian fountain. "Raymond was riveted to the spot with astonishment. He believed that he saw a vision of angels and would have prostrated himself at their feet, had not one of them advanced and stayed him. The lady inquired into the cause of his manifest terror, and the young man, after a hesitation, told her of his dreadful misfortune."

The mysterious girl "listened with great attention, and at the conclusion of his story recommended him to remount his horse and return to the castle, as though unconscious of what had taken place. All the other huntsmen had that day lost themselves in the woods and were returning singly to the castle, so no suspicion would attach to him. The body of the Count would be found, and from its proximity to the boar, it would be concluded that he had fallen before the tusk of the animal, to which he had given a death blow.

"Relieved of his anxiety, Raymond was able to devote his attention exclusively to the beauty of the lady who had proved to be as wise as she was beautiful. During the rest of the night they conversed intimately and before the sun arose they knew they loved each other."

The rest of the story is familiar: Completely captivated by the "fair unknown," Raymond asks her to be his and she agrees wholeheartedly.

She then tells him that her name is Melusina and that she is a water-fairy of great wealth and power whose secret identity must be kept from all mortals. Also, for reasons she cannot divulge, she asks Raymond to promise her complete privacy every Saturday night: a breaking of his vow will force her to leave him forever.

Raymond agrees, of course, and keeps his promise, until one Saturday, when, goaded by an evil brother and his own mounting curiosity, he peeks through the keyhole of her bathroom door and sees that she is a mermaid with the monstrous tail of a fish or serpent. "Silently he withdrew. No word of what he had seen passed his lips; it was not loathing that filled his heart but anguish that he might lose the most beautiful wife who had been the charm and glory of his life.

"Some time elapsed, however, and Melusina showed no sign of having been observed during her transformation bath. But one day, news reached Raymond and Melusina that one of their sons, Geoffrey of the Tooth, had murdered his brother Freimund. When Melusina approached to comfort her husband, he turned savagely upon her and shouted: 'Away, foul serpent, contaminator of my race!' "

At once Melusina fainted; when Raymond, aghast at his words, revived her and begged forgiveness, she merely uttered a terrible wail of agony and "swept out of the window, never to return."

56

"At once Melusina fainted." Here, as in the case of Freud's two public "faintings in Jung's presence," Melusina's traumatic fall into unconsciousness obeys the classic psychoanalytical pattern: Whenever a person's powerfully repressed emotions (fear or desire) are *suddenly released or revealed*, the hysterical symptom (fainting, in this case) appears. The hysteric fainter is one who, finding himself/herself unable to face the consequences of the suddenly revealed inner state, escapes by falling instantly into a temporary sleep-oblivion-simulated death called *fainting*.*

---

*As explained by Dr. A. A. Brill in his *Lectures on Psychoanalytical Psychology*. (New York, 1956.)

57

> It is my experience, and one to which I have
> found no exception, that every dream deals with
> the dreamer himself. Dreams are completely
> egotistical.
> —Freud, *The Interpretation of Dreams*

Not long after my return from Vienna, while still wondering what role, if any, the haunting Melusinas might have played in Freud's psyche and writings, I scanned his books dealing with dreams and was astonished to find one in which *Freud himself entered the Melusina fairy tale* in the role of a "someone" who is unquestionably the vow-breaking Raymond.*

Here, from his essay "On Dreams" (1900), is Freud's brief résumé of his Melusina-Raymond-Freud night vision: "I once had a dream of a sort of swimming pool in which the bathers were scattering in all directions; at one point on the edge of the pool someone was standing and bending forwards as though to help her out of the water. The situations were put together from a memory I had had at puberty and from two paintings, one of which I had seen shortly before the dream. One was a picture from Schwind's series illustrating the legend of Melusina, which showed the water nymphs surprised in their pool;† the other was a picture of the Deluge by an Italian master."

As usual, Freud links this mythic Melusina reference to a personal emotional crisis: ". . . in the first place there was an episode from my engagement. . . . Behind this . . . lay an exactly similar scene from the time of our engagement which estranged us for a whole day." The incident being recalled took place nearly fifteen years before Freud wrote his dream essay. I marvel at Freud's persistence, his remarkable pre-Proustian remembrances of things past.

---

*Melusina and Raymond's "favorite son" was *Freimund*. The similarity of the names Raymond, Freimund, and Sigmund (born in *Frei*berg) may have played some part in helping Freud, also a favorite son, identify with the myth.

†My examination of the Moritz von Schwind painting of "Melusina Surprised at Her Bath" shows her as the *only* surprised and anguished fish-tailed bather among the many allegorical bathers in the large swimming pool referred to by Freud. Was the plurality of Melusinas suggested to Freud by the four Melusinas that stared at him perpetually from across the narrow Berggasse? I wish I knew.

58

Freud's further identification with the fugitive Raymond, who finally reaches the therapeutic fountain in a state of extreme anxiety, is mirrored in Freud's account of his dramatic dream "My Son, the Myops": "I was sitting at the edge of a fountain and was greatly depressed and almost in tears . . . a female attendant (appeared) . . ."

Though Freud assigns other more important explanations for his presence at the dream-fountain (which is near a "mental hospital"), the dream and its analysis do remind one of Raymond's therapeutic encounter with the crypto-analytical Melusina.

59

A comparative reading of the *Melusina* fairy tale as transcribed from earlier sources in the fourteenth century and retold by Baring-Gould in 1880 suggests, astonishingly, that the anonymous creators of *Melusina* intuitively anticipated the basic concept and *modus operandi* of psychotherapy. Or, reversing the comparison, Freudian therapy seems to derive in part from the treasury of ancient folk wisdom found in the Melusina legend.

Since, as we have noted above, Freud said he had seen and identified with the Schwind murals in Vienna illustrating Raymond surprising Melusina at her bath, we may assume that he also saw its companion mural, showing the moonlight encounter between Raymond and Melusina at the forest fountain. I believe further that Freud knew the popular version of the fairy tale, as familiar to Europeans as *Cinderella, Little Red Riding Hood,* or "the princess whose lips dropped pearls and roses."

In any case, some may agree with me that the following comparisons between the Viennese Odd Couple Melusina and Sigmund are thought provoking:

> 1. *The Melusina Fairy Tale:* Raymond has suffered a severe trauma. He is *suffering terrible guilt feelings* because he has unintentionally *killed his surrogate father* (and unconsciously killed in

symbolic form his true father, who had rejectingly given him away for adoption). The hunted boar, in Freudian terms, may have been a disguised form of his true father.

Freudian Psychotherapy: After discovering the role of the universal Oedipus complex as a major factor in neuroses, in drama and fantasy, Freud routinely isolates the Oedipal elements in his patients, or in his analyses of literary works and historical personalities. Every human is profoundly affected by his/her relationship to parents.

2. *Melusina:* Fleeing in wild confusion (derangement), lost in a dense forest, a well-known metaphor for mental bewilderment, Raymond is magnetically drawn to the therapeutic arena. He sees three beautiful maidens (the Three Fates?) at an artesian fountain, a classical symbol of purifying, regenerating wisdom issuing from Mother Earth. It is a place of symbolic rebirth.

   Freud: After becoming figuratively "lost in the (mental) woods," desperate patients finally arrive at the therapeutic arena, Freud's consulting room. They come to this fount of healing and wisdom seeking psychic regeneration or rebirth. (Outside, across the narrow street the Melusinas sympathetically watch their comings and goings.)

3. *Melusina:* Baring-Gould writes: "She inquired into the cause of his manifest terror."

   Freud: Like every other analyst, Freud also inquired into the cause of the manifest distress displayed by the patient at the first session. The same sympathetic questions were asked: "What is your problem? How can I help you?"

4. *Melusina:* After hesitating, her patient Raymond, who effected an immediate transference because of her mystery and beauty, told her of his "dreadful misfortune."

   Freud: Similarly, after hesitating, Freud's patients told this awesome authority figure (some refer to him as though he were a "Supreme Being") of their real or imagined misfortunes and problems.

5. *Melusina:* "She listened with great attention."
   Freud: In the long history of that rare art, *no one* ever listened more attentively to another person than did Freud.

6. *Melusina:* After listening sympathetically, analytically, to Raymond's recital, Melusina believes in his innocence and offers guilt-relieving explanations. The telling of the story, her sympathy and belief as well as her quasi-legal advice cure him instantly. (This happens only in fantasies, of course.)
   Freud: After listening to his patients far longer than Melusina did, Freud tried to help them in a variety of guilt-relieving ways. In many cases, like Melusina, he suggested techniques for dealing with personal and social problems; he collaborated in various rehabilitative actions.

7. *Melusina:* The patient Raymond is, in Baring-Gould's exact pre-Freudian words, "relieved of anxiety."
   Freud: The *relief of anxiety* is, of course, one of the principal aims of Freudian as well as all other psychotherapeutic methods based on his work.

8. *Melusina:* She advised him to act as though "unconscious" of his actions or his inner sense of terror or guilt.
   Freud: He advised his patients to act publicly as if unconscious of their grave problems, not to discuss them.

9. *Melusina:* Raymond falls in love with Melusina, his analyst-advisor.
   Freud: His method requires the temporary transference of love from the patient to the doctor.

10. *Melusina:* After their prolonged mouth-to-mouth session, Raymond asks his "therapist" to be his.
    Freud: A serious problem arising from the patient-doctor relationship was the sometime sexual advances of the patient. Freud's friend and colleague, Dr. Josef Breuer, quit analysis because, says Jones, one of his patients hysterically accused him of causing her phantom pregnancy.

If this ten-fold comparison between the mythic Melusina and the utterly real Dr. Sigmund Freud is valid, then, with due respect for the far greater complexity of Freud's scientific methods, I nominate Melusina as one of the first psychotherapists of either sex. Perhaps she was the very first woman lay analyst. (I know of only one other figure in either the real or the fantasy world who may have anticipated a part of the Freudian method for curing severely maladjusted men and women: he was the remarkable fourth-century miracle-worker St. Nicholas of Myra (later Santa Claus).*

60

Here is an odd and amusing coincidence: The name of the alleged pre-Freudian "psychoanalyst," Melusina, is similar to the first name of one of Freud's most distinguished disciples, Dr. Melanie Klein:

M   E   L   (US)   I   N   A
M   E   L   (US)   A   N   I   E

Fantasy: When Melusina saw Melanie arrive at Freud's front door, did she wink or wave her tail at her? Or did she jealously ignore this latest usurper of her role as pioneer analyst of either sex? Also: Did Freud accept her as a pupil and later colleague because . . . ? No, that's stretching the "fantasy" too far!

61

Pleased at the fulfillment of my detective guess that Melusina had entered Freud's therapeutic methods and nocturnal dream theater, I turned my attention to other aspects of his life. But then one day while browsing through his *Collected Letters*, I stumbled upon another Melusina reference: a letter written to his future wife in which *Freud openly identified her and himself with Melusina and her husband.*

Moreover, a close study of this Melusina reference, when seen in the

---

*Those interested in St. Nicholas as protopsychoanalyst may consult my essay in *Confessions of a Trivialist.* (New York, Penguin Books, 1972.)

context of Freud's "secret engagement," has led to an even more exciting discovery: Obeying his syndromic habit of reliving scenes (abreaction) from certain historical, mythic, and fictional sources, young *Freud had twice physically "acted out" the climactic incident in Goethe's version of the ancient Melusina legend.*

In this remarkable letter, written just two days after his unannounced betrothal, Freud began by thanking Martha Bernays for sending him a *miniature* likeness of herself. (The word "miniature" is important to the Melusina-Freud revelations that follow.)

> Your lovely photograph . . . the more I stare at it the more it resembles the beloved object. . . . But the precious picture does not move, it just seems to say . . . I am but a symbol, a shadow cast upon paper. . . . I would like to give the picture a place among my household gods* that hang above my desk, but while I can display the severe faces of the men I revere, the delicate face of the girl I have to hide and lock away. It lies in your little box and I hardly dare confess how often during the past twenty-four hours I have locked my door and taken it out to refresh my memory.

With this tender prologue about a *miniature image concealed in a box,* the compulsive mythographer launches another of his identification dramas, which, just a month later, exploded into an act of self-revealing hysteria.

The letter continues:

> And all the time I kept thinking that somewhere I had read about *a man who carried his sweetheart around with him in a little box* . . . and having racked my brains I realized that it must be *The New Melusina,* the fairy tale in Goethe's *Wilhelm Meister's Wanderings.* I took down the book and found my suspicions confirmed. The most tantalizing superficial allusions kept appearing here and there; *behind the story's every feature lurked a reference to ourselves;* and when I remembered what store my little girl sets by my being taller than she is *I had to throw the book away, half-amused, half-annoyed, and comfort myself that my Martha is not a mermaid* but a lovely human being. As yet we don't see humor in the same things, which is why you may be disappointed when you read this little story. And *I prefer not to tell you all the crazy and serious thoughts that crossed my mind while reading it.* [Italics mine.]

---

*Instead of referring to his little gallery of photographs in a neutral manner, syndromist Freud here likens himself to an ancient Roman with "household gods." Not a very Jewish thing to do.

Wondering "What were the 'crazy and serious thoughts' that crossed Freud's mind as he read the story behind whose every feature lurked a reference to himself and his 'little girl,' " I read Goethe's story and found that Freud had damned good reason to "throw the book away."

In the classic "story-within-a-story" referred to by Freud, Goethe merged the well-known d'Arras version of *Melusina*, as told above, with the equally well known pre-Wagnerian legend of Tannhäuser, mixed with story elements taken from the fairy tale *Tom Thumb* and Swift's *Gulliver's Travels*. (Soon, after placing the essential details of the d'Arras and Goethe versions of *Melusina* firmly in the reader's mind, I will show their acute relevance to Freud's conscious and unconscious suffering during his betrothal.)

Goethe introduces his "New Melusina" as a mysterious beauty of great wealth who travels alone "without servants or maid" in a splendid "double coach with four horses." Upon her arrival at a country inn, Redcloak, a "gay young blade" on the make, seeing that she is alone, leaps forward to help her down from her carriage. She graciously accepts his help, asks him to carry her little strongbox, and then invites him to dine with her. That night they become lovers, and she invites him to accompany her on her travels.

At a business conference the next morning Redcloak is told:

> If you mean to attach yourself to my service, here are the terms. I am come hither to visit with a lady friend from time to time. Meanwhile I desire that my carriage and this box be taken forward. Will you do this for me? You have nothing to do but carefully lift the box in and out of the carriage seeing that no harm comes to it. Guard it with your life.
>
> When you enter an inn, it is to be put into a chamber by itself, in which you must neither sit nor sleep. You lock the chamber door with this key, which will open and shut any lock. It has the peculiar property that no lock shut by it can be opened in the interim.

Redcloak scrupulously obeyed her instructions and traveled alone to the agreed-upon destination. But during one long stretch, delayed, he did not arrive at a scheduled inn until well after dark. As he rode along with the box securely fastened to the seat next to him, he suddenly became aware of a light inside the box. He had always been most curious about the contents of the mysterious box ("Does it contain precious gems?") and, as he says, "set about investigating. I postured myself as well as might be so that my eye was in immediate contact with the chink from which the light emanated. But how great was my astonishment when a fair apartment, well lighted and furnished with much taste and costliness, met my inspection; just as if I had been looking down through a dome into a royal suite! A fire was burning in the grate, and before it stood an armchair."

Holding his breath, Redcloak continues his observation:

> And now entered from the other side of the apartment a lady with a book in her hand, whom I recognized as my mistress Melusina, though her figure was contracted into the extreme of diminution.
>
> She sat down in the chair by the fire to read, and trimmed the coals with the most dainty pair of tongs; and in the course of her movements, I could see that this fairest little creature was in a family way . . . the next moment, when I bent down to look again and convince myself that it was no dream, the light within the box had vanished and my eye rested on empty darkness. . . . How amazed, nay, terrified, I was, you may easily conceive.

Redcloak's amazement and terror soon yield to his greater love and dependency upon Melusina, and, in the words remembered almost verbatim by Freud, he says to himself, "Is it so great a misfortune, after all, to have a wife who, from time to time, becomes a dwarf one must carry about with him in a casket? Were it not much worse if she became a giantess, and put her husband in a box?" (The reader has already observed all of the Freud and Ibsen imagery in Goethe's earlier fantasy, especially the images of a woman and a man reduced to the size of dolls, living in a doll's house.)

When the weeping, distraught Melusina reappears, she confirms her lover's worst fears: his discovery of her secret compels her to leave him forever. Redcloak begs her to remain with him; in the ensuing dialogue she explains who she really is and why she must part from him forever.

Melusina is the daughter of King Eckwald, "dread sovereign of the race of dwarf fairies," a race with grave biological problems. Through constant inbreeding the royal family had become weakened, growing smaller and smaller. To meet this crisis, royal princesses were sent regularly into the world of mortals to breed with human studs. Now, mission accomplished, Melusina was returning to her Lilliputian kingdom.

62

Behind [*The New Melusina's*] every feature
lurked a reference to ourselves.
—Freud, letter to Martha Bernays, June 19, 1882

Martha presented him with an [engagement] *ring*
. . . Freud wore it on his *little finger.*
—Jones, *The Life and Work of Sigmund Freud*

I was directed to hold out *the little finger* of my
right hand. . . . Melusina quite softly pulled the
ring from her finger and let it run along mine.
—Goethe, *The New Melusina,* from *Wilhelm Meister's
Wanderings*

In a scene staged by Goethe in a rural setting suggestive of the Garden
of Eden, the love-maddened Redcloak begs the fairy princess to take him
with her. She finally agrees and *signals their betrothal by silently placing on
his little finger the magical size-changing ring given her by her father.*
"That instant," recalls Redcloak, "I felt a violent twinge in my finger,
the ring shrank together and tortured me horribly, I gave a loud cry. . . ."
An instant later he finds himself reduced to grasshopper size, standing
alone among blades of grass now taller than trees; soon, Melusina,
similarly reduced, joins him and they embrace joyfully in their new-found
mini-world. Bidding him follow her, she leads him to a gigantic structure
which he recognizes as the portable doll's house. "Go to it, my friend,"
says Melusina, "and do but knock on it with your ring and thou shalt see
wonders."

He obeys, and at once the box expands in all directions to become a
vast palace into which they walk hand in hand. At the end of a long
corridor they enter an apartment which Redcloak recognizes as the "royal
suite" he had seen while peeping into the portable strongbox; astonished,
frightened, he realizes that he too has become a mini-person living within
a doll's house.

The stirring music of a military band is heard; and soon, at the head of
a magnificent procession, King Eckwald appears to congratulate his
daughter on the completion of "Operation Pregnancy" and to welcome
Redcloak as his son-in-law. He "orders the nuptial ceremony to take place
on the morrow."

"A cold sweat came over me as I heard him speak of marriage," says Redcloak. And then, in a strange *non sequitur* that reminds one of Freud's "aversion to music" and the fatal siren songs that lure men to their deaths, Redcloak adds: "For I dreaded marriage even more than music, which had of old appeared to me the most hateful thing on earth."

The rest of Goethe's *The New Melusina* is derived mainly from the German legend of Tannhäuser, the knight-crusader and minnesinger who lived with Venus deep within the Venusberg, or *"Mons Veneris."* Finally sated with Venus's divine lovemaking, the luxurious life free from all care, and the promise of immortality, Tannhäuser escaped to Rome, where he confessed his sins to Pope Urban VI. When the pope heard Tannhäuser had been the pagan goddess's lover, he said sternly: "I can no more pardon you than this staff I hold can bear blossoms." Three days after Tannhäuser left Rome to return to the Venusberg, the miracle occurred: the papal staff began to send forth green shoots. Messengers were sent to find Tannhäuser, but he was never seen again. (When Richard Wagner brought the score of his opera *Venusberg* to Dresden for publication, he was told that the local medical students and faculty were laughing their fool heads off at Wagner's *"Mons Veneris."* The name of the opera was changed at once to *Tannhäuser*.)

63

After King Eckwald forced Redcloak to marry Melusina, the highly reluctant bridegroom found himself thinking only of his terrible mistake in allowing love to imprison him in the miniature fairy kingdom. "I felt within myself a scale of bygone greatness, and it rendered me restless and cheerless. I had an ideal of myself, and often in my dreams I appeared as a giant. In short, my wife, my ring, my dwarf figure, and so many other bonds and restrictions made me utterly miserable, and I began to think only of obtaining my deliverance.

"Persuaded that the whole magic of my captivity lay in the magic ring," Redcloak borrowed tools from the court jeweler and, after secretly working for some time, finally cut through and broke the ring asunder. At once he shot up to normal size, and hastened to join human society. Many years later, as a "surgeon-barber," he met and told Wilhelm Meister the amazing story of his love affair with Melusina.

64

> And the Lord God commanded the man, saying, of every tree in the garden thou mayest freely eat; but of the tree of good and evil thou shalt not eat of it, for the day thou eatest thereof, thou shalt surely die.
>
> She took the fruit thereof, and did eat, and she gave it also unto her husband, and he did eat . . . so the Lord God drove out them and he placed at the east of the Garden of Eden the cherubim, and the flaming sword which turned every way, to guard the Tree of Life.
> —Book of Genesis

Like every "accident," slip of the tongue, dream, fantasy, or bungled action dissected and explained by Freud after he discovered the secrets of the stratified mind, his own "accidents," fantasies, and actions at the beginning of his long secret engagement may be observed on at least two levels. On the surface: an "innocent," conventional young man eager and willing to assume the roles of lover, husband, father, and bourgeois householder.

But, as I learned at the end of the "Melusina-Freud" trail, there was another man inside: a highly reluctant Sigmund, who, like many young men before and after him, dreaded the ego-diminishing, imprisoning chains of love and matrimony and who "acted out" that dread in scenes he wrote, directed, and acted in his private romantic theater. (However, as all who knew him testify, Freud did overcome his private resistances to assume the roles the majority of his internal Parliament voted for. From all accounts Freud was as successful in marriage as any man of his towering genius and tumultuous but controlled personality—and sexual complexity—could possibly be. And, says Jones, all of his six children adored him.)

As background to the "hysterical attack suffered by Freud" I have been hinting at, here, taken from Jones's biography, is a brief account of the early rounds of the Sigmund Freud–Martha Bernays engagement.

One day in April 1882, more than a decade before he began the creation of psychoanalysis, the twenty-six-year-old Freud came home and met two visiting girls, Martha and Minna Bernays. But instead of merely nodding and then rushing into his room to study, as he usually did, he was "arrested," says Jones, "by the sight of a merry maiden [Martha] peeling an apple; then, to the general surprise of the family," he joined the group. (Was he *arrested* by a scene which reminded him unconsciously of the apple incident in the Garden of Eden? Did this modern Eve coyly tempt him with a slice, and did he accept and eat of the (forbidden) fruit of the tree of good and evil? Or, using his own later mode of thinking, was it also the sight of the phallic knife cutting into the fruit (breast, testicles, seed-womb) that *arrested* him? I ask these loaded questions because, as we shall see, the "cutting knife" image was repeated at least four times during the first phase of Freud's engagement: three times "innocently," the fourth time violently and most revealingly.

65

> I was wandering in the Garden of Eden all the
> while with Dora . . . she was a Fairy, a Sylph.
> —Charles Dickens, *David Copperfield*

The provocative questions above are not merely rhetorical or fanciful; they were suggested by a letter Freud wrote just a few months after he first met the "merry maiden peeling an apple." After returning from a visit to Martha in Wandsbek, a suburb of Hamburg, Germany, the newly betrothed Sigmund ecstatically recalled a walk through a public *garden* and identified, again, with legendary characters:

> Oh, the Prater [Vienna park] is a *paradise*, but the Wandsbek *grove* is more beautiful because *we were alone like Adam and Eve.* . . . Eve wore a brown dress as befitted the changed conditions and a great big hat that wanted never to stay on, and the Almighty had placed seats under *the lovely trees, all of which were ours,* and *nowhere could be seen an angel with flaming sword.* [The

knife image again.] Only one little angel with emerald eyes and two sweet lips, which, refusing to be closed, had to be closed with kisses. [Italics mine.]

The infatuated young man ended this letter with more of the mythic same, which I include as prelude to his later violent reenactment of the climactic scene in the Melusina fairy tale.

Ah, the magic carpet that carried me to you is torn, the winged horses which gracious fairies used to send, even the fairies themselves, no longer arrive; the magic hoods are no longer available, the whole world is prosaic. All that it asks is, "What do you want, my child?" You shall have it in time. Patience is the only magic word.

An added verification of Freud's pomological awareness may be seen in his *Interpretation of Dreams* (1900), where Freud quoted and stressed the following lines from Goethe's *Faust:*

FAUST
(dancing with Young Witch)

A *lovely dream* once came to me,
And I beheld an *apple-tree,*
On which two lovely apples shone.
They charmed me so, *I climbed thereon.*

THE LOVELY WITCH

Apples have been desired by you
Since first in Paradise they grew;
And I am moved with joy to know
That such within my garden grow.

Freud interprets: "There cannot be the faintest doubt what the apple-tree and the apples stand for."*

---

*The amusing use of the erectile words "stand for" in this context, probably those of the translator, remind me of the first "dirty joke" I ever heard. When I was seven, a kid on the block asked me: "Who was the first carpenter?" When I said, "I give up," he told me: "Eve was the first carpenter because she made Adam's banana stand."

From those close to Freud during his engagement we learn, via Jones, that though he was smitten with Martha Bernays at first glance, he did nothing about it for several weeks, because (his consciously expressed reasons) he was profoundly embarrassed by his dire poverty as a medical student, with four more years to go before he could begin earning a living. Though, like many doctors, he could have married into a rich family, he had romantically chosen a girl as poor as himself.

But love and optimism (and courage) prevailed, and Freud began his courtship in the conventional Viennese manner: each morning he sent a symbolic red rose with snippets of discreetly amorous verse. Then, continuing his syndromic habit of identifying with mythic figures at a time of high emotion, he "offered his first compliment, which he later recalled . . . of likening Martha to the fairy princess from whose lips fall pearls and roses . . . and from which came his favorite name for her: 'Princess.' " With himself as "Prince Charming," of course. (Though all this sounds quite normal and innocent, it was the necessary prelude to the developing *Melusina* drama.)

The first phase of the courtship consisted of a series of walks in public *parks, gardens, woods,* which Freud's vivid self-dramatizing imagination transformed into "Garden of Eden" complete, as we have seen, with a hovering deity and "angels with flaming swords." The first of these little psychodramatizations took place on the last day of May 1882, when, according to Freud's unpublished diary (read by Jones), the young couple had their first serious talk while returning from (Mount) Kahlenberg, a part of the famous Vienna Woods. During this walk Freud, perhaps thinking of Adam and Eve after they became conscious of their nudity, became quite upset when Martha refused his offer of some oak leaves he'd picked. "It made him hate oak trees," says Jones, quoting Freud.

On the following day, with Martha's mother as chaperone, Sigmund and his "fairy princess" walked in the beautiful Prater *gardens,* which he later, quoted above, called "a paradise." On June 10, the Garden of Eden "schtick" was repeated: "In a garden in Mödling they came across a double almond [another seed-womb] which the Viennese call a *Vielliebchen* [much beloved sweetheart] and which exacts a forfeit in the form of exchanged presents. Sigmund promptly sent his gift: a copy of *David Copperfield.*"

66

... my wife Dora seemed to me by one consent to be regarded as a *pretty toy* or *plaything* . . . my aunt called her Little Blossom . . . her maid treated her like a pet child. I sometimes awoke, as it were, to find that I had treated her like a plaything too.

"Will you call me a name I want you to call me?" inquired Dora, without moving.
"What is it?" I asked with a smile.
"It's a stupid name," she said, shaking her curls for a moment. "Child-wife."
—Charles Dickens, *David Copperfield*

Young Freud's sentimental present to his "sweet darling girl," "his little treasure," just four days before his *secret engagement*, proves to be yet another of his unwitting reenactments from fiction during an emotional "high."

In *David Copperfield*, "Freud's favorite Dickens," according to Jones, we find some exact parallels to Freud's real-life situation: David Copperfield becomes "secretly engaged" to Dora, a tiny, infantile girl whom he thinks of as an Eve with whom he is "wandering in the Garden of Eden all the while . . . she was a Fairy, a Sylph." When it becomes painfully obvious that Dora knows nothing about housework, David (like Sigmund) gives his fiancée a book. About cooking. But the childish Dora, who reminds one strongly of Nora in Ibsen's later *Doll's House*, gives the book to her dog to play with. She is, like Nora, called a "reckless spendthrift" by her patronizing husband. She fails utterly as a housewife, and then, realizing she can never attain emotional maturity, simply fades away into death. This leaves Copperfield free to marry the girl he really loves. (All sorts of nasty death wishes floating around here.)

But in the real-life situation in Vienna we find no Dickensian tragedy and much more comedy, for at least one of the messages conveyed by Sigmund's highly ambivalent book-gift was perceived by Martha (no Nora or Dora she); and she countered effectively by sending the young doctor a cake she'd baked and with it a pointed, clever note suggesting that he "dissect" it, anatomize it, and devour it as he did everything else. How cleverly this "sweet little darling," this "little fairy princess," flashed the "cutting knife" image!

67

Though convinced that Freud had the "doll's house" couples of Goethe, Dickens (whom he loved), and Ibsen in mind when he thought of his relationship to his future wife, I still searched among his writings, hoping to find the clincher: his own exact words which would bring together and verify all these seeming connections. Finally, in the Jones biography there appeared Freud's letter to his fiancée, openly admitting his "doll's house" and "Melusina" thinking. While admitting to a "clumsy, self-tormenting kind of deeply rooted love," Freud scolded himself as if he were the contrite husband of Nora at the end of Ibsen's play. *"The loved one,"* he wrote, *"is not to become a toy doll,* but the good comrade who still has a sensible word left when the strict master has come to the end of his wisdom. *And I have been trying to smash* her frankness so that she should reserve her opinion until she is sure of mine." (Italics mine.)

68

We may say that hysteria is a caricature of an artistic creation.
—Freud, *Totem and Taboo*

Being persuaded that the whole magic lay in the ring I wore *on my little finger,* I resolved on breaking it asunder . . . the golden hoop leaped suddenly from my finger.
—Goethe, *The New Melusina,* from *Wilhelm Meister's Wanderings*

And now we come to the climax of our Freud and Melusina explorations: About a month after confessing to his future wife Martha that "crazy and serious thoughts" crossed his mind while reading *The New Melusina,* "behind whose every feature I see ourselves," Sigmund Freud also syndromically smashed the betrothal ring slipped on his little finger by his own "little fairy princess." (Like Melusina's ring, Martha's ring had once been worn by her father.)

What happened, says Jones, was that a surgeon stuck a knife (the fourth "cutting knife" image) into Freud's throat to cauterize an anginal abscess, "*and in his pain Freud banged his hand on the table, breaking the ring.*"*

Though some may dismiss this hysterical reflex action as an "accident," as the pre-Freudian Freud did at the time (the later Freud would have disagreed emphatically), the deadly accuracy of his ring-smashing tells me that during his paroxysm of pain he reverted to his syndromic habit: his hysteria "caricatured," parodied, reenacted the climactic scene in which Redcloak smashed his wife's ring to escape captivity in her fairy doll's house. Yes, Freud's hysteria caricatured Goethe's artistic creation.

Any doubt I may have had about the accidentality of Freud's hysterical ring-breaking was erased by Jones's further comment: "Sure enough, a year later, and again during an anginal attack, the ring broke again, and this time the pearl was lost."

Then, to add to this serio-comic picture of a hysterical pre-psychoanalytical Freud who performed exactly like one of his later, more irrational patients, Sigmund compounded his parapractic offense against the innocent Martha by primitively blaming *her.* After the incident in the surgeon's office, Freud wrote to Martha: "Now I have a tragically serious question for you. Answer me on your honor and conscience whether at eleven o'clock last Thursday you happened to be less fond of me, or more than usually annoyed with me, or perhaps even untrue to me—as the song has it. Why this tasteless ceremonious conjuration? Because I have a good opportunity to put an end to a superstition. At the moment in question my ring broke where the pearl was set in.

"I have to admit that my heart did not sink. I was not seized by forebodings that our engagement would come to no good end, no dark suspicion that you were at that moment occupied in tearing my image from your heart. A sensitive man would have felt all that, but my only thought

---

*After his escape from Melusina and King Eckwald, Redcloak became a "surgeon-barber" (doctor). A nifty link to the surgeon who operated on Freud's throat. Freud, a doctor, also studied surgery.

was that the ring would have to be repaired and that such accidents can hardly be avoided."*

I have had the same response each time I've read, reread, and copied the above: "Freud invented or defined the words 'ambivalence' and 'paranoia' as the perfect descriptives for such confusions and rationalizations within his own and other minds."

69

This interpretation of Freud's ring-smashing is, of course, elementary. In his *Lectures on Psychoanalytical Psychiatry*, Dr. A. A. Brill, the first American psychoanalyst and English translator of Freud's books, tells the not unusual case of a woman who lost several valuable jewels, *including a ruby from a ring* given her by her husband: "For some time she had told her husband she was seriously thinking of leaving him. It is therefore safe to assume that these jewels symbolized her desire to get rid of her husband. The husband, an intelligent layman, knew the meaning of these losses without any interpretation. He said to her: 'You dislike me, so you lose the jewels which were worn by my mother and my grandmother.' " (Freud lost the pearl "stone" from the ring formerly worn by his fiancée's father.)

"What did my patient mean," asks Dr. Brill, "by losing the stone? We know that the evolution of the marriage ring goes back to the time when the ceremonials of coitus at marriage were no longer tolerated in public. Instead, a symbolic coitus was performed by putting a ring on the finger. That is the origin of the wedding ring. People have always looked upon the wedding ring as a symbol of marital fidelity, and a woman feels badly if she loses her ring. In analysis one often finds all kinds of symbolic action expressed by the marriage ring. The ring is a symbol of union between husband and wife, and (to belabor the point) when a woman (or man) loses a wedding ring it may be assumed that there is something wrong with the marriage. . . . I have seen too many women (and men) who have used the wedding ring as an expression of their marital status."

*Letters of Sigmund Freud, edited by Ernst L. Freud. (New York, Basic Books, 1960.)

70

If anyone were to ask if Freud's hysterical smashing or breaking of his engagement ring was an isolated act, the answer would be: "No, it is quite similar to another hysterical incident he analyzes in his *Psychopathology of Everyday Life.*"

During his well-known discussion of the "accidents" which prove to be acts of *unconscious deliberation*, Freud tells of several of his own "accidents" involving personal talismanic objects. But the one most relevant to the smashing of his love-binding ring has to do with his personal attack on the love-goddess herself!

Freud remembers: ". . . one morning while in my bathrobe and slippers, I followed a sudden impulse as I passed a room, and hurled a slipper from my foot against the wall so that it brought down a beautiful little marble Venus from its bracket. . . . As it fell to pieces, I recited quite unmoved some verses from [Wilhelm] Busch:

> *Ach! Die Venus ist perdu!—**
> *Klickeradoms!—von Medici!*"

Freud continues: "This crazy action and my calmness at the sight of the damage are explained in the then existing situation. We had a very sick child in the family, of whose recovery I had personally despaired. That morning I had been informed that there was a great improvement. I know that I said to myself, 'After all she will live.' My attack of destructive madness served therefore as a grateful feeling toward fate, and afforded me the opportunity of performing 'an act of sacrifice,' just as if I had vowed, 'If she gets well, I will give this or that as a sacrifice.' That I chose the Venus . . . as this sacrifice was only gallant homage to the convalescent. But even today, it is still incomprehensible to me that I decided so quickly, aimed so accurately, and struck no other object in close proximity."

Afterthought: Could this be another of Freud's reenactments of a scene from an ancient Roman book well known to him? Suetonius tells of the Roman householders who reacted to grave domestic misfortune by smash-

---

*Alas! The Venus is lost!

ing "the god that failed" on the cobblestones in front of the house. They then calmly transferred their piety to a new and, it was hoped, more dependable god.

71

> I was very incompletely dressed and was going upstairs . . .
> —one of Freud's dreams, in *The Interpretation of Dreams*

After "shooting" the Medusas in telephoto closeup (taking care to look at them *only in the mirror* of the reflex camera!), I entered, through the large double door of Berggasse 19, into a high-ceilinged corridor—at the other end of which, opening into a garden, was another double door decorated with etched-glass mythological figures. (What, more of them? The man was besieged!)

But before looking at the mythic figures more closely, I obeyed my notebook's instructions: "Be sure to look at staircase, shown in the house plans, leading up to Freud's apartment. And take a good look at the door on the first landing. This was the entrance to the rear ground-floor professional suite used by Freud for sixteen years beginning in 1891. He conducted his first analyses there; in the ground-floor study he wrote his revolutionary, seminal books: *The Interpretation of Dreams*, *The Psychopathology of Everyday Life*, and *Wit and Its Relation to the Unconscious*. By an odd coincidence (?) this same flat, as I told Henry Koerner, was occupied previously by another revolutionist: the Marxist Viktor Adler, a leader of the Austrian Socialist Party and the Second International. Though Freud was skeptical of Marxist solutions to basic human problems, he and Adler were friends."

My notes continued: "Freud immortalized the Berggasse 19 staircase in one of his own naughty dreams, indexed in his 'dream-work' as: 'Undressed, running up stairs, 238–40, 257.' Though rather prosaic at first reading, this highly condensed dream increases in interest when reconstituted and analyzed by the dreamer. Fellow 'syndrome-watchers' will recognize it as another significant example of an unconscious nocturnal fantasy which triggered Freud into associating himself with (a) a fairy-tale monarch and (b) one of the greatest heroes in world literature."

This "staircase dream," told in a letter to Fliess and repeated in *The Interpretation of Dreams*, is a brief one:

> I was very incompletely dressed and was going upstairs from a flat on the ground floor to a higher storey. I was going up three steps at a time and was delighted with my agility. Suddenly I saw a maid-servant coming down the stairs—coming towards me, that is. I felt ashamed and tried to hurry, and at this point the feeling of inhibition "set in." I was glued to the spot and unable to budge from the spot.

Freud's analysis begins: "The situation in the dream is taken from everyday reality. I occupy two flats in a house in Vienna, which are connected only by the public staircase. My consulting room and study are on the upper ground floor and my living rooms are one storey higher. When, late in the evening, I have finished my work down below, I go up the stairs to my bedroom. On the evening before the dream, I had in fact made this short journey in rather disordered dress—that is to say, I had taken off my collar, tie and cuffs. In this dream this had been turned into a higher degree of undress, but, as usual, an indeterminate one."

He continues: "The staircase up which I was going, however, was not the one in my house. At first I failed to recognize it, and it was only the identity of the person who met me (on the stairs) that made it clear to me what locality was intended. This person was the maid-servant of the old lady I was visiting twice a day in order to give her her injections; and the staircase, too, was just like the one in her house which I had to go up twice a day.

"Now how did this staircase and this female figure come to be in my dream? The feeling of shame at not being completely dressed is no doubt of a sexual nature; but the maid-servant whom I dreamt about was older than I am, surly and far from attractive. The only answer to the problem that occurred to me was this: When I paid my morning visits to this house it was my rule to be seized with a desire to clear my throat as I went up the staircase, and the products of my expectorations would fall on the staircase . . . and the concierge, an equally elderly and surly woman (but of cleanly instincts, as I was prepared to admit) . . . would lie in wait for me to see if I should make free of the stairs, and if she found I did she would grumble audibly; and for several days afterward she would omit her usual greeting when we met. . . ."

After offering several "meanings" to the dream, including its "wishful" and "exhibitionistic" characteristics, Freud quits his technical, scientific mode of explanation and switches to the first of his syndromic identifications with a remembered figure from folklore:

"There can be no doubt that the connections between our typical dreams and fairy tales and the materials of other kinds of creative writing are neither few nor accidental. . . . We possess an interesting piece of evidence that the dream in the form in which it appears—partly distorted by wish-fulfillment—has not been rightly understood. For it has become the basis of a fairy tale which is familiar to us all in Hans Christian Andersen's version, *The Emperor's New Clothes*, and which has been recently put into verse by Ludwig Fulda in his dramatic fairy tale *The Talisman*. Hans Andersen's fairy tale tells us how two imposters weave the Emperor a costly garment which, they say, will be visible only to persons of virtue and loyalty. The Emperor walks out in the invisible garment, and all the spectators, intimidated by the fabric's power to act as touchstone, pretend not to notice the Emperor's nakedness. *This is the situation in our [my] dream.*" (Emphasis mine.)

But there are more syndromics (the man was tireless!) to report. Not satisfied with his identification with the balls-naked Emperor and the little boy who exposed his nudity and the collective delusion, Freud escalated his quite ordinary dream to a loftier Greek plateau: "One of my friends [to whom he told this dream] has drawn my attention to the following passage in Gottfried Keller's novel *The Green Henry:*

I hope, dear Lee, that you may never learn from your personal experience the peculiar and *piquant* plight of Odysseus when he appeared naked and covered with mud, before Nausicaa and her maidens."

I wonder: Has any psychoanalyst written about Freud's "use" of *The Emperor's New Clothes* story as a nifty paradigm of his lifelong role as the "boy who reveals the naked truth to a population which collaborates in its suppression"? (The folktale doesn't say what happened to the indiscreet "boy," but I would imagine he was rewarded with a swift kick in the ass.)

72

". . . spitting is sperm ejaculation."
—Freud, in a letter to Karl Abraham, 1908

An amusing little psychomystery: Though Freud's explanation of his own staircase dream is, as always, convincing to me, I see that he has omitted or censored certain basic explanations of the kind he offered when analyzing the "running up staircase" dreams of others.

Since I do not wish here (or elsewhere) to rush in with "wild analyses" where, for reasons of his own, Freud desisted, I shall offer some observations of these dreams in the form of comments and questions addressed to those qualified to evaluate them.

My questions and comments are based on the statements made by Freud and his disciple Marie Bonaparte on the sexual symbolism of *staircases, neckties,* and *spitting.* Thus, in his *Interpretation of Dreams* Freud wrote: "Steps, ladders, staircases, or, as the case may be, walking up and down them, are representations of the sexual act . . . the rhythmic movement, the increased breathlessness . . . the act of mounting."

In another book,* Freud offers an illustrative example: "A gentleman who had passed a night in intercourse with a lady [patient] described her as one of those motherly women in whom the wish for a child breaks irresistibly through in intercourse with a man. The circumstances of this meeting, however, called for a precaution which prevented the fertilizing semen from reaching the woman's uterus. On waking up after this night, the woman reported the following dream:

An officer in a red cap was running after her in the street. She fled from him, and ran up the stairs with him still after her. Breathless, she reached her flat, slammed the door behind her and locked it. He stayed outside, and when she looked through the peep-hole he was sitting on a bench outside and weeping."

Freud then tells his lecture audience: "You will doubtless recognize the officer in the red cap and the breathless climbing upstairs as represent-

---

The Complete Introductory Lectures on Psychoanalysis. (New York, 1966.)

ing the sexual act. The fact that it was the dreamer who locked herself up against her pursuer will serve as an example of the reversals that are so common in dreams, for it was the man who had avoided the consummation of the sexual act. In the same way her grief was displaced onto the man, for it was he who wept in the dream—and this was simultaneously a representation of the emission of semen."

After pausing to recall that American pornographers often depict a drop of semen running down a penis as a "tear," we return to Freud's (and Marie Bonaparte's) explanations of *neckties* and *spitting:* ". . . the necktie," said Freud, "dependent and peculiar to men . . . often appears as a penis." And, in her book about Edgar Allan Poe, Princess Bonaparte wrote: "A man's mouth becomes, through its phallic tongue and ability to spit, a male potency symbol." Also, as quoted in a letter from Freud to Karl Abraham (above): ". . . spitting is sperm ejaculation."

Some perhaps rhetorical questions may now be asked: "Does this picture of an undressed Freud 'delightedly' running up the stairs three at a time while holding in his hand his necktie and accompanied by the image of (disgusting) spitting add up to a dream paradigm of (a) his solitary masturbation as boy or man? And being caught at it? Or, since he was on his way to inject an old lady (mother substitute), was the dream one of (b) symbolic incest, or was it (c) one of premature emission *(ejaculatio praecox)* to *avoid* incest? (I leave "d" and all the rest of the speculative alphabet to the reader's imagination.)

73

A closer look at the two etched-glass figures on the double door opening from the corridor into the rear garden revealed that one was the ecological Pomona, divine protectress of gardens, as well as of forests and their fauna. Her equally lovely companion, holding aloft her symbolic pitcher, with bow and arrows slung on her back, was Diana, Roman counterpart of the Greek Artemis. As Diana she was, like Pomona, a fertility goddess; she was also a guardian of vegetation; and, though a patroness of hunters, she punished all wanton destroyers of wildlife.

Diana was worshipped everywhere in the Roman world, especially in the sacred oak grove at Nemi, near Rome, the starting point of Sir James Frazer's *The Golden Bough*, a book greatly admired and quoted by Freud in his *Totem and Taboo*.

As Artemis, the goddess performed many vital functions, the more positive of which remind one of Freud's self-assigned tasks as healer, fertility consultant, and moral umpire and guide. As the goddess of chastity, Artemis strove, as Freud did, to protect her suppliants from the deranging assaults of her rival Aphrodite (Venus). But when her male and female protégés fell victim to the love-goddess, Artemis did not rescue them (as Freud tried to do). Instead, she became a vengeful, malign Cupid-in-reverse who shot the sexual offenders with her fatal arrows.

Artemis was also the divinity of fertilizing waters. (This explains the pitcher she holds aloft at the entrance to Freud's garden.) In another randomly selected part of her complicated legend, we learn of another of her draconian reprisals against those who offended her. When Niobe, mother of fourteen children, mocked Leto as "the mother of only two children: Artemis and Apollo," and demanded that *she* be worshipped instead, Artemis reacted infamously. To punish the hubristic mother, she put an arrow through the heart of each of the fourteen children, causing the eternally weeping Niobe to turn to water-dripping stone. (This last detail of petrification links the "inside" Artemis to the Medusas on the front façade of Freud's residence.)

But when later the *Britannica* informed me that "Artemis was sometimes represented in Arcadian art as half-human and half-fish" (mermaid), and that she was also merged with Medusa and worshipped here and there as Artemis-Medusa, I exclaimed, as anyone might: "Melusina again! Medusa again! No wonder Freud thought and dreamed and wrote about them. He was surrounded at all times by these haunting mythic figures!"

But the pretty rococo pictures acid-engraved in the glass garden doors were not intended to be merely decorative. Like all the rest of Vienna's abounding apotropaic art, these household votaries were part of symbolic mythic drama, for just inches away from their lovely feet were two large and ugly mustachioed Satans, the spittin' images of Kaiser Wilhelm II. Together, the goddesses and devils look straight into the eyes of the residents and visitors to remind them of the eternal antitheses: love, fertility, unity, against death, sterility, and destructive disunity—exactly like the Eros-Thanatos and other oppositional pairs in Freud's psychoanalytical philosophy. And of course Freud saw these large, compelling images every time he entered the hall or opened the doors to the garden.

74

The image of the fertility goddess Diana-Artemis armed with bow and arrow and linked visually, inseparably, with Satan reminds me of an advertising card in my collection of printed ephemera. Issued in the 1880s by a New York manufacturer of industrial grinding machinery, this card, a masterpiece of pre-Freudian insight, shows Cupid (Eros) working contentedly alongside Satan in a factory. The grinning King of Devils is sharpening the arrowlike point of his obviously phallic tail on a spinning emery wheel; Cupid, working at a second wheel *on the same shaft driven by the same engine,* is also sharpening an arrow. Behind his back an apprentice devil is stealing an arrow from his quiver. This "comic" visual parable recalls, does it not, Freud's explanations of the transformations of the libido—the interrelatedness of the diverse good and evil, love and death responses "driven" by the same libidinal motors?

The question asked previously about the propinquitous Medusas and Melusinas must, I feel, be repeated here. What influence, if any, did the persistent images of Pomona, Diana-Artemis, and Satan have on the exceedingly myth-conscious man who was exposed to them for nearly half a century?

When I wrote to Miss Anna Freud asking her if her father had ever mentioned any of the above-mentioned household mythic figures to her, she replied that he had never done so, nor did she remember them. But, she added, she did remember a "stone figure of a woman," still standing in the rear courtyard, a "figure that had once been part of a fountain in the garden."

75

As I opened the double glass door and walked out, I was shocked to see that the "lovely garden with flowering chestnut trees" described by Freud's visitors had vanished completely, replaced by garages and a wall-to-wall expanse of rat-gray cement, the ugliest of paving materials. Obviously Pomona and Diana had lost their magical protective powers, leaving the landlord free to destroy the trees, remove the fountain, and throw out every flower, plant, and blade of grass.

The reader may be thinking, as I am: "Yes, we understand the utilitarian needs—and greeds—which motivated the landlord. But one senses that he may also have shared Vienna's great hostility to Freud; that he unconsciously wanted to eradicate every life-enhancing organism associated with his tenant."

Certainly poets have always known that such *chopping down of trees, uprooting of living floral growth,* and *ripping out of a regenerating fountain* are acts of symbolic castration and hysterectomy.

There was one survivor in this gutted place: the niche-enclosed sculptured pagan Diana, who, exactly like her twin on the double glass door, holds aloft her pitcher of life-giving water. (She is the "fountain figure" mentioned in Anna Freud's letter.)

76

"My Son, the Myops"
—one of Freud's dreams, in *The Interpretation of Dreams*

Just now, while thinking of the provocative objects and images in Freud's immediate environment, I was suddenly startled to perceive that all of the Berggasse house and garden elements were duplicated in the dream Freud called "My Son, the Myops": the *double doors,* one at the front *gateway* to his apartment house, the other at the entrance to the rear garden and decorated with the figures from *ancient Roman* mythology; the image of the eternally *weeping Niobe, protectress of young people,* turned to dripping stone *when her children were murdered;* and, major image, near this fountain and these double doors a doctor (Freud) who has his office where mental patients, some who prove to be incurably insane, come to be treated—all this in the larger arena of Viennese anti-Semitism.

Now, after a detailed comparison of Freud's dream and the above elements from his immediate domestic environment, I strongly suspect that the dream Freud thought had taken place in Siena was staged by his tricky unconscious in the garden at the rear of Vienna's Berggasse 19.

To test this suspicion, let us together read the dream in question, beginning with Freud's introductory remarks: "Another time I had a dream that a man I knew on the staff of the University said to me: 'My son, the Myops.' Then followed a dialogue made up of short remarks and rejoinders. After this, however, there was a third piece of dream in which I myself and my sons figured."

Freud then offers the main part of the dream:

> On account of certain events which had occurred in the city of Rome, it had become necessary to remove the children to a place of safety, and this was done. The scene was then (shifted) to the front of a gateway, double doors in the ancient style (the "Porta Roman" at Siena, as I was aware in the dream itself). I was sitting on the edge of a fountain and was greatly depressed and almost in tears. A female figure—an attendant or nun—brought two boys out and handed them to their father, who was not myself. The elder of the two was my eldest son; I did not see the other one's face. . . .

Freud begins his analysis: "This dream was constructed on a tangle of thoughts provoked by a play I had just seen, called *Das neue Ghetto* (*The New Ghetto*).* The Jewish problem, concern about the future of one's children, to whom one cannot give a country of their own, concern about educating them in such a way that they can move freely across frontiers— all this was easily recognizable among the dream thoughts."

Freud continues: " 'By the waters of Babylon we sat down and wept.' Siena, like Rome, is famous for its beautiful fountains. . . . *If Rome occurred in a dream, it was necessary for me to find a substitute known to me.* [Italics mine.] Near the Porta Romana in Siena we had seen a large

---

*Written by Theodor Herzl, the founder of the Zionist movement, this play about Vienna's anti-Semitism compares the city to the "walled-in" ghettoes of medieval Italy. The "Vienna-Italy" link plays a dominant role in the "Myops" dream.

and brightly lighted building. We learned that it was the *Manicomio*, the insane asylum. Shortly before I had the dream, I heard that a man of the same religious persuasion as myself had been obliged to resign the position he had painfully achieved in a state asylum."

77

> GARDEN, transitively, a place of exceptional fertility.
> —*Oxford Unabridged Dictionary*

Here are some of the linked images from the "Myops" dream which indicate (to me) that this night-vision actually "took place" at Vienna's Berggasse 19, and not in "Rome-Siena," as Freud says it did.

First, "Rome and Siena": Did Freud really dream about these two Italian cities? I do not think so. Nor, apparently, did he. In the lines quoted above, he says quite clearly that whenever he dreamed of "Rome" he always found it necessary to determine which locality *known to him* was the "real" city he dreamed about. He then refers his reader to page 193 of the "dream-work," where he offers the example of a dream about Rome which was not about Rome because it was plastered with German posters. It was, he guessed, the city of Prague in the Austro-Hungarian Empire. (In that dream, "Prague"=Vienna.)

Freud says also: ". . . the situation of removing my children to safety from the city of Rome was related to . . . some relatives who had [left] Vienna for another country."

Finally, as the reader will recall from an earlier part of the present book, Freud's compulsive encirclements of Vienna's vanished walls seem to have been in part a reenactment of Hannibal's long, unsuccessful encirclements of the walls of Rome. Rome was, to Freud, a Vienna "displaced-downwards."

The foregoing tells me: Though Freud understood clearly that "Rome" in dream and fantasy was a codeword for a city "known" to him, he seems to have missed the last step in deduction—to recognize that "Rome" was Vienna.

"Siena": With the above in mind, it is safe to assume that "Siena," which rhymes so perfectly with the name of Freud's city, is another example of a "downward-displaced" Vienna. If, for the sake of idea exploration, this not-unreasonable assumption is made, it enables the rest of the elements in the "Myops" dream to fall perfectly into place. Or so it seems to me.

Second: The setting of Freud's dream, he says, was shifted from Rome to the *"front of a gateway [with] double doors in the ancient style."* This corresponds exactly to the elements in Freud's residence: its front *double door* opening into the corridor and the stairs, the second *double door* at the *gateway* to the garden, a "Roman" double door *decorated with figures of Roman goddesses* (ancient style). Later I saw another set of soundproof double doors between Freud's waiting room and his consulting room.

The third set of similarities between Freud's "Myops" dream and his domestic environment is revealed in the line: *"I was sitting on the edge of a fountain and was greatly depressed and almost in tears."* This recalls our earlier exploration of Freud-Raymond's healing encounter with Melusina at her fountain, arena of crypto-analysis.

Now, in the "Myops" dream, a fountain is again the scene of psychotherapy, since Freud practiced that science just a few feet from his backyard fountain attended by the Melusina-like Diana, another rescuer of suffering humans attacked by Aphrodite.

Yet another glance at Freud's dream shows that the "Siena" dream-fountain was quite close to the "double door of the Porta Romana." This fits the Vienna backyard situation precisely: Freud's fountain was also close to the gateway decorated with Roman mythological figures.

The fourth cluster of similarities arises from a consideration of the line "By the waters of Babylon, we sat and wept." These lines quoted by Freud, says Dr. Alexander Grinstein,* come from Swinburne's poem *Super Flumina Babylonis* (1869); they, in turn, are copied almost verbatim from Psalm 137:

> By the waters of Babylon
> There we sat down, yea, we wept,
> When we remembered Zion . . .

When Freud's conscious offering of Swinburne's poem is fully considered, it strengthens the "Rome-Siena-Vienna" hypothesis; it offers as well another example of Freud's syndromic insistence, since he obviously

---

*On Sigmund Freud's Dreams. (Detroit, Wayne State University Press, 1968.)

identifies himself with the Jews exiled in Babylon and then later throughout the world.

In his amplification of Freud's dream, Grinstein explains: "It is a direct association with his emotional state in the manifest (part of) his dream where he 'was greatly depressed and almost in tears.' The mood of Swinburne's poem fitted in with his feelings of isolation in Vienna and a longing to be away from the city."

Though it was now obvious to me that Freud *knew* he was reenacting in his dream a scene from a well-remembered poem and Biblical Psalm, I, recalling Freud's other multiply-inspired restagings, continued the search for more possible literary sources for the "manifest" part of his many-layered dream. (For an understanding of the deeper layers of the "Myops" dream, one must, of course, read Freud's unmatchable analysis in his *Interpretation of Dreams.*)

Recalling also his constant recourse to Shakespeare for illustration (Freud seems to have memorized his plays *in toto*), I made a mechanical search of various concordances on the off-chance of finding at least one reference to someone "weeping at a fountain." What I found was astonishing.

Yes, astonishing. Though now accustomed to finding verifications of the "Freud Syndrome" at every turn, I was not prepared to find two dramatic lines so perfectly related to Freud's "Siena-Vienna" dream of *sitting at the edge of a Diana-fountain . . . almost in tears.*

In the first, from *As You Like it*, Shakespeare has his heroine Rosalind say: "I shall *weep* for nothing, *like Diana at her fountain.*" This suggests, doesn't it, that Freud's unconscious memory got the idea of weeping at his own Diana-fountain from his beloved Shakespeare's simile? (A footnote in the *Pelican Shakespeare:* "Stow's *Survey of London* [1598] says that six years earlier 'a fountain of Diana was set up in West Cheape with water rilling (flowing) from her breasts.' Out of delicacy Shakespeare changed the figure to 'weeping.' ")

The second "weeping at a fountain" quotation, from *Titus Andronicus*, supplements the first from *As You Like It*, and adds powerful elements which echo Freud's fatherly dread of the atrocities which might be inflicted on his sons and daughters if Vienna's anti-Semitism ever reached the murderous pogrom stage, as it frequently did in nearby Poland and Russia.

In *Titus Andronicus*, we find King Titus overwhelmed with horror and grief because his beloved daughter Lavinia has been raped; her tongue has been cut out and her hands amputated (to prevent her from telling or writing the names of the rapists). This prompts Titus to lament:

> Gentle Lavinia, let me kiss thy lips,
> Or make some sign how I may thee ease.
> *Shall* thy good uncle and thy brother Lucius
> And thou and *I sit about some fountain,*
> Looking downwards to behold our cheeks
> How they are stained, like meadows not yet dry
> With miry slime left on them by a flood?
> *And in the fountain shall we gaze so long*
> Till the fresh taste be taken from that clearness,
> And *made a brine-pit by our bitter tears?* [Italics mine.]*

78

The captioned objects in the front hallway (entrance) of the Freud Museum are:

403. Cabin trunk, used for the last time in 1938.

404. Photo of Anna Freud unveiling the statue of her father, by O. Nemon, in London, 1970.

405. Cane, hat, and sporting cap of Freud. [Wired to the coat-rack to foil souvenir hunters.]

406. Suitcase and traveling bag with initials: S. F.

407. Map of Vienna, circa 1890, on which points of interest from Freud's biography are marked.

408. Map of Silesia and Moravia (1888) on which Freiberg, Freud's birthplace, is pointed out.

---

*Significantly, *Titus Andronicus* takes place in Rome, which, as we have seen, is, for Freud, really Vienna. More "displacement downwards."

409. Walking flask used by Freud on Sunday hikes.

410. Clothes hanger used by Freud during his years at the General Hospital in Vienna.

411. Next to entrance: Ashtray of copper and brass (Vienna Jugendstil period), circa 1905, which had been here.

412. Opposite: Original doorplate of Freud's office. [It reads: "Prof. Dr. Freud."]

79

As Hans Lobner, the youthful co-curator of the Freudhaus, led the way into the room next to the front hallway, he said: "As you can see, this was Freud's waiting room. The original furniture, the prints, the books in that cabinet and the objets d'art from Freud's collection in those cases were all returned from London by Anna Freud."

"Was this the room where the Psychological Wednesday Society met?"

"Yes." He handed me a catalog. "This tells you all the things in the collection. I will be back in a few minutes to show you the rest of the rooms."

As he was leaving, I caught sight of a copy of a familiar picture. "Isn't that Henry Fuseli's 'The Nightmare'? That must be the print given to Freud by Ernest Jones when he—Jones—wrote his analytical study of nightmares."

"Yes, I believe it was. Are you interested in nightmares?"

"Not especially. But I *am* interested in Fuseli. I've discovered that Ibsen may have based his *Rosmersholm* on an incident in Fuseli's friendship with Mary Wollstonecraft. And I think there's a connection between Ibsen's *Rosmersholm* and Freud's relationship to . . ."

Ignoring the reference to Freud, the curator said, "Ibsen? We are standing just a few feet from him!" Taking a key ring from his pocket, he walked to a cabinet, opened the glass doors and pointed to a set of Ibsen's

Collected Works. He then took out one of the books. "Here is Freud's own copy of *Rosmersholm*."

I held the book once held and read by Freud, an eerie feeling, and thought: "Freud, who greatly admired and emulated his spiritual twin Ibsen, world-famous moral liberator . . . who reenacted much of *Hedda Gabler* when he fainted in Bremen in 1909,* and *consciously* identified with the male-chauvinist husband in *Doll's House*, seems also to have restaged the basic situation—without the tragic ending—of Ibsen's *Rosmersholm*, or Rosmer's home, right here in this house . . . with his sister-in-law, Miss Minna Bernays. After the death of her fiancé in 1896, this dynamic, intellectual, attractive thirty-one-year-old woman moved in with the Freuds to be, like 'Rebecca West' and Mary Wollstonecraft, a 'spiritual' companion to Freud, displacing her sister. She not only occupied the adjoining bedroom reachable only through Freud's *schlafzimmer* but, says Ernest Jones, traveled alone with this husband many times on week-long excursions. And apparently with her sister's consent. I can't think of any woman in fiction or real life who would consent to such an arrangement. And this happened at the turn of the century! Though, like Freud's relationship to Wilhelm Fliess and those questionable 'Congresses' held so frequently away from either man's familiar surroundings, these Sigmund-Minna trips arouse suspicions of sexual hanky-panky. But from all indications Freud seems to have been a man who, to use his own word, sublimated a great deal of his sexual-emotional life into his great work. Yes, except for the tragic ending, Freud seems to have reenacted *Rosmersholm* in his own home."

In the first volume of his Freud biography, Ernest Jones, who observed the Sigmund-Minna relationship for thirty years, has much to say about that relationship. Here, with my interpolations, is a part of it:

When there were six children, his sister-in-law, Minna Bernays [1865–1941], joined the family [as companion and "second mother" to the Freud children] and remained with them until her death.† Previous to this, after the

---

*This "discovery" is dealt with in Part Three of this book.
†As we all know, this was a common arrangement in the nineteenth century. Unmarried women, especially those educated "above their station," often "buried themselves" in extended family groups.

death of the man she was engaged to, she had [like Mary Wollstonecraft and "Rebecca West"] been a lady's companion, an occupation she never found congenial. As a girl she had gone about her housework with a duster in one hand and a book in the other, so that it was not surprising that intellectual, and particularly literary, interests absorbed her life.

After describing her domestic skills, Jones tells his reader:

> She and Freud got on excellently together. There was no sexual attraction on either side, but he found her a stimulating and amusing companion and would occasionally make short holiday excursions with her [sometimes for more than a week] when his wife was not free to travel. All this has given rise to the malicious and entirely untrue legend that she displaced his wife in his affections. [The same "malicious and entirely untrue legend" afflicted Rosmer and Rebecca West.] Freud always enjoyed the society of intellectual and rather masculine women, of whom there was a series in his life. It is perhaps surprising that "Tante Minna" never helped Freud in his literary work, for instance by learning shorthand and typing.

Those familiar with the specific Freudian symbol *pen=penis* may find the following Jonesian gratuitous remark amusing and revealing:

> But Freud could never be parted from his pen, which he used for both his *private* correspondence and his scientific writings: *He evidently thought best when he had it in hand.* [Italics mine.]

In his highly informative *Freud and His Followers,** Dr. Paul Roazen has written of the Sigmund-Minna relationship. Speaking of Freud's confession that his sexual desires had dwindled after the birth of the sixth child (he was forty), Roazen writes:

> In 1969 an article appeared asserting that Jung had claimed that Minna had spoken to him of her anxiety about Freud's love for her and the intimacy of their relationship. It might be attractive to think of Freud and Minna having had a grand passion for each other. Freud once wrote that, unlike Minna's

---

*(New York, Alfred A. Knopf, 1974.)

fiancé and Martha, who were completely good people, he and Minna were, in Jones's gloss, "wild, passionate people, not so good." Supposedly Freud meant to explain why he was suited to Martha, and Minna to her beau, by the contrasts in their natures. But an entirely different (and prophetic) construction might be put on this characterization.

Roazen speculates further: "The evidence for the premature falling off of Freud's sex life might be interpreted in a quite different light; instead of merely the cooling of his ardor for Martha, what might have happened is that he transferred his physical and/or emotional needs to another woman, Minna. (An old neighbor of the Freuds thought Minna was prettier than Martha.) In the case of such a prolific and self-investing writer as Freud, it may well be that if an affair with Minna ever took place, evidence for it exists somewhere in unpublished letters. . . . On balance, however, and in a tentative spirit, I would be inclined to reject the notion that a physical relationship existed between Freud and Minna. She did indeed speak to Jung about Freud's involvement with her; his attentions did worry her. But according to Jung's account it was Freud's attentions to her that were worrisome, not an actual affair."

Roazen concludes:

The important matter is what Minna meant to Freud, the power she gained over him, and not so much the specifics of a possible sexual liaison between them. Freud seemed to have a split in his love life, his sexuality remaining with Martha, and his spiritual involvement shifting to Minna.

The words used by Roazen to describe the possible inner relationship between Sigmund Freud and Minna Bernays—"spiritual involvement"—will remind some readers, as it did me, of the "spiritual concubine" nature of the relationships in the lives of Mary Wollstonecraft and "Rebecca West."

There is only one person who, at this time of writing, probably knows the true facts about the Minna Bernays–Sigmund Freud relationship: Miss Anna Freud. But in this, as in all other personal matters relating to her father, she has, like him, remained discreetly silent.

80

> NIGHTMARE, from the Teutonic *mare*, or goblin, female spirits or monsters supposed to beset people and animals by night, settling on their chests when they are asleep, and producing a feeling of suffocation.
> —*Oxford Unabridged Dictionary*

A Necessary Digression

Fuseli's painting, which created an international sensation in the 1780s, shows a voluptuous maiden in a revealing *negligee* sprawled over the edge of her bed in the throes of a suffocating nightmare. Through the medium of Fuseli's imagination *we* "see" what *she* "sees": a hideous naked goblin squatting heavily on her breast; and, at the same instant, thrusting violently through the vaginoid opening of the blood-red curtain, the head of a terrified and terrifying white horse. The goblin's angry, thwarted look suggests that the sudden arrival of the spectral horse has stopped him from sexually assaulting the helpless, perhaps dead, girl.

As I looked at this arresting decoration in Freud's waiting room, I wondered: "Was Fuseli inspired by similar 'scenes' from the then-fashionable Gothic horror novels and their illustrations? Or did he intend this to be a visual parable of a virgin's dread of rape? Fuseli was a tiny 'gnomish' man. Could this be some sort of self-projection of himself as a little ape-goblin seated on his mother's breast, about to commit some unspeakable act? I wonder what Freud thought about this picture given to him by Jones.

"But more relevant to this visit, we may ask why Freud displayed so violent and disturbing an image where no patient entering his consulting room could fail to see it. Other doctors hang happy or tranquilizing pictures. But not Freud, master strategist. He probably put this Grand Guignol shocker here to agitate, stir up his patients and, amusing thought, challenge them to bring him deeper dreams which might even hasten the healing process. Dreams *really* worth listening to!"

Then, paradoxically, Fuseli's horror print evoked several far from horrible associations which, when explored, confirmed an earlier suspicion, hinted at above, that Freud had restaged an important part of another Ibsen drama *(Rosmersholm)* in his private life.

In an essay about Mary Wollstonecraft's daughter Mary Shelley, creator of *Frankenstein,** I wrote: "A few months after the publication of her revolutionary *Vindication of the Rights of Woman* (1792), Miss Wollstonecraft, then thirty-three, fell in love with the runty fifty-one-year-old Johann Henry Fuseli, William Blake's friend and imitator. (His famous 'Nightmare' is swiped in part from Blake's engraving 'Death of the Wicked Strong Man.') Fuseli once said: 'Blake is damned good to steal from!' But obscure, completely isolated Blake forgave him and wrote a grateful if confused eulogy:

> The only man that ever I knew
> Who did not make me almost spue
> Was Fuseli; who was both Turk and Jew.
> So, dear Christian friends, how do you do?

"The Anglo-Swiss Fuseli was of course neither a Turk nor a Jew, but a self-defrocked Lutheran minister turned radical. Mary Wollstonecraft had a penchant for homely men of genius, and, forgetting her own dictum—'Nothing can more destroy peace of mind than platonic attachments. They are born in false refinement, and frequently end in sorrow, if not in guilt'—she Wollstonecraftily offered herself to Mr. Fuseli as his 'spiritual concubine.' But Mrs. Fuseli knew a husband stealer when she saw one and kicked her out of the house.

"Thwarted, Miss Wollstonecraft crossed the English Channel to Paris to witness and write about the "enthralling" French Revolution. There she met and fell in love with the American adventurer Gilbert Imlay and bore him an unlicensed child. Later, in London, when Imlay cruelly deserted their 'free love association' to live with a younger woman, the 'emancipated' Miss Wollstonecraft leaped from the Putney Bridge into the Thames. But, ironically, the voluminous air-filled dress and petticoats imposed on women by the male-dominated society kept her afloat, and she was removed from the water by passing boatmen.

---

*In *Life* Magazine, March 1968.

"While still damp, Mary, desperately seeking love, met, slept with, and then, contrary to her libertarian principles, married William Godwin, another most unworthy man. Soon afterwards she died in giving birth to the future authoress of *Frankenstein*, Mary Wollstonecraft Shelley."

81

Recently, while rereading Ibsen's *Rosmersholm*, I was struck by its resemblance-in-depth to the real-life Wollstonecraft-Fuseli episode. I now conclude that the pro-feminist author of *Doll's House* was familiar with the episode and may have based his *Rosmersholm* on the premise: "What would have happened if the Fuselis had indeed invited Mary Wollstone-craft into their home as a member of a platonic or spiritual ménage à trois?"

Observe the similarities: In *Rosmersholm*, the beautiful, dynamic Rebecca West, an emancipated intellectual "idealist," has been living in the home of Johannes and Beata Rosmer as Johannes's intellectual companion. Like *Johannes* Fuseli, *Johannes* Rosmer is a self-defrocked Lutheran minister. Earlier, Rosmer's wife Beata, realizing that the superior Rebecca has succeeded in stealing her unwitting husband from her, emulated Wollstonecraft's leap into the Thames with a similar leap off a bridge into a river millrace. At the drama's climax, Rebecca, consumed by guilt, confesses to Rosmer her responsibility for his wife's suicide. The play ends with their joint suicide by drowning: hand in hand, they leap off the same symbolic bridge into the same symbolic river. Except for the two endings, the basic situations are almost identical.

82

Many random "waiting-room" associations came to mind as I looked about the room waiting for the curator's return. One in particular was a paragraph (copied into my notebook) from Martin Freud's *Sigmund Freud, Man and Father.** In this nostalgic memoir, which consists mainly of a

---

*Published in England as *Glory Reflected*.

reliving of the idyllic summers enjoyed by the Freud family, Martin takes a brief vacation from vacations to speak about his father's early psychoanalytical circle:

> We were aware of the Wednesday night meetings in the waiting room of the Berggasse flat, where great minds, led by my father, strove to bring to the surface knowledge long suspected but still fugitive and still unrecorded with that precision science demands. We heard people arriving, but we seldom saw them. The inevitable curiosity of a boy allowed me to inspect the arrangements in the waiting room before the guests arrived. Near each chair on the table was always an ashtray from father's collection, some of them Chinese jade. I saw the necessity of this multiplication of ashtrays one night when, on returning from a dance, I looked into the waiting room from which the guests had only just withdrawn. The room was thick with smoke, and it seemed to me a wonder that human beings had been able to live in it for hours, let alone speak in it without choking. I could never understand how father could endure it, let alone enjoy it; which he did. It is possible that to some of his guests the smoke-filled atmosphere was an ordeal, but it is certain they thought the price low for the high privilege of a close personal contact with a great teacher.

As I sat in that "Berggasse flat waiting room," reading about the meetings held there about seventy years earlier, I wondered: "Do I detect a faint whiff of disguised Oedipal hostility in what I've just read? Here is a son who says he never sat in on his father's Wednesday night seminars but, on one occasion, went 'dancing' instead. He found the 'smoke-charged atmosphere' 'choking,' and wonders how his father 'could endure, let alone enjoy it.' "

The *choking* and *unendurable* smoke may actually be Martin's own psychological smoke screen for his underlying negative feelings, not toward the dense tobacco fumes, but toward the highly controversial Freudian theories discussed in the room . . . the sulfurous ideas which were responsible for his father's severe rejection in Vienna. This may be a loving, loyal, but troubled son speaking. In England, Martin Freud's book is called *Glory Reflected:* He did bask in the reflected light of his father's success in later years, but there must have been a great many hours of reflected shame and humiliation during the early years in Vienna.

83

The walls of the waiting room held about eighty objects. On the longest wall: a scramble of Freud portraits, framed diplomas, awards, testimonials, alternating with group photos of Freud and his colleagues, now all dead. Opposite this photo-Pantheon, in glass-front cabinets, some forty items from Freud's fine collection of concretized myth: small clay, bronze, marble icons from Egypt, Greece, Etruria and Rome, interspersed with such items as a "*sacred bull,* seventh century, B.C.*,*" two *dancing satyrs* of the same century, a "*phallic pendant,* Egyptian bronze" (worn to avert the evil eye and/or VD), and, as I noted with sharp personal interest, a "*Gorgoneion,* bronze, Roman, sixth century, B.C.*"* Its face, with protruding clit-tongue, was a twin of my own lost-and-found and exiled Etruscan coin. All these ancient artifacts, one reflected, were talismans owned by common people who needed to hold divinity in their hands.

Here, as in the front of the house and in the rear garden, as well as in Freud's personality and work, "myth" and "reality" had become extremely hard to separate. Soon, to this over-stimulated visitor, the waiting room began to resemble a gigantic surrealist assemblage, the smallest segment of which was myself.

But the opposition of mythic artifacts on one side of the room and the real images on the other side became further confounded by the presence of more mythic images among the photographs. Over a large picture of Freud and colleagues in Worcester, Massachusetts (1909), for example, there hung four eighteenth-century prints of dancing nymphs personifying *Fire, Water, Earth,* and *Air.*

84

Standing before a superb statuette of "*Enthroned Demeter,* Boeotian, fifth century before Christ," I mused: Those closest to Freud tell us that he spent all of his long working days and nights for more than forty years completely surrounded by his large collection of things which had "died" and been resurrected archeologically. He used his collection as a part of his resurrective therapy; he "fondled choice pieces"* while talking (but never while listening); he discussed them with art scholars and dealers, read about them avidly, and even took new acquisitions to the dinner table, where he devoured them (visually) along with his favorite meal of *Rindfleisch.* †

Freud, profound iconographer, must have regarded this ancient "Enthroned Demeter" with great admiration and respect, since she symbolizes the triumph of indomitable love over death . . . which is, after all, the ultimate goal of psychoanalysis.

Demeter was an even greater fertility goddess than the downstairs Pomona and Diana; with Dionysus she governed all vegetation, especially vineyards. But she was worshipped in the ancient world and is remembered now mainly for her dauntless rescue of her beloved daughter Persephone. When Hades, king of the underworld, fell madly in love with Persephone, kidnapped her, and made her the mistress of his dreadful domain, Demeter strove desperately to bring her back to life. When all else failed she went on strike, halting the growing of all vegetation on earth. Finally, under great pressure, Zeus reluctantly forced Hades to return Persephone to her mother for all but the winter months.

85

Demeter and Baubo

Freud's passionate, lifelong preoccupation with mythological characters, his assiduous collection and study of their images, his deep, precise knowledge of their iconographic meanings, his curative use of that knowledge are shown once again in a paper he published in 1916.

Here, in the flattened language of the Abstract published by the U.S. Public Health Service, is his "A Mythological Parallel to a Visual Obses-

---

*We may guess what he would have said if one of his patients, while talking, had played with similar hard, rigid objects!

†Boiled beef. His son Martin says he ate it three or four times a week.

sion."* As may be seen, Freud was thoroughly acquainted with the Demeter figure in his collection and, characteristically, extracted an amusing erotic episode from her great story:

> A mythological parallel to a visual obsession is presented. In a patient of about 21 years, the products of conscious mental activity become unconscious not only in obsessive thoughts but in obsessive images. The two could accompany each other or appear independently. At one particular time, whenever the patient saw his father come into the room, there came into his mind, in close connection, an obsessive word and an obsessive image. The father was *"father-arse"*: the accompanying image represented his father as the naked lower part of a body provided with arms and legs, but without the head or upper part. The genitals were not indicated, but the facial features were painted on the abdomen. "Father-arse" was soon explained as a jocular Teutonization of the honorific title of patriarch. The obsessive image is an obvious caricature. It recalls other representations which, with a derogatory end in view, replace a whole person with one of his organs; it reminds us, too, of unconscious fantasies which lead to the identification of the genitals with the whole person, and also of joking figures of speech such as "I'm all ears."

Enter two characters from the mythology always at the threshold of Freud's consciousness. The Abstract quotes him: "According to a Greek legend, Demeter came to Eleusis in search of her abducted daughter Persephone; she was given lodging by Sysaules and his wife Baubo; but in her great sorrow she refused to touch food or drink. Thereupon her hostess Baubo made her laugh by suddenly lifting up her skirts and exposing her body. In the excavations at Priene in Asia Minor some terra-cottas were found which represented Baubo. [Like the obsessive images seen by Freud's patient.] They show a woman's body without a head or chest and with the face drawn on the abdomen: the lifted dress frames the face like a crown of hair."

When curiosity led me to find photographs of these ancient Baubo figures, I found that the "Abstracter" did not describe them accurately. The "face" is not "drawn on the abdomen." It is created by means of an amusing, ingenious visual pun in which the parts of the body "stand in" for facial features: Baubo's breasts become her "eyes"; her belly button is her "nose"; her chin-cleft becomes a hairless "pubis." The photographed

*(Washington, D.C., U.S. Government Printing Office, 1971.)

images reminded me that many of us high-school art students drew "Baubos"; that, later, in the *Dictionnaire Abrégé du Surréalisme*, Paris, 1938, I'd seen René Magritte's funny Baubo variations. (In American slang, breasts are sometimes called "eyes," as in the "What beautiful *eyes* you have!" of the low burlesque skits.)

86

Seated at the elegant little table in the waiting room (my rear end faints whenever it sees a chair) and looking rapidly from wall to wall, I began to feel like a spectator at a jai alai match. Finally, dizzied by the extreme incongruities of the room's imagery, I imagined that the *"Hellenistic Aphrodite*, fifth century, B.C.," was actually glaring across the room at a photo of unsmiling men at "The Psychoanalytic Congress, the Hague, 1920: J. van Emden, E. Jones, S. Freud, S. Ferenczi, and Dutch psychoanalysts." If Aphrodite (Venus) is indeed staring at these gents, she may be thinking: "If it weren't for me, none of these psyche-repairmen, especially that 'S. Freud,' would be in business. And what do I get from them? Nothing. Not one of them has ever sacrificed anything to me, not even a scrawny rooster! And I shan't ever forget what Freud did to my image right here in this house. Of course he repaired it. But the damage to my pride remains, and I shall certainly talk to King Hades about the matter."

(My coupling of "Aphrodite" with the word "sacrifice" probably came from an unconscious recall of Freud's impulsive "act of sacrifice," his smashing of the pagan "marble Venus" at the time of his daughter's illness. Was the Aphrodite of the waiting room the *same* one he attacked with his bedroom slipper? A substitute?)

87

Myth and reality merged again, farcically, at the American School in Rome in June 1951 at a third-graders' performance of *Persephone*, with our daughter Ruth Amber in the title role.

The ten-minute-long scripted drama began as an unrelieved tragedy. But soon, because the kids were obviously bored and perhaps scared by all the talk about death, the drama collapsed into a wild and funny improvisation.

At the climax the seven-year-old Persephone and the eight-year-old Demeter, spurning the male-chauvinist help of descending (and condescending) Zeus, took matters into their own little hands. They rescued Persephone from her infernal imprisonment by a direct assault on King Hades: they whacked him, knocked him down, sat on him, tweaked his nose, and then took turns jumping up and down on his gilded cardboard crown. At last, to thunderous applause led by Ruth Amber's proud Mom and Dad, they strutted offstage hand in hand.

88

Soon one playful fantasy spawned another, and all the portraits and photos of Freud were staring empathetically at an engraving (after Rembrandt) of Moses. In this crude print the great lawgiver, Freud's major "identification" figure, has just returned from his summit powwow with Jehovah, stone steno-pad in hand. He has just learned that his "stiff-necked" people have reverted to the bestial worship of the Egyptian god Apis in the form of a golden bull-calf. He is about to smash the offending idol and the tablet of the Commandments and to order the execution of 3,000 idolaters.

In his *Erotica Judaica*,* Allen Edwards explains the reasons for Moses's drastic reprisals against the Hebrew backsliders: "While Moses meditated in the mountains, consulting his Yahwic oracles, the Hierarch Aaron was induced to fashion an image of Apis (Egyptian bull-god of fertility) from the molten gold earrings of the womenfolk.

"During the sacrificial feast, an orgy of eating and drinking and copulating, a sacred auto-erotic-homosexual ritual erupted among a vast number of males (who apparently outnumbered the females) 'cocked up to

---

*(New York, Julian Press, 1967.)

pound repeatedly' *(yiqqumŭ li-tzahiq)*. Linked like huge [daisy] chains of flesh about the idol, these zealots performed the circular dance *(hagg)*, sanctified to arouse the procreative power of Apis with the seminal libations of repeated masturbation and round-robin sodomy. The ceremony was the *sine qua non* of all phallic worship."

Another, delayed afterthought: All this "smashing" and "breaking" of false idols by Moses, with whom Freud identified so powerfully, suggests that Freud's "accidental" breaking of the "beautiful little marble Venus" from his collection of non-Jewish art, an "act of sacrifice" during his daughter's illness, may also have been an act of propitiation to the Hebrew God whose commandment he had violated:

"Thou shalt have no other gods before me. Thou shalt not make unto thee any graven images, or any likeness of anything that is in the heavens above, or that is in the earth below, or that is in the waters beneath the earth. Thou shalt not bow down to them, nor serve them: for I the Lord thy God am a jealous God, visiting the iniquity of the fathers upon the children even unto the third and fourth generation of them that hate me." (Exodus 20: 3, 4, 5.)

In Freud's waiting room Rembrandt's "Moses" seemed to be stiffly averting his gaze from all the forbidden graven images cherished by Freud, especially the propinquitous *sacred bull*.

89

Some weeks after returning from Vienna, I read a personal memoir by Dr. René Laforgue,* France's first psychoanalyst and a long-time friend of Freud, and learned that during a discussion of a Schwind painting at a seminar in his waiting room, Freud could not resist "playing" one of the painted characters.

We have already seen above how Freud, incited by Schwind's picture of "Raymond Surprising Melusina at Her Bath," dreamed he was the vow-breaking Raymond; now he was reenacting another of the artist's

---

Freud As We Knew Him, edited by H. M. Ruitenbeck. (Detroit, Wayne State University Press, 1973.)

paintings,* with himself in another antiheroic role—and doing so quite consciously.

As Dr. Laforgue tells it: "One day one of Freud's collaborators told the story of Schwind's painting of 'St. Hieronymous.' It took place at Freud's house at the close of a lecture by one of his pupils on the Ego. After giving his opinion on the discourse, Freud spoke about Schwind's painting, which shows the saint selling his soul to the devil to get the materials for the construction of a cathedral. Freud asked his listeners who, in their opinion, represented the saint and who the devil. Naturally, everyone replied that Freud was the saint. 'You don't know then that I am the devil?' he exclaimed. 'During my lifetime *I have had to play the role of the devil* in order that others might construct cathedrals with the materials I brought.' [Italics mine.]†

> "Even if this anecdote is not authentic," says Laforgue, "and there is not reason to doubt the person who told it—it corresponds to reality. It is Freud, the atheist, to whom we are beholden for our knowledge of the role of faith and myth in the development of the ego, on both the individual and collective planes."

90

Notes written after my first visit to Berggasse 19 read: "Hotel de France, 6:00 P.M. Except for a small table and mirror, Freud's consulting room and study have none of the original furnishings and only a few unimportant pieces from his art collection. I seriously miss seeing the art collection, especially one particular image I had hoped to see: the enormous Ernst Koerner print that hung on the wall behind Freud and directly over the head of his reclining patients. This etching, which I've studied in several books, depicts the façade of Ramses II's Great Temple at Abu Simbel on the Nile, 250 miles south of the Mediterranean. This picture is, I believe, the key to one of Freud's most profound reenactments.

"Faced with the problem of re-creating Freud's professional suite, but

---

*A third picture by Schwind may be seen in Freud's *General Introduction to Psychoanalysis:* "The Dream of the Prisoner."

†This is repeated for emphasis.

unable to use its original furnishings, the museum curators hit on a clever idea: they obtained the photographs of the rooms made by Edmund Engelmann a month before the Freuds escaped, had huge wall-to-wall murals made from them, and installed them in the proper position. Then, above these murals they exhibited about four hundred Freud-related photographs, documents, and memorabilia. In glass-topped cases are displayed first editions of books and papers written by Freud and others.

"As we entered the consulting room, the curator said: 'As you can see in the photomurals, the famous couch stood there against that wall; and, of course, Freud sat at the head of the couch in that corner.'

"After gazing in awe at the mural and then at the now-empty space occupied by the great man for more than thirty years, I, wishing to show off my knowledge of the room, pointed to a white object under a table filled with Egyptian statues. 'That must have held the water for Freud's Chow dog. I read somewhere that the Chow had Pavlovian reflexes: he lay at the foot of the couch during the entire session, and when the hour was up, he would get up and walk to the door. I wonder: If the patient ignored the signal and kept on talking, did he growl menacingly, bare his teeth?'

" 'Oh, no!' said the curator defensively. 'He was a *good* dog! Very *friendly!* But that reminds me, a former patient who visited here told me that once when he was having a hard time expressing himself and could feel Freud's impatience, suddenly the dog jumped up and ran to the door. He must have heard something. To the patient's astonishment, Freud also jumped up and, imitating the dog, also ran to the door. He then turned and said to the patient, "You see, the dog and I are trying to escape from you because you are boring us. But if you promise to do better we will return and listen to you." ' "

91

"Cipion" Freud

Freud's actorlike mimicry of his pet Chow may be related to his life-long syndrome. (What, *"syndromic" dogs* too?) In a bit of information that reveals his indefatigable mythomania, we learn from Jones about:

". . . Silberstein . . . who was Freud's bosom friend in schooldays. They learnt Spanish together and *developed their own mythology* and private words, mostly from Cervantes." (Emphasis mine.)

"In another book they found a philosophical dialogue between two dogs who lay before the doors of a hospital, and they appropriated their names for themselves. Silberstein became 'Berganza,' and Freud was 'Cipion' and used to sign his letters to his friend *'Tu fidel Cipion, perro en el Hospital Sevilla.'* "

Was the pet Chow that lay at the foot of the couch and ran to the door of Freud's consulting room a reincarnation of "Cipion-Sigmund"? This notion is verified by the strong similarities and by the presence in Freud's workrooms of sculptures of several Egyptian dog-headed humans, a link between the boy and the man.

92

As I entered the Freudhaus for my third visit, the young curator greeted me with good news: "The people now living in the other half of Freud's apartment invite you to look at it." A moment later we crossed the hallway, to be admitted by a large, robust and friendly man in his early thirties. As we walked through the foyer and into the living room he said, redundantly, "This is the living room." He seemed embarrassed.

As I looked around the spacious, high-ceilinged room and compared it mentally with a photograph made shortly before Freud's 1938 "exodus," it was obvious that no physical trace of Freud's occupancy remained. Freud's home reminded me of theaters where once-great actors had played in great dramas to huge audiences. Now all had vanished.

The present occupant's uneasiness disturbed me, and I thought: "Will he allow me to see the other rooms? I'd like to locate, if possible, the spot near the bedroom where Freud, perhaps imitating the enraged Moses and/or Suetonious's disenchanted Roman, smashed one of his pagan household icons and spoke the line: *'Ach! Die Venus ist perdu!— Klickeradoms!—von Medici!'*

"And will I be permitted to look at the former bedroom of Freud's sister-in-law Minna Bernays, which she could enter or leave only through the bedroom of Freud and her sister? A most peculiar arrangement, suggesting a household for three. I already know that Freud once reenacted an entire scene from Ibsen's *Hedda Gabler* when he fainted in Bremen in 1909. Now, standing here in Freud's living room, I suspect . . . no, more than suspect, that Freud reenacted part of Ibsen's *Rosmersholm* as well—with himself as Johannes Rosmer and with Minna Bernays as his 'spiritual concubine' Rebecca West. But I sense that this embarrassed man won't let me go beyond this room." A moment later he said: "I'm sorry, but we have family visitors, and it won't be possible to show you the other rooms. You understand . . ."

As I thanked him and lingered for a last look around the room, I thought sourgrapedly, "Well, the other rooms are probably as devoid of Freud as this one. But all is not lost. With the help of the two eyewitnesses Martin Freud and Ernest Jones, I will still be able to reconstruct some of the dramatic scenes enacted right here in this living room during Freud's last days in Vienna in the spring of 1938."

93

Every reader over fifty will remember the terrible events of 1938: after outwitting, humiliating, frightening the Western democracies into becoming helpless spectators of his actions, Hitler decided to conquer Austria. All through 1936 and 1937 his deadly propaganda machine, aided by Austrian "fifth columnists," built up to a Wagnerian climax of attacks on left-wing parties and the Austrian Jews, especially those in Vienna. When Chancellor Schuschnigg defied Hitler and ordered a plebiscite on independence to be held on March 9, 1938, Hitler moved at once to forestall the predicted vote against him.

"The first months of the year," writes Jones in his biography of Freud, "were filled with the apprehension of a German invasion. . . . Like so many Austrian Jews, Freud had hoped that Chancellor Schuschnigg would conjure up some device for warding off the danger. As late as February, Freud wrote to Eitingon (in Palestine), 'Our brave, and in its way honest, government is at present more energetic in defending us against the Nazis . . . although in view of the newest events in Germany, no one can be sure what the outcome will be.'"

Then, in what appears to be another of Freud's syndromic references to characters in a classical work of fiction, Freud adds: " 'One cannot avoid thinking occasionally of Meister Anton's closing words in one of Hebbel's dramas, "I no longer understand this world." ' "

Writing to Marie Bonaparte just one month before Hitler's triumphal entry into Vienna, Freud, still clutching at straws, said: "It undeniably looks like the beginning of the end for me. But we have no other choice than to hold out here. Will it be possible to find safety in the shelter of the Catholic Church? *Quién sabe?*"

94

The "Hebbel drama" referred to in Freud's letter to Max Eitingon is, I find, *Maria Magdelena*, written in 1844. It is not, as I imagined before reading it, a drama about the Christ-redeemed harlot; its symbolic "Magdalene" is Clara (no last name), a middle-class German girl of the 1840s who, jilted by her fiancé when he made her pregnant, and rejected by her father, Meister Anton, drowns herself. Hebbel's moral: It was her father's "selfish pride and weakness" which led his daughter to make the mistakes that led to her self-destruction.

As I read this play, keeping in mind Freud's propensity for identification with fictional characters when in crisis, I wondered: "Was Freud's recall of the closing words in *Maria Magdelena* a random one, or was he in his hour of great apprehension identifying with Meister Anton?" Freud was writing to Eitingon, who had wisely anticipated the coming horrors and emigrated to Palestine with his family, long before the threatened invasion. Was Freud thinking he was another Meister Anton, that his own weakness and selfish pride (in staying in Vienna, his headquarters) might cause the death of his beloved daughter Anna and others? If so, then we have another (tragic) example of Freud's syndromic replay of a literary work.

Also: The symbolic, ironic title *Maria Magdelena* implies a similarity between the Biblical harlot and Anton's sexually "sinful" daughter, with Anton as a crucified Christ. Possible equation: If indeed Freud was thinking of himself as another Meister Anton, and that character is a secular Christ, then, deep down, is Freud thinking of himself as a "Christ crucified"? Once before, during a talk with his friend Ludwig Binswanger, Freud referred to himself in another context as a "Christ on Calvary."* Again, as related above, he metaphorically wore the "Iron Crown of Lombardy," with its reminder of the crucifixion.

95

Freud's Living Room as Arena

When, on March 12, 1938, the Freuds, who knew that Hitler's armored divisions were approaching Vienna, heard newshawks shouting headlines, they immediately bought a paper and handed it to Sigmund Freud: "He read the headlines through," writes Martin in his memoirs; "and then, crumpling it with his fist, he threw it into a corner of the room. Such a scene might not be unusual in any happy land not enduring political convulsions; but father's self-control seldom, or never, permitted him to show emotion: and thus all of us remained silent in the living room, well aware that a turn of events which would allow him to fling a paper from him in disgust and disappointment must have alarming implications."

Martin continues: "We did not dare question him as he now sat deep in thought, thoughts which, doubtless, saw foundations crumbling and normal security fading into uncertainty, but we too had to know what was happening, something I sensed in the others when, after a few moments, I crossed the room and picked up the crumpled paper. The front page . . . expressed jubilation; enslaved Austrians were apparently greeting liberators . . . all this, we knew, was bad for Austria; but as I read through the paper, I saw that the tragedy had narrowed down to us—that we Jews would be the first victims. Anti-Semitic propaganda was cleverly distributed throughout the general news items. Mean and dastardly crimes, allegedly committed by Viennese Jews, were reported, and, following closely the example of Streicher's *Stürmer*, given pornographic flavor."

After dutifully presenting his father's reactions to the catastrophic

---

*Ludwig Binswanger, *Sigmund Freud, Reminiscences of a Friendship*. (New York, Grune & Stratton, 1957.)

news, Martin recalls his own responses in terms that remind one of "Joseph K," the victim in Kafka's enigmatic *The Trial:* "My feelings," writes Martin, "if I may express what I felt, were of horror and a strange perplexity. I, as a respectable barrister and the eldest son of a man of worldwide reputation, nurtured insecurity; and, not affected by my father's fame, I could only imagine myself enduring a nightmare, as an innocent man standing on the dock to be condemned by judges unconcerned with a trial, and sentenced to death in dishonor."

On the following morning the anticipated reign of terror that soon engulfed all the Jews of Austria moved from Freud's living room to the nearby office of the *Psychoanalytic Press,* where Martin, its manager, was feverishly selecting financial records for burning. Suddenly a gang of Austrian Nazis with rifles burst in. As Martin tells it: "There were a dozen of them, an odd medley shabbily dressed, including a fat boy of perhaps fourteen who nevertheless took a full part in the discussions and had a vote. The most aggressive was a small haggard-looking man who, unlike the others, was armed with a revolver. Whenever I showed no desire to cooperate, he displayed a bloodthirsty spirit by dragging out his pistol and noisily pulling out and pushing in the magazine as he shouted, 'Why not shoot him and be finished with him? We should shoot him on the spot!' "

For almost the entire day, while Martin was forced to remain in his chair with rifles held against his stomach, the invaders ransacked the premises looking for hidden cash and "incriminating documents." But, as in Poe's *Purloined Letter,* they overlooked completely a group of important papers lying exposed on a shelf near the door.

Recalling all this eighteen years afterwards, Martin wrote: "One of the curious aspects of this raid was the fact that across the narrow street from the office there lived a staunch Nazi who, now seated at his window, enjoyed a grandstand view of the proceedings, something I was unaware of at the time."

After placing the money from the safe in neat uncounted piles on the table, the invaders left, leaving Martin guarded by the trigger-happy "small haggard-looking man." But as soon as they were left alone, the little man's belligerency wilted as he told a long whining tale of personal misfortunes and financial bad luck. Understanding correctly that the man was hinting, "I can be bribed," Martin gave him all the cash he had—and was at once allowed to go to the hallway toilet. There he tore the important papers (which he had picked up on his way) into bits and flushed them down the john.

The incipient tragedy now turned into Kafkian comedy: As Martin's newly purchased friend stood guard outside the toilet door waiting for him to come out, several of his comrades returned to the office and pocketed some of the money. At once the ever-watchful Nazi seated in the window across the narrow street phoned headquarters. In a few minutes his district commander arrived to take charge, declared the raid "unauthorized," and searched the pockets of the raiders for the money belonging to *"Der Fuehrer."* When Martin's bribe was found in the schlemielian guard's pocket, it was assumed to be the confiscated money, and the guard was immediately stripped of his prized revolver. But was he shot on the spot? Court-martialed? Severely reprimanded or slapped on the face as in an old war film? No, says Martin; he was arrested and made to stand in the corner with his face to the wall.

Then, after violently "chewing out" the free-lance looters, the district commander curtly ordered Martin to report to the Gestapo headquarters on the following day and released him. Outside, Martin met his sister Anna; together they dashed up the street to be with their parents.

At Berggasse 19, Martin was relieved to learn that though a similar raiding party had confiscated 6,000 schillings ($840.00) and Mrs. Freud's household money, they had behaved decently, being under the command of an officer presumably ordered not to harm or harass the "man of worldwide reputation" or members of his household.

"I think mother's attitude had some effect," says Martin. "Deeply concerned for father at this time, barely recovering from one of his [cancer] operations, and forced to spend much time resting on the sofa in his study, she called on that inner strength she shared with him, and remained perfectly calm."

He adds:

> It was no small thing to a woman of mother's housewifely efficiency to see her home invaded by a pack of irregulars, yet she treated them as ordinary visitors, inviting them to put their rifles in the hallway umbrella-stand. Though the invitation was not accepted, her courtesy and courage had a good effect. Father too had retained his invincible poise, leaving his sofa where he

had been resting to join mother in the living-room, where he sat calmly throughout the raid.

Ernest Jones, who had arrived from London to be with Freud and who had himself undergone a brief arrest, tells it somewhat differently: "Mrs. Freud, fetching her household cash, placed it on the table and said, 'Won't the gentlemen help themselves?' Anna Freud then escorted them to a safe in another room and opened it. The loot amounted to 6,000 Austrian schillings ($840.00), and Freud ruefully commented that *he* had never been paid so much for a single visit. They were debating their prospects for continuing their petty burglary when a frail and gaunt figure appeared in the doorway. It was Freud, aroused by the disturbance. He had a way of frowning with blazing eyes that any Old Testament prophet might have envied, and the effect of lowering mien completed the visitors' discomfiture. Saying they would call another day, they hastily took their departure."

They returned of course. A week later, the Gestapo ransacked the house and then arrested Anna. Her brother, a terrified witness, tells of the glimpse he had of her being taken away: ". . . Anna being driven off in an open car escorted by four heavily armed S.S. men. Her situation was perilous; but far from showing fear, or even much interest, she sat in the car as a woman might sit on her way to enjoy a shopping expedition."

To this Ernest Jones adds, "This was certainly the blackest day in Freud's life. The thought that the most precious being in the world, and also the one on whom he so depended, might be in danger of being tortured and deported to a concentration camp, as so commonly happened, was hardly to be borne. Freud spent the whole day pacing up and down and smoking an endless series of cigars to deaden his emotions. When she returned at seven o'clock that evening, they were no longer to be restrained. In his diary for that day, however, March 22, there is only the laconic entry '*Anna bei Gestapo.*' "

After four months of tortured waiting, while all around them the Jews of Vienna were daily being carted off to torture, deportation and extermination, Freud and his family were finally, in June 1938, given permission to leave Vienna.

In his last confrontation with the enemy, Freud was told he could have the vitally important visas for himself and family if he agreed to sign a formal release written by the Gestapo:

I, Professor Freud, hereby confirm that after the Anschluss of Austria by the German Reich I have been treated by the German authorities and especially the Gestapo with all the respect due to my scientific reputation, that I could live and work in full freedom, that I could continue to pursue my activities in every way I desired, that I found full support from all concerned in this respect and that I have not the slightest reason for any complaint.

Freud signed it, of course, but, Viennese to the last, he could not refrain from giving himself a good exit line. Turning to the leather-coated officers, he asked if he might add a word of his own. After some discussion they agreed, and Freud wrote, "I heartily recommend the Gestapo to everyone."

96

After spending a few days in Paris with Princess Marie Bonaparte, the heroine of their rescue, Freud met his son Ernst; together they took the boat-train for Calais and Dover. The eighty-two-year-old Freud, with only one more year to live, stood the journey well, "aided by doses of nitroglycerin and strychnine" administered by a physician who accompanied him to London.

As might be expected, the dramatic journey into exile provides us with one of the most remarkable of Freud's syndromic reenactments, this time a multiple one. Says Jones: "During the night journey from Paris to London, Freud dreamed that he was landing at Pevensey. When he related this to his son Ernst, he had to explain that Pevensey was where William the Conqueror landed in 1066. That does not sound like a depressed refugee, and indeed it foreshadowed the almost royal honors with which he was greeted in England."

97

William the Conqueror

Although Freud explained the topmost layer of his "Pevensey" dream as relating to the landing there of William the Conqueror, there are, I find, several additional possibilities for exploration which supplement Freud's explanation. I say this because, while I was thinking and writing about Freud's dramatic nocturnal fantasy, the name "Shakespeare" flashed before me repeatedly.

So, recalling Freud's passionate love of Shakespeare's plays, I brooded on the matter for a bit, and then remembered the possible link between Shakespeare and the "William the Conqueror" in Freud's dream. It was the well-known anecdote about Richard Burbage and Shakespeare recorded by their contemporary John Allingham, an anecdote I'd read in George Brandes's *William Shakespeare,* a book owned, admired, and referred to by Freud.

In his journal for March 13, 1602, Allingham wrote:

Upon a time when Burbidge played Rich, 3, there was a Citizen grone so farr in liking with him, that before shee went from the play shee appointed him to come that night unto hir by the name of Ri:the 3. Shakespeare ouerhearing their conclusion went before and was entertained (in her bed) ere Burbidge came. Then message being brought that Rich, the 3rd was at the dore, Shakespeare caused return to be made that William the Conqueror was before Rich, the 3rd. Shakespeare's name was William.

If we obey Freud's instructions to look for the sexual wishes concealed within many dreams, we may ask: Does the historical William the Conqueror seen by Freud mask an additional underlying image of himself as the sexual "William the Conqueror" of that English "Citizen," Mother England herself? A vagrant and perhaps farfetched analysis which, I hope, provokes similar exploratory fantasies in the imaginative reader. (It's a pity Freud is no longer here to respond to the questions raised by his dream-identification with William the Conqueror.)

98

> See them guarded, and safely brought to Dover.
> —Shakespeare, *Henry Sixth, Part I*

> There is a litter ready, lay him in't, and drive
> towards Dover.
> —Shakespeare, *King Lear*

> (Freud) crossed on the ferryboat to Dover.
> —Ernest Jones, *The Life and Work of Sigmund Freud*

As I continued to write and reverize about Freud's identification with the two "William the Conquerors," a dense cluster of ideas and images evoked by the Shakespearean associations began to circle around the dream Freud had while traveling in his wagon-lit to Dover:

"Freud, the helplessly sick old man driven from his home by evil, power-mad usurpers . . . exiled, *he makes his way to Dover* with his wife and daughter Anna . . . enroute *he is met by his son Ernst who accompanies him to Dover* and then to London . . . of whom do Freud and his tragic situation remind me? He has spoken of himself as a self-exiled *Oedipus,* as an expatriated or exiled '*Old Jacob,*' as the permanently exiled '*Wandering Jew,*' and the exiled '*Chief Rabbi of Jerusalem*' at the time of the Roman conquest. . . . But now two other exiled characters come vaguely to mind . . . *aged fictional characters who were also on their way to Dover.*"

Then I remembered: "In this tragic episode Freud closely resembled Shakespeare's *King Lear* and his fellow victim, *The Duke of Gloucester.* In fact, the similarities between Freud and these two fictional characters are so striking that one may suspect that in 'going to Dover' Freud was performing another of his unconscious reenactments."

99

> Go thrust him out at gates, and let him smell his
> way to Dover.
> —said of blinded Gloucester, *King Lear*

To show the similarities among *King Lear, Gloucester,* and Freud, here are the related incidents from the fictional and real-life tragedies.

The Duke of Gloucester: Blinded, ruined, and exiled from his home by Lear's dreadful daughters *Goneril* and *Regan* (the combined names seem to equal *gonorrhea*), the aged Gloucester *decides to go to Dover* and leap to his death from the white cliffs. He does try "to smell his way to Dover," but cannot find his way. Finally, he meets his exiled and hunted son Edgar, who pretends to be a mad fool out of Bedlam. The blind man begs the disguised Edgar to lead him to his fatal destination.

GLOUCESTER: Know'st thou the way to Dover? . . .
Dost thou know Dover?

EDGAR: Ay, master.

GLOUCESTER: There is a cliff, whose high and bending head
Looks fearfully in the confined deep.
Bring me to the very brim of it,
And I'll repair the misery thou dost bear
With something rich about me. From that place
I shall no leading need.

EDGAR: Give me thy arm.
Poor Tom shall lead thee.

But instead of leading his sightless father to the cliffs of Dover, Edgar, double-talking all the way, continues to walk on the flat plain. Finally, believing that he is standing on the "brim" of the high cliffs, Gloucester "leaps" and faints. When revived, he is easily convinced that he not only had leaped, but had also been saved by a divine miracle.

At that moment King Lear appears. Driven insane by the massive brutality inflicted upon him by his daughters and their consorts, exiled from court, stripped of his title and wealth, he is wandering alone *in search of Dover*, where he hopes to find his one loyal daughter Cordelia, and her husband, the king of France, who have arrived with an army to avenge the wrongs done him.

We return to Freud to summarize: Like Lear and Gloucester, he was, we repeat, an old and helplessly sick man who was driven into exile by evil, power-mad villains. Like the Shakespearean characters, *Freud is on his way to Dover.* Just as Gloucester was met by his son Edgar (acting as Tom the Fool), so did Freud meet his son Ernst while on his way to Dover;

his son accompanied him the rest of the way to Dover and London. Like Lear, Freud chose to "go to Dover" in the hope of finding peace and security with his family. Like Lear and Gloucester, the aged psychoanalyst was on the verge of death. Earlier, like Lear and Gloucester, Freud *also fainted* twice during power crises.

100

Inner voice: "But how could this be a 'reenactment'? Freud's situation was not a fantasy like all the others we've discovered, borrowed from history, myth, or fictional works. In this situation Freud and all the other Austrian Jews were the palpable victims of a vast political reign of terror expressed *physically* in house and business raids, beatings, murder, and extermination in German death camps and exile. This was an *enactment!*"

Another inner voice answered: "True enough. But the logical validity of this reenactment, if that was what it was, pivots on *Freud's choice of destination*. He could have chosen to stay in France, or he could have gone to Canada as his brother Alexander did. He would have been welcome in Scandinavia or in the United States; instead, he chose to go to England by way of Dover."

101

The Consulting Room

While wandering physically and mentally about the space once vitally occupied by Freud, his patient-bearing couch, his therapy-related collection, and his canine votary, I mused: So this is the world-famous room where couch number one, now in London, used to stand. Hilda Doolittle was cured in this room of her terrifying hallucinations . . . a genius capable of responding to Freud and his icons on an Olympian level, she called this room his "Inner Sanctum" . . . to her he was a "Supreme Being," a god in human form, and a high priest of the "mysteries" as well. She was perhaps the only one who perceived that his cigar-smoking may have been a part of the magical-scientific-religious healing arts practiced here, and there is more than a trace of wit in her remark: "From his niche rises *the smoke of burnt incense*, the smoldering of his mellow, fragrant cigar." But now her image as she lay on the couch, the couch itself, and all the talismans that surrounded her and her "blameless physician" have vanished with all the rest.

Another visitor to this room and the adjoining study also perceived Freud as a descended deity. Writing at about the same time as Doolittle, Dr. Maryse Choisy Clouzet, a French psychoanalyst, said: "Never did my heart beat for a lover as it did the day I walked up the Berggasse. Was that really a steep climb? Or did it only appear so to me because I was at last going to see my God (at that time) who by some miracle had become accessible?"*

How much therapy did this great healer actually do in this room? Let's see, now . . . after moving here from the downstairs he had used for seventeen years, Freud worked with his "cases" until he left Vienna in 1938. Since he didn't become a psychoanalyst until about 1893, and didn't acquire a full caseload for some years, it's hard to arrive at an exact figure. Jones says that Freud saw ten to eleven patients a day for more than forty years. Even with the time lost during the First World War and the long summer vacations, we may estimate that Freud conducted his therapeutic sessions for 90,000–100,000 hours. If these separate hours were to be joined into one continuous single session, we see that Freud listened and talked to his patients *twenty-four hours a day for about ten years!*

My rumination continued: Here in this extraordinary environment, Freud integrated his psychiatric work with his art collection, his library, and something else quite magical. . . . It's that "something else" I've come here to try to learn about. In this room and the adjoining study . . . actually one large room, since he always left the doors wide open . . . Freud surrounded himself and his patients with his large collection of Egyptian, Greek, Etruscan, Cypriote, and Roman sculptures and artifacts. There were some fine Oriental pieces as well. Behind him at his listening post, suspended over the heads of his reclining patients, where they could not

*Maryse Choisy, *Sigmund Freud: A New Appraisal*. (New York, Philosophical Library, 1963.)

avoid looking at it, Freud hung an enormous print of the Great Temple built by Ramses II on the Nile at Abu Simbel. . . . This was the temple recently taken apart and reassembled on the cliffs above to escape the waters rising behind the new Aswan Dam.

Atop the cabinet at the foot of the couch rested a large 3,000-year-old model of an Egyptian funerary ship manned by slaves . . . probably taken from the tomb of an aristocrat. On the study desk, plainly visible to Freud and his patients through the open door, stood a number of Egyptian gods in human form. Together with the Vishnu, Athena, and Osiris figures he handed Hilda Doolittle, they, his peers, communed with him as he worked far into the night on his books, monographs, and correspondence. In this consulting room, on the table between him and the outer doors, he placed in his direct line of vision many more Egyptian figures, all lined up like palace sentries. Did he consciously or unconsciously intend them to be his own private Swiss Guard? I have several (to me) plausible reasons for thinking he did. The first is one that may seem trivial: after visiting the Vatican in 1907 he jokingly signed a letter to his family with the word "Papa." He signed other letters from Italy and other places with the same word, but *without* the quotation marks. In many languages the word *papa* means *father*; to Freud, fluent in Italian, the word was meant, I think, to be an obvious pun (ambivalence) meaning: "I am not only your father, but everyone's Holy Father as well." Several commentators mindful of the "confessional" and other spiritual and psychological similarities between Catholicism and Freud have called Freud a "Pope." Freud's awareness of the well-known comparison is illustrated in the already quoted remark he made to his friend Ludwig Binswanger. When Binswanger asked him why Jung and Adler had broken away from him, Freud replied, "Precisely because they too wanted to be Popes."

102

The overwhelming presence in Freud's healing chamber of funerary imagery formerly buried and then resurrected as life-enhancing instruments leads me to suspect that Freud, who identified with the Hebrew-Egyptians Joseph and Moses, also identified with the Egyptian aristocracy who surrounded themselves in their tombs with replicas of their families, gods, animals, vehicles, ships, and slaves to serve them in the afterworld.

Did Freud really create this entirely mythicized environment to serve as the dramatic arena in which he starred as a reincarnated high priest, nobleman, or Pharaoh? My accumulated data and observations tell me that it was the last, that in his "deepest being" Freud identified with the Pharaoh Ramses II.

103

Recently, while reading Jack Spector's *The Aesthetics of Freud*, I found that he had reacted similarly to the clearly necrophilic aspects of Freud's collection when he saw it in London. After speaking of "the dominance of the theme of death and burial" in the large collection, Professor Spector adds, "Perhaps more significant than any of the themes so far discussed is that of death. This subject, partly hidden, partly obtrusive, pervades the whole collection. . . . One can easily list the more obvious instances: all the Egyptian works, the little marble name plates from a Roman sarcophagus, the Greek and Roman burial urns, especially those containing ancient bones, the Kaulbach engraving from the *Totentanz* [dance of death] series . . ."

Mr. Spector ends his comment with the reminder that Sigmund Freud is presently a consubstantial part of his collection: his ashes now repose in a "Grecian urn given him by Princess Marie Bonaparte." That "Grecian urn" (actually a Roman Apulian vase) was once prominently displayed in Freud's study or consulting room.

Another keen-eyed observer who spotted the preponderance of therapeutically employed death objects with which Freud surrounded himself was the novelist Arnold Zweig. In 1929 he wrote to Freud perceptively, revealingly, ". . . during our conversations in your flat in Vienna, among all the treasures and sacred objects which the tombs have had to yield up to you who opened so many a tomb . . ."

The direct impact of the enveloping Egyptian images—each a negotiable unit of profound human experience, especially those related to death and rebirth—is revealed in the dream interpretation arrived at by Freud and the most perceptive Hilda Doolittle. After equating herself with a "dream-doll" and with the infant Moses, she tells of the "Egyptian impact." In so doing she reveals Freud's main reason for staging his therapy in his crowded museum of antiquity:

> The doll is the dream or the symbol of the dream of this particular child [herself], as these various Ra, Nut, Hathor, Isis, and Ka figures that are dimly apprehended on their shelves or on [Freud's] table are the dream or symbol of the dream of other aspiring and soaring souls. . . . The childhood of the individual is the childhood of the race, we have noted Freud has written somewhere. The child in me has vanished and is yet not dead. This contact with the Professor [Freud] intensifies or projects this dream of a Princess, the River . . . the child Moses. The river is an Egyptian River, the Princess is an Egyptian lady. Egypt is present.

Then, perhaps mistakenly identifying the Abu Simbel picture she has seen daily for many months, she adds, "Egypt is present, as I say, actually or by inference in the old-fashioned print or engraving of the Temple of Karnak, hanging on the wall above me, as well as the egg-shaped Ra or Nut or Ka figures on the Professor's desk in the next room" (visible through the always-open doors between the treatment room and Freud's study).

Afterword: Freud's print of the Karnak temple may have hung over the couch when Hilda Doolittle graced it in 1933–34. Several Egyptologists have said that of the many self-glorifying monuments built by Ramses II, the two most magnificent were the temples at Karnak and Abu Simbel. From this we may deduce that of the multitude of pictures of Egyptian monuments to choose from, Freud selected for his healing arena one or the other of the Ramsesian architectural masterpieces. It would seem that Ramses the Great was vitally important to him.

104

Now, as we continue to think about the Abu Simbel print and its owner, more questions arise: "Why did Freud acquire this outsize picture and hang it in his 'Inner Sanctum' where the patient was forced to look at it a great many times? Was his interest in the print aesthetic? A part of his well-known archeological interests? His Egyptomania? Or did he, in addition, have deeper hidden motives for making this the dominant object in his psychoanalytical theater?" To find some possible answers we must first examine the print, and then learn something about the Abu Simbel temple and the Pharaoh who built it.

First, the picture itself: Engraved by the Berliner Ernst Koerner in 1906, it shows the only façade of a "Great Temple" at the edge of the fructifying Nile. Dwarfing all other façade elements sit four gigantic identical statues of Ramses II, guarding the vast structure carved out of the mountain. Wearing a false beard (once painted black) the quadruplicated Ramses sits with his hands on his lap, serenely welcoming his suppliants. He faces eastward, we're told, awaiting the morning sun, confident that its life-giving rays will conquer the symbolic night-death and resurrect him for another day. High above him, a line of carved baboons join him in waiting for the revivifying light. This play of life-versus-death symbolism is repeated in the objects Ramses holds crisscross on his chest; the symbols of the murdered and resurrected Osiris, god of the tombs in which the living-dead await rebirth. All royal Egyptians who died "became" Osiris. Everything here is resurrectional.

At the feet of one Ramses-Osiris lies the greater part of his body, fragmented by rocks fallen from the high cliff above. In ancient times crowds of pilgrims seeking spiritual (psychological) and physical regeneration prostrated themselves before the enthroned Ramses before entering the inner temple to pray before nine more images of the deified Ramses.

105

He sits among mortal men like a descended god;
He hath a kind of honor sets him off
More than a mortal seeming.
—Shakespeare, *Cymbeline;* Posthumous, as described by Iachimo

The Great Temple at Abu Simbel

Early in the thirteenth century before Christ, Ramses II ordered his architects to build the Great Temple for the celebration of his *sed,* or the thirtieth anniversary of his reign. In remote times the *sed* ended with the ritual murder of the king and the crowning of his successor. But in Ramses's time the sacrificial ritual had long since been replaced by one in which the symbolically slain Pharaoh replaced himself.

Pilgrims who entered the inner temple found themselves in a vast corridor flanked by eight thirty-foot-high Ramses statues, each holding the symbols of the murdered and resurrected Osiris. These guards of honor protected the innermost sanctuary in which the Pharaonic megalomania reached its climax: seated on a low throne on equal terms with the major gods Ptah, Amun, and Re-Hakarti was the deified Ramses. He too sat with his hands folded in his lap, staring toward the eastern horizon. The temple, Egyptologists tell us, was constructed on an east-west axis so that a great symbolic resurrectional event could take place. Amelia Edwards, who witnessed the yearly event in the 1870s, wrote: "It is fine to see the sun come over the hilltops, but something finer takes place on certain mornings of the year, in the heart of the Great Temple. As the sun rises above the trees, one long level beam strikes through the doorway, pierces the heart of the inner darkness like an arrow and penetrates to the sanctuary. No one who has watched the coming of the shaft of sunlight can doubt that the excavation was directed at one special angle to produce it."

106

A tentative summary of Freud's relationship to the print of Abu Simbel, the dominant object in his "Inner Sanctum," is, roughly:

Item: Freud habitually identified with ancient great heroes and kings, real and fictional, among them Hannibal, Alexander the Great, King Lear, Odysseus.

Item: Freud, a passionate amateur Egyptologist, knew all about Ramses, the great Abu Simbel temple, and the elaborate symbolic religious thinking which prompted Ramses to build his self-monument.

Item: Freud, who, as we know, identified profoundly with the Hebrew-Egyptians Moses and Joseph, certainly knew that "Ramses" was the name of not only the Pharaoh but also the district and town where Joseph settled his father Jacob and their family. Ramses was also the starting-point of the Moses-led Exodus.

Item: A strategist who was never aimless in such grave matters, Freud acquired and carefully positioned the enormous Egyptian print on the wall behind his chair and directly over the couch, forcing the patients to look at it. Thus we see that Freud and Ramses would be constantly seen, subliminally, as almost identical figures seated in exactly the same position, facing in the same direction. When, as was the case a great many times, Freud sat silently with his hands in his lap, listening to his suppliants, the mutual resemblance must have been amazing. In this extraordinary visual equation Freud and Ramses become as one.

Item: If Freud's consulting room is visualized as an unconsciously choreographed arrangement, with the dramatistic Freud as a "Pharaoh" surrounded by his Egyptian "next world" objects; seated before the Abu Simbel print as a "fifth Ramses"—then Freud's reclining patients may be seen in a related double role.

First: Lying prostrate directly below the Egyptian temple, at the feet of the seated Ramses figures, they merge visually, as in a collage, with the ancient suppliants who prostrated themselves before the man-god Ramses before entering his temple of spiritual regeneration. Second: They are at the same time lying "at the feet of" Dr. Sigmund Freud for exactly the same reason: they are pilgrims who have come to the room Doolittle called the "Inner Sanctum" as suppliants seeking spiritual (psychic) regeneration. Yes, the art of healing was practiced in the ancient religious and now in Freud's modern secular temples.

Item: A mind-boggler. If all of this seems valid, this "item" may be the most therapoetic of all. If Sigmund Freud lay on that celebrated couch to rest or conduct his great self-analysis, then, with a further stretch of fantasy, we may see him as *the second Ramses from the left*, whose broken fragments lie on the ground before the other intact Ramses statues. (I *said* this would be a mind-boggler!)

107

Recently, while studying the photographs of Freud's consulting room and a copy of the Abu Simbel print on the wall behind him, I found my attention being drawn time and again to the two figures of the falcon-headed Re, ancestor of all the Pharaohs. One of these figures stood on the table directly in front of Freud's listening post; the other guarded the entrance to Abu Simbel's inner temple.

Finally, after some brain-wracking, I perceived the reasons for this special interest when I recalled that figures exactly like these appeared in one of Freud's childhood dreams. Soon it became apparent that the dream, when thought about, helped verify the hypotheses that Freud identified with one of the Pharaohs, probably Ramses II, and with the patriarchal Moses, whom he believed to have been an Egyptian nobleman.

The dream, from *The Interpretation of Dreams:* "It is dozens of years since I myself had a true anxiety-dream. But I remember one from my seventh or eighth year, which I submitted to interpretation thirty years later. It was a very vivid one, and in it I saw *my beloved mother, with a peculiarly peaceful, sleeping expression on her features, being carried into the room by two (or three) people with birds' beaks and laid on the bed.* I awoke in tears and screaming, and interrupted my parents' sleep. The strangely draped and unnaturally tall figures with falcons' heads were derived from the illustrations to Phillipson's Bible. I fancy they must have been gods with falcons' heads from an ancient Egyptian funerary relief."

My interpretation of this nightmare, based on Freud's unconscious "syndromic" thinking, runs along these lines: First, if Freud's dream-mother is being laid to rest by falcon-headed figures representing the great Egyptian god Re, she was not Freud's real mother, a lower middle-class Galician *yiddeneh*, but an Egyptian princess or queen. And, obviously, if Freud's "mother" was a member of the high nobility, her dreamer-son would also be a scion of the nobility, perhaps an heir to the throne—like Ramses II, whom he imitated in his physical self-positioning in his consulting room that was so much like a royal tomb filled with funerary art and objects.

And if his dream-mother was a royal princess, she might very well have been the same princess who rescued the infant Moses. (In his *Collected Lectures,* Freud wrote: "In myths a person who rescues a baby from the water is admitting she is the true mother. There is the well-known comic anecdote according to which an intelligent Jewish boy was asked who the mother of Moses was. He replied without hesitation: 'The Princess.' 'No,' he was told, 'she only took him out of the water.' 'That's what *she* says,' he replied, and so proved that he had found the correct interpretation of the myth."

In a footnote to this "comic anecdote," James Strachey, editor, adds: "Freud used this 'correct interpretation' of the myth as the basis of his last work, *Moses and Monotheism*, 1939."

108

A star witness: Some time after setting down my speculations about Freud as a conscious or unconscious mimic of the man-god in the Abu Simbel picture, I found that an observer close to Freud had spotted the print and intuitively recognized its significance. She was Mrs. Lou Andreas-Salome—whom we have met as a "character" in Carl Jung's "Elijah" dream. Mrs. Salome, who saw the Abu Simbel print during her many private discussions with Freud in his consulting room, ends her *Freud Journal* with words which show that she had given much thought to the role the Ramses figures played in Freud's thought and in his psychiatric arena:

"And all the vanished persons of the past arise anew, whom one had sinned against by letting them go; they are there from all eternity— peaceful, monumental, and one with being itself, as the rock figures of Abu Simbel are one with the Egyptian rock, and yet, in the form of men, sit enthroned over the water and the landscape."

109

> Thou shalt not have any other gods before me.
> Thou shalt not make unto thee any graven images, or any likeness of anything that is in the heavens above, the earth beneath, or that is in the water beneath the earth.
> —Exodus 20: 3, 4

I believe that I may have found the precise "identification" link between Freud the Jew and Freud the crypto-Pharaoh who surrounded himself with Egyptian, Sumerian, Hittite, and other non-kosher "graven images." It is the fact given by Ernest Jones that Freud's hidden first name was *Schlomo* or Solomon. Like many Jews of his and earlier generations, Freud was named after the wisest of Hebrew kings.

Recalling Freud's statement that a man's name plays an important if not decisive part in shaping his character and lifelong behavior, I reviewed King Solomon's life and found that "Solomon" Freud may have (in part) collected "idolatrous" objects in syndromic imitation of King Solomon, who also violated the strict commandments against having images of "other gods." If this is so, then we may add to the long list of Freud's compulsive restagings from ancient history: Schlomo Freud=King Schlomo.

The pertinent quotations from the Old Testament's I Kings are these:

1. But King Solomon loved many strange women, together with the *daughter of the Pharaoh* [this is a definite link between Freud, his Pharaoh-like consulting room, and his famous identification with Moses, whom he believed to be the son of an Egyptian princess], women of the Moabites, Ammonites, Edomites, Ziddonians, and Hittites.

4. And it came to pass, when Solomon was old, that his wives turned his heart after other gods; and his heart was not perfect with the Lord, his God, as David his father.

5. For Solomon went after Astoroth, the goddess of the Ziddonians, and after Milcom, the abomination of the children of Ammon.

7. Then did Solomon build a high place for Chemosh, the abomination of Moab, in the hill that is before Jerusalem, and for Molech, the abomination of the children of Ammon.

9. And the Lord was angry with Solomon, because his heart was turned away from the Lord God . . .

10. And commanded him concerning this thing, that he should not go after the other gods: but he kept not which the Lord commanded.

In his *Bible Dictionary*, William Smith summarizes: "King Solomon fell from the loftiest heights of his religious life to the lowest. Before long the Hebrew priests and prophets had to grieve over the rival temples to Molech, Chemosh, and Astoroth, forms of ritual not only idolatrous, but cruel, dark, and sexually impure. Solomon found himself deeply involved in the fascination which led to the worship of strange gods."

Like the Golden Calf, Astoroth, better known as Astarte or Ishtar, was a fertility goddess worshipped orgiastically. In his *Erotica Judaica* Allen Edwardes explains: "She was the Semitic Aphrodite or Venus. She is said to have sprung from the prepucial or circumcisional blood of Al or Cronus."

We must not, however, think of Freud's collection too narrowly. Though his collection held many "idols" identical with those worshipped or tolerated by Solomon, Freud had other important therapeutic and intellectual reasons for gathering effigies of phallic or fertility gods: they were essential to his profound explorations of the origins of our behavior.

The resemblances between the two Schlomos—Solomon and Freud—go beyond their common rejection of Jehovah and the possession of forbidden gods. Many of King Solomon's celebrated proverbs exalt the pursuit of wisdom above all other qualities or possessions. One proverb seems to describe his Viennese namesake's vocation and method perfectly: ". . . thou criest after wisdom and understanding and *searchest for them like a hid treasure.*" To Freud, lifelong reader of the Old Testament, this may have been a poetic directive.

PART THREE

Why Freud Fainted

Richard III: I swoon with the dead-killing news.

As You Like It: Now counterfeit to swoon, why not fall down?

King John: Did your brother tell you how I counterfeited a swoon?

Antony and Cleopatra: He sleeps—swoons rather.

Expectation fainted, longing for what it had not.

Othello: O, for a chair, to bear him easily hence!—Alas he faints!

Titus Andronicus: . . . if fear hath made thee faint.

1

"Life imitates art."
—Oscar Wilde

We may say that hysteria is a caricature of an artistic creation.
—Freud, *Totem and Taboo*

Although, by his own admission, Sigmund Freud fainted hysterically five times, the best documented and important of his psychosomatic attacks, "in the presence of Carl Jung," occurred in Bremen in 1909, and in Munich three years later. The first, two years after they met; the other before they parted as enemies in 1913.

Though other psychoanalysts were present on both of these remarkable (understatement) occasions, it has generally been assumed that the "attacks" were Freud's direct response to his conflicts with the increasingly intransigent Jung. And this may indeed have been the major cause.

However, as my "detective" explorations of these cryptic events will suggest, there may have been more, much more, to these "attacks" (interesting choice of words) than was reported by Ernest Jones, the various memoirists, or by Freud himself.

Along with a great many others, I bought the "eagerly awaited" Jones biography of Freud in 1953. After reading the story of the great man's Jewish origins, childhood, student days, struggles with poverty and discrimination, betrothal, marriage, his switch from pure research to medical practice, I came to "Chapter XII, *The Fliess Period* (1887–1902)."

There I was astonished to learn that my great hero Sigmund Freud was actually *human*, that he had suffered from a severe emotional-mental psychoneurosis lasting about ten years, that this unnamed illness was linked by him and Jones to what appeared to be a heavily sublimated or repressed platonic (?) or overtly homoerotic (?) relationship with a man named Wilhelm Fliess; that, according to *Freud's own written diagnosis* (letter), the transfer of his feelings for Fliess to Carl Jung played an important part in his faintings first in Bremen and then in Munich. Especially the latter.

2

As background for my informal inquest of the circumstances surrounding Freud's mysterious "losses of consciousness" in the two German cities, I present some key excerpts from eye-witness accounts, from sources close to the central figure—and, later, from letters Freud wrote at the time.

The first excerpt, from Jones's biography:

> However unpalatable the idea may be to hero-worshippers, the truth has to be stated that Freud did not always possess the serenity and inner sureness so characteristic in the years when he was well known. The point has to be put more forcibly. There is ample evidence that for ten years or so—roughly comprising the nineties—he suffered from a very considerable psycho-neurosis. An admirer might be tempted to paint this in darkest colors so as to emphasize by way of relief Freud's achievement in self-mastery by the help of the unique instrument he himself forged.* But there is no need to exaggerate; the greatness of the achievement stands by itself. After all, in the worst times Freud never ceased to function. He continued with his daily work and with his scientific investigations. His care and love for his wife and children remained unimpaired, and in all probability he gave little sign of neurotic manifesta-tions to his surroundings (with the sole exception of Fliess). Nevertheless, his sufferings were at times very intense, and for those ten years there could have been only occasional intervals when life seemed much worth living. He paid heavily for the gifts he bestowed on the world, and the world was not very generous in its rewards.

---

*His epochal self-analysis.

Jones then reminds his audience of the benefits to them of Freud's suffering:

Yet it was just in the years when the neurosis was at its height, 1890–1900, that Freud did his most original work. There is an unmistakable connection between these two facts. The neurotic symptoms must have been one of the ways in which the unconscious material was indirectly trying to emerge, and without that pressure it is doubtful if Freud would have made the progress he did. It is a costly way of reaching that hidden realm, but it is still the only way.

Was Freud *conscious* of all this? Yes, says Jones, "Freud of course recognized the existence of his neurosis, and several times in the [Fliess] correspondence used that word to describe his condition. . . . It consisted essentially of extreme changes of mood, and the only respects in which the anxiety got localized were occasional attacks of dread of dying *(To-desangst)* and anxiety about travelling by rail *(Reisefeber)*. He refers to Fliess's having witnessed one of the worst attacks of the latter in Berchtesgaden at the time of their first 'Congress' in 1890, probably when they were parting."

The second excerpt relates to Freud's intimate relationship with Wilhelm Fliess during his ten years of intense psychoneurotic suffering:

We come here to the only really extraordinary experience in Freud's life . . . for a man of nearly middle age, happily married and having six children, to develop a passionate friendship with someone intellectually his inferior, and for him to subordinate for several years his judgments and opinions to those of the other man: this is also unusual, though not entirely unfamiliar.

The always protective Jones then lifts his worthy subject off the subtly suggested homoerotic hook and adds deserved high praise: "But for this man to free himself by following a path hitherto untrodden by any human being, by the heroic task of exploring his own inner mind: that is extraordinary in the highest degree."

3

(Freud's acute anxiety attack in the German railroad station when he had to part with Fliess—did he faint then as he had done on two other similar occasions?—reminds one of Jung's fainting attack in a Swiss railroad station long afterward. The only connection I can think of is that Jung, intimately conversant with Freud's psychological history, and having read about Freud's *Reisefeber* or railroad anxiety and "Hannibal-Rome complex" in *The Interpretation of Dreams*, "used" this information in 1949 unconsciously while he was buying his ticket to Rome in the Swiss station—as another of his imitations of Freud.)

According to Ernest Jones, the only biographer given access to Freud's private papers, Freud met Fliess, a Berlin nose-and-throat specialist, when he came to Vienna in 1887 to do postgraduate work. During that brief period a mutual friend, Dr. Josef Breuer, who later collaborated with Freud on *Studies on Hysteria* (1893), touted Fliess onto Freud's pre-psychoanalytical lectures on physiology and neurology. The two young men (Freud, thirty-one; Fliess, twenty-nine) discovered many intellectual interests in common and began what Jones calls a "passionate friendship." (Later, Freud said of Fliess: "I loved him very much.")

A voluminous correspondence began when Fliess returned home—an outpouring of letters, manuscripts, reprints, etc., in which Fliess told Freud about his theory that the nose played a major role in the causation of a great many diseases; he also propounded his system of mystical numerology which, he insisted, could be used to predict the course of human conditions both normal and abnormal, and even predict the time of a person's death. (I have often wondered what Freudian psychologists think when they read that Freud twice asked Fliess to operate on his nose. Or that, long before "Bremen" or "Munich," *Freud fainted* dead away when he witnessed a bloody operation Fliess performed on a woman's nose. As everyone knows, to Freud a nose was a you-know-what symbol.)*

Freud's letters to Fliess are among the important documents in modern cultural history. They tell, step by step, the development of psychoanalysis from 1887 until the publication of *The Interpretation of Dreams* in 1900. Jones believes that the "passion" began to ooze rapidly from the Freud-Fliess friendship when Freud neared the completion of his

---

*The reader will recall that during two minor surgical operations on his throat (1882–1883) Freud hysterically smashed his engagement ring. Point? Freud utilized such surgical nose-and-throat intrusions symbolically.

"dream-work." Though there were other reasons, it seems that Freud, no longer needing Fliess as his sounding board, ditched him.

4

The most extraordinary feature of what Jones calls "the only really extraordinary experience in Freud's life" was, I find, their manner of meeting. Says Jones, always stressing the "intellectual" aspects of their relationship, "The two men met fairly often in Vienna, and occasionally in Berlin, but whenever possible they would meet for two or three days elsewhere away from their work, where they could concentrate on the development of their ideas. These special meetings Freud half jocularly, half sadly, called 'Congresses.' Fliess was, as he put in an allusion from Nestroy, his 'sole public.' And this was literally so. There was no one else, no one at all, with whom he could discuss the problems that so preoccupied him."*

Pausing for a moment to note that here again, in a strong emotional context, Freud "identified" with a literary figure, this time the nineteenth-century Austrian playwright Nestroy, we continue with Jones's account of the "intellectual" meetings: "We know of several of these meeting places, but the list is probably incomplete. The first one certainly took place in Salzburg in August 1890. Then there were 'Congresses' in Munich (August 1894), Dresden (April 1897), Breslau (December 1897), and in or near Ausee (July 1898); and the final one, where the break took place, in Achensee, Tyrol (September 1900). They never met again. In later years an international Psychoanalytical Congress was held in four of these six towns; the one arranged to take place in a fifth town also, Dresden, was prevented by the outbreak of the First World War."

---

*Freud's wife Martha seems to have expressed no objections to these extraordinary and frequent "intellectual" trysts. But Fliess's wife became, says Jones, "increasingly jealous of the close relations between the two men and did her best—spurred on by Breuer!—to disrupt them. Ultimately Freud summed her up as a 'bad woman,' but doubtless she had her point of view."

5

. . . the importance of being Ernest Jones

Jones's dead-earnest listing of these Fliess-Freud "Congresses" has incited another rumination loaded with presently unanswerable questions: Now why did these "passionate friends" deem it so necessary to leave wives, family, patients, research projects, and familiar environments to travel to these distant powwows? While working as a photographer in Berlin in 1946–47, I traveled by train to the places listed by Jones: Munich, Salzburg, Nuremberg, and the Austrian Tyrol. And what excruciatingly long and boring trips they were . . . eight to twenty-four hours long. Now that's a helluva long way to go for intellectual discussions, even those as great as these must have been. Jones's use of the word "passionate" begins to seem like an understatement. Also, his professional attitude toward the Freud-Fliess relationship is puzzling. Here is a first-rate Freudian analyst who elsewhere exposes such "arrangements" with merciless objectivity; yet in this case, perhaps feeling the need to protect Freud and a therapy beneficial to mankind, he says nothing about the sexual implications of these "two- and three-day" flights from conjugality. I suppose he expects the trained or perceptive reader to read between the lines understandingly, sympathetically, and then, for the good of all suffering humanity, to join the benign conspiracy of silence. And, incidentally, surely Jones knew; but did Freud, fluent in English, know that in English the word "congress" is a well-known euphemism for sexual intercourse?*

But something Jones *does* say immediately after listing the numerous out-of-town "Congresses" did make me sit up and take notice: "It is understandable that such meetings played a central part in Freud's otherwise isolated intellectual life. *They were oases in the desert of loneliness.*" (Italics mine.)

Have you, reader, ever seen these italicized words before? No? Well, they are a slight variation of the epigram uttered by Oscar Wilde during his 1882 American tour as advance man for the Gilbert and Sullivan operetta

---

*The Oxford Unabridged Dictionary defines "congress" as: "sexual union, copulation, coition."

Patience, based on Wilde's homosexual "aestheticism." When he was asked the trite reportorial question, Wilde answered: "The American woman? She is a charming *oasis in the* bewildering *desert* of common sense." (My emphasis.)

Is Jones's variation of Wilde's famous witticism as innocently sympathetic as it seems at first glance? Or was it an inadvertent or parapractic spilling of diagnostic beans, revealing his private view of the Freud-Fliess relationship as "Wildean"? My guess is that Jones's use of that figure of speech was far from innocent.

6

. . . oases in the desert of . . .

This line was instantly familiar to me because, in my recent book about Arthur Conan Doyle and Sherlock Holmes,* I offered my discovery that Doyle used a variation of the oft-quoted "oasis" crack to identify one of his comic characters as an "Oscar Wilde."

This, in part, is what I wrote:

> Doyle's *The Sign of Four*, bought by a Lippincott editor at a dinner in which Oscar Wilde was commissioned to write *The Picture of Dorian Gray* (that was *some* dinner!), begins with the arrival of Miss Mary Morstan at 221B Baker Street.
>
> Mary, later Mrs. Watson, tells Sherlock Holmes that she has received a very frightening note from a mysterious stranger asking her to meet him at a London theater. She begs Holmes to go with her.
>
> At the theater they are met by a go-between who takes them in a hansom-cab to a suburban street of abandoned homes. There they are led to a magnificent apartment in one of the houses. In that "Arabian Nights" setting they meet the writer of the frightening note. He is Thaddeus Sholto, a superaesthete who not only talks like Oscar Wilde, but also has facial features and mannerisms which identify him as the man Doyle dined with and later called in his memoirs "the champion of aestheticism."
>
> The obviously effeminate and effete Sholto identifies himself as a carica-ture of Wilde with his first remarks: "Pray step into my sanctum. A small

---

Naked Is the Best Disguise. (New York, Bobbs-Merrill, 1974; Penguin Books, 1975.)

place, but furnished to my liking, *an oasis of art in the howling desert of London."* [Italics mine.]

Then, after describing himself as an "aesthete," an obvious link to Wilde, the talkative Sholto ends his monologue with some remarks about his painting collection, remarks that seem irrelevant, even pointless, until one realizes that the entire parody of Wilde was written by Doyle for the sake of his final jokes about Wilde's well-known sexual preferences:

> I may call myself a patron of the arts. *That is my weakness.* That landscape is a genuine Corot [core-oh], and though a connoisseur might perhaps throw a doubt upon that Salvatore Rosa, *there cannot be the slightest doubt about the Bouguereau* [bugger-oh]. I am partial to the *French* [orogenital, fellatio] *school.** [My emphases and interpolations.]

To ensure that his readers, who knew Wilde from the numerous caricatures in the contemporary press, would easily recognize Sholto as Wilde, Doyle described him as having ". . . *a pendulous lip,* a too-visible line of *yellow and irregular teeth, which he feebly tried to conceal by constantly passing his hand over the lower part of his face."* When we compare this with Wilde and Doyle biographer Hesketh Pearson's description of Wilde, we see the visual proof of Doyle's sly intentions:

> Wilde had *thick purple-tinged lips, uneven discolored teeth* . . . it was noticed by many that *when talking he frequently put a bent finger over his mouth which showed he was conscious of his unattractive teeth.*

7

We continue with more background material taken from Jones's biography:

> The Fliess story is dramatic enough; so indeed is the minor one of how the world came to know of it. Freud destroyed the letters Fliess sent him, but Fliess preserved Freud's. Some time after Fliess's death in 1928 his widow

---

*I apologize to all Frenchmen for Doyle's use of the word "French" in this context.

sold the packet of 284 extremely private letters, together with the accompanying scientific notes and manuscripts Freud had from time to time sent him, to a bookseller in Berlin, Reinhold Stahl by name. But she sold them under the strict condition that they were not to pass to Freud himself, knowing he would immediately destroy them. Freud and his wife had both been very fond of Frau Fliess in the early days, but as time passed she became increasingly jealous of the close relations between the two men and did her best . . . to disrupt them. Ultimately Freud summed her up as a "bad woman," but doubtless she had her point of view. At all events her final thrust was a shrewd one.

Stahl fled to France during the Nazi regime and there offered the documents to Mme. Marie Bonaparte, who at once perceived their value and acquired them for £100 ($500.00). She took them with her to Vienna, where she was doing some post-graduate analysis with Freud, and spoke of them to him.

Now comes Freud's self-revealing reaction: "He was indignant about the story of the sale and characteristically gave his advice in the form of a Jewish anecdote. It was the one about how to cook a peacock. 'You first bury it in the ground for a week.' 'And then?' 'Then you throw it away!' "

Jones completes his account of this "Fliess" incident: "He offered to recompense Mme. Bonaparte by paying half the expenses, but fearing this would bestow on him some right in the matter, she refused. She read to him a few of the letters to demonstrate their scientific value, but he insisted they should be destroyed. Fortunately she had the courage to defy her analyst and teacher. . . ."

When I read this account of the sale of Freud's letters and his "characteristic Jewish anecdote," I laughed. This is funny and amazing. Here we have Freud, of all people, revealing himself in a spontaneous outburst worthy of his most unsophisticated patient. And it goes unnoticed. In Freud's symbology a bird, especially one with "cock" as part of its name, signifies an erect penis or "fucking." In his analysis of his "Bird-Beaked Figures" dream, Freud recalled: ". . . an ill-mannered boy, son of a concierge . . . it was from him that I first heard the vulgar term for sexual intercourse (*Voglen,* from *Vogel,* or bird) instead of which educated people use the Latin word 'to copulate.' "

And Ernest Jones, who repeats the "peacock recipe" without comment, certainly should have recognized it as an unconscious self-revelation, because, using Freud's symbolism and methods, he had once written an essay about the Catholic belief, now abandoned, that the Virgin's Conception was effected by God's Word transformed into a bird and its song.* The music entered the Virgin's ear (displacement upwards of the vagina) and impregnated her. In this essay Jones wrote: "Birds have always been favorite baby-bringing symbols and are still used for this purpose in the familiar stork legend; winged phalli were the commonest Roman fertility amulets. . . . the reptilian neck of birds, the power of rapid intrusion, are features that inevitably recall a snake, thus explaining why this part of the bird is unconsciously conceived in terms of phallic symbolism."

And Marie Bonaparte, to whom Freud gave the "peacock recipe," wrote in her study of Edgar Allan Poe: "We know that flying, to all races, unconsciously symbolizes the sex act, and that antiquity often represented the penis erect and winged."

". . . winged phalli looking like cocks . . ." This fourth example of cock-as-phallus symbolism comes from a letter sent to Freud by Jung in 1907. Later, in a different context, I will quote more of the letter, but here, to show that Freud was quite used to getting verifications of such symbolism from his disciples, are Jung's words: "Do you know Kaulbach's pornographic picture 'Who Buys Love-Gods?' (Winged phalli looking like cocks, getting up to all sorts of monkey-tricks with the girls.)"

A footnote in The Freud/Jung Letters, † source of this quotation, adds: "A drawing (undated) by Wilhelm von Kaulbach (1805–74). . . illustrating Goethe's poem 'Wer Kauft Liebesgotter?' Reproduced in Eduard Fuchs's [!] Das Erotische Element in der Karikatur, Berlin, 1904."

When we apply Freud's own symbolic vocabulary to his responses to the suddenly surfaced letters he wrote to Fliess, several interpretations come to mind. One would be: "My relationship to Fliess is now as dead as he is. Yes, dead and buried. If exhumed, it will prove to be a rotten and

---

*"The Madonna's Conception Through the Ear," 1914.

†Edited by William McGuire; translated by Ralph Manheim and R. F. C. Hull. (Princeton, Princeton University Press, 1974.)

inedible phallic peacock. Don't attempt to cook and eat it. Throw it into the garbage where it belongs!"

8

My recognition of the symbolic meaning of Freud's "peacock" is based also on several non-Freudian sources. The first, of course, is the common knowledge of the meaning of "cock" in American slang. The second is D. H. Lawrence's use of the word in the 1930s, a daring usage at that time. Another was the "dirty joke" circulated in Cleveland's Glenville High School: "What's the difference between a rooster and a 'loose woman'?" Answer: "A loose woman says, 'Any cock will do!' "

And that reminds me of Herman Melville's allegorical "cock" in his astonishingly naked parable *Cock-a-Doodle-Do!* written in the 1850s. In that piece of tragic "obscenity" masquerading as a humorous sketch, Melville, as narrator, tells of his sudden obsession with an unseen neighborhood rooster with the loudest crowing he has ever heard.

He soon spends all his time searching for the bird, but cannot find it. Finally, he tracks it to the shack of a handyman-woodcutter named "Merrymusk" (another of Melville's allegorical sexual names), and asks him: "My friend, do you know of any gentleman hereabouts who owns an extraordinary cock?" The lecherous eyes of Merrymusk twinkle brightly as he answers with an even more flagrant double entendre: "I know of no *gentle*man who has what might be called an extraordinary cock."

This heavy-handed wordplay leads to tragedy of an inexplicable nature: When the narrator (Melville) offers five hundred dollars for the unseen cock, the impoverished Merrymusk refuses to sell. Finally, the continual crowing of the phallic bird mysteriously causes the death of Merrymusk and his entire family. Some highly imaginative Melvilleans have guessed that this is a parable of Melville's secret sexual life.

(How did Melville "get away with" such a parable printed in the 1850s? Or did he? Was it the transparent "obscenity" of this and other parables, including parts of *Moby Dick*, that helped bring about his literary and personal "oblivion"? I think so.)

9

"Dear Professor Freud . . .
Ever sincerely yours,
JUNG"
—*The Freud/Jung Letters*

While searching for psychological clues to Freud's first syncopicol-
lapse, I have found a small piece of information that may have played a
significant part in that incident: It is a subtly hostile passage in a letter
Jung wrote to Freud shortly after their first highly euphoric meeting in
1907.

Jung begins this letter, quoted in part previously, with several titillating little case histories. One is that of a "hysterical patient who is obsessed
with a Lermontov poem about a prisoner who releases his 'beloved bird
that is his sole companion.' " Jung asks, " 'What is the patient's greatest
wish?' She: 'Once in my life I would like to help someone reach perfect
freedom through psychoanalytical treatment.' In her dreams she is condensed (identified) with me. She admits that her greatest wish is to have a
child by me who would fulfill her unfillable wishes. For that purpose I
would naturally have to 'let the bird out first.' (In Swiss-German we say:
'Has the birdie whistled?')

"A pretty little chain, isn't it? Do you know Kaulbach's pornographic
picture 'Who Buys Love-Gods?' (Winged phalli looking like cocks, getting
up to all sorts of monkey-tricks with the girls.)"

Jung next regales Freud, the perfect audience for such tidbits, with the
piquant case of a girl with an "itching anus . . . who relieved it by sitting
with her bare behind on the stove. . . . At twenty she had a bad attack of
diarrhea. Her mother wanted to fetch a doctor, but the patient fell into a
state of nervous excitement because she didn't want to be examined,
fearing that the doctor would look at her anus. But what a frightful tussle it
was until the whole story was out!"

Then, abruptly switching psycho-channels from the titillating "winged
cocks" and "itching anus," Jung links Freud to a pair of eighteenth-
century Viennese doctors now regarded as charlatans: the hypnotist Franz
Mesmer, and Franz Josef Gall, reader of head bumps, or phrenology

specialist. (Mesmer, Gall, and Freud graduated from the Vienna University Medical School.)

I believe this unflattering juxtaposition, crudely linking Mesmer and Gall to Freud, and to the cities of Vienna, *Bremen*, and Zurich (Jung's home), helped predispose Freud to faint during his angry confrontation with Jung in Bremen. I base this belief on Freud's axiom that the unconscious mind never forgets anything, especially insults or belittling comparisons.

The jocular—or jugular—passage in Jung's letter reads:

> . . . fearing that the doctor would look at her anus. But what a frightful tussle it was until the whole story was out!
>
> Now for a bit of historical mysticism!
>
> *Vienna* has produced 3 anthropological medical-reformers: Mesmer, Gall, Freud. Freud (in keeping with the times) went unrecognized. Mesmer and Gall then went to Paris.
>
> Mesmer's views remained confined to Paris until Lavater of *Zurich* imported them into Germany, at first *Bremen*. Hypnotism revived in France and was imported into Germany by Forel of *Zurich*. [Freud started as a hypnotherapist.] Forel's first pupil of many years' standing was Delbruck of *Bremen*; he is now director of the asylum there.
>
> *Freud* first met with clinical recognition in *Zurich*. The first *German asylum* to recognize Freud was *Bremen* (independently of all personal relations with us). Apart from Delbruck, the only German assistant at the Burghölzli [asylum-hospital in Zurich] is Dr. Abraham of *Bremen*.
>
> You will say that thinking in analogies, which your analytical methods train so well, yields poor fruit. But I have enjoyed it.

Though Freud responded scrupulously to almost every comment in his correspondents' letters, his answering letter to Jung said nothing about the dubious and insulting "Mesmer-Gall" comparisons. But from a letter he wrote many years later we learn of his "strong desire for vengeance" against Stefan Zweig for linking him to Mesmer.

Responding to Arnold Zweig's joking complaint that Freud had mistakenly given him the title of "Doctor," Freud acknowledged that he had parapractically confused Arnold with someone who had deeply offended him. In a matching light tone he wrote:

Dear Arnold Zweig:

I hasten to confess to you how ashamed I am of my mistake. I had the feeling of uncertainty, it's true, as I wrote the title [Doctor] down, but since there were obviously unknown forces involved, it is not surprising that I quickly silenced these warnings. The analysis I immediately carried out on the *Fehlleistung* (slip) naturally led on to delicate ground: it revealed the other Zweig, whom I knew to be engaged at this moment in Hamburg working me into an essay which is to bring me into public notice with Mesmer and Mary Baker Eddy. During the past six months he has given me great cause for annoyance, but my original strong desire for vengeance has now been completely banished into the unconscious, and so it is possible that I wanted a comparison and to establish a compensation.*

Jung and his earlier comparison of Freud with Mesmer are not mentioned in the letter, but Freud's use of the words "strong desire for vengeance that has now been completely banished into the unconscious" evokes for me the faint ghostly presence of Jung looking over Freud's shoulder as he wrote to Arnold Zweig.

10

That Freud may have regarded his clandestine-seeming meetings with Fliess guiltily, and associated them with death or death wishes, is suggested by certain details in his *"Non Vixit"* dream of 1898. In this dream, which reads like the script of a scene in a surrealist film, Freud tells of meeting a friend he calls "Fl." (identified by Dr. Alexander Grinstein as Fliess):

My friend Fl. [Fliess] had come to Vienna unobtrusively in July. I met him in the street in conversation with my (deceased) friend P. [Josef Paneth], and went with them to some place where they sat opposite each other as though they were at a small table. I sat in front at its narrow end. Fl. [Fliess] spoke about his sister and said that in three quarters of an hour she [would be] dead, and added some such words as "that was the threshold." As P. failed to understand him, Fl. turned to me and asked me how much I had told P. about

---

*The Letters of Sigmund Freud and Arnold Zweig, edited by Ernst L. Freud; translated by Elaine and William Robson-Scott. (New York, Harcourt, Brace, Jovanovich, 1970.)

his affairs. . . . I tried to explain to Fl. that P. (could not understand anything at all, of course, because he) was not alive. But what I actually said . . . was "*non vixit.*" I then gave P. a piercing look. Under my gaze he turned pale; his form grew indistinct and his eyes a sickly blue—and finally he melted away. I was highly delighted at this. . . .

All of this suggests, does it not, that Fliess came to Vienna and met Freud secretly ("unobtrusively"), that Freud met him away from home ("on the street"), that Fliess was worried that Freud had told his friend P. about "his affairs" (these secret meetings?). To silence the already dead man, Freud turned his Medusan look of annihilation on Josef Paneth (P.) and melted him away. Another thing: Freud said (elsewhere) that he identified with the name "Joseph" because, like himself, that Biblical figure was a great dream interpreter. Also, that Freud may have been "P." in this dream is suggested to me by his great observation in his "dream-work" that in many dreams the characters are split fractions of the dreamer's psyche. (Of course I do not insist on my interpretation of this or any other dream dreamed by Freud. As with the rest of this book, I wish only to share my explorations.)

11

CORIOLANUS: What cause do you think I have to swoon?

KING LEAR: Look there, look here!
He faints! My lord, my lord!

We come now to the hysterical or psychosomatic faintings we have referred to so often, the first of which occurred in Bremen, Germany, on August 20, 1909.

But first the background: In the previous December Freud was invited by Clark University, Worcester, Massachusetts, to participate as lecturer at the school's twentieth-anniversary celebration. Though delighted with this international recognition of psychoanalysis, Freud, feeling he could not afford to lose three weeks' practice in July, declined the invitation. But later, when the festivities were advanced to September and the honorarium was increased to about $800, he accepted and invited his brother Alexander and Dr. Sandor Ferenczi to accompany him. Only Ferenczi was able to go. Later, when he learned that Jung had also been invited, they arranged to travel together.

In the following August *Freud spent some weeks* with his family *in the Austrian Tyrol and then crossed the border to Munich, where he took the overnight train that carried him northwest through Germany to Bremen, a North Sea harbor.* (I have italicized the details of this journey for use in my revelation of what was perhaps the most astonishing of Freud's syndromic reenactments. I can hardly wait to tell you.)

After checking into the Bremen hotel where he met Jung and Ferenczi, Freud insured his life for twenty thousand marks ($4,764) and invited his traveling companions to what was intended to be a celebratory luncheon. After a "kidding" argument over the manner of celebrating their forthcoming recognition in America, and another far more serious dispute, Freud suddenly lost consciousness and fell to the floor of the public dining room.

Now we hear from Ernest Jones. In the first volume of his authorized Freud biography, Jones offered his first meager version of the Bremen happening: "Freud had a poor night on the train from Munich to Bremen, which partly accounted for a curious incident. . . . He was host at a luncheon in Bremen, and after some argument he and Ferenczi persuaded Jung to give up his principle of abstinence and join them in drinking some wine. Just after, however, Freud fell down in a faint, the first of two such attacks in Jung's presence. In the evening Jung played the host, and the next day they went on board."

Later, in the second volume of his Freud biography, while relating the 1913 Munich repetition, Jones amplified his earlier version but, as we shall shortly see, left out a highly important element which contributed to the "fainting in Jung's presence." (Ferenczi was also there. Why doesn't Jones include him as a "presence"?)

Say Jones: "Ferenczi, on hearing of the [Munich] incident, reminded Freud of the similar one that happened in Bremen when the three men were setting out for America . . . the occasion was, just as now, when Freud had won a small victory over Jung. Jung had been brought up in the fanatical anti-alcohol tradition of the Burghölzli [hospital in Zurich] . . . and Freud did his best to laugh him out of it. He succeeded in changing Jung's previous attitude towards alcohol—incidentally with serious aftereffects on the relationship with Bleuler—but then fell to the ground in a faint. Ferenczi was so far-seeing as to wonder beforehand whether Freud would not repeat this in Munich, a prediction which was confirmed by the fact."

Recently, while seeking more information than Freud-protecting Jones seemed willing to divulge, I pursued this intriguing matter and found that Jung had, after reading Jones's truncated versions, written his own account in his memoirs. I saw at once that his version omitted any mention of what Jones called the "laughing" Freud-Jung "argument over the drinking of wine." As may be seen, Jung's version (below) injects a psychological element that would have been far more likely to induce an hysterical fainting attack than would a jolly little argument over wine-drinking. But these two elements, along with others discovered later, were only a part of the many stimuli, acting concurrently, which felled Freud. Though seemingly trivial and innocent, the wine-pushing scene was the clue that led to the discovery that Freud's Bremen fiasco may have been (in part) his reenactment of the major elements of a world-famous drama.

Jung's version of the occurrence at Bremen, in his memoirs written a half century afterward, is most interesting:

> The year 1909 proved decisive in our relationship. I had been invited to lecture on the association experiment at Clark University in Worcester, Massachusetts. Independently, Freud had also received an invitation, and we decided to travel together. We met in Bremen, where Ferenczi joined us. In Bremen the much discussed incident of Freud's fainting fit occurred. It was provoked—indirectly—by my interest in "peat-bog corpses." I knew that in certain districts of Northern Germany these so-called bog corpses were to be found. They were the bodies of prehistoric men who either drowned in the bogs or were buried there. The bog water in which the bodies lie contains humic acid, which consumes the bones and simultaneously tans the skin, so that it and the hair are perfectly preserved. In essence this is a process of natural mummification, in the course of which the bodies are pressed flat by the weight of the peat. Such remains are occasionally turned up in Holstein, Denmark, and Sweden.

Then, referring to the effects of the wine he'd drunk at Freud's insistence, Jung continues: "Having read about these peat-bog corpses, I recalled them when we were in Bremen. But, being a bit muddled [the wine] . . . confused them with the mummies in the lead cellars of the city

[Bremen]. This interest of mine got on Freud's nerves. 'Why are you so concerned with these corpses?' he asked me several times. He was inordinately vexed by the whole thing, and during one such conversation . . . he suddenly fainted. Afterward he said to me that he was convinced that all this chatter about corpses meant that I had death-wishes toward him. I was more than surprised by this interpretation."

12

Fugal Repetition (Replay)

"At once Melusina fainted." Here, as in the case of Freud's two public "faintings in the presence of Carl Jung," Melusina's fall into unconsciousness obeys the classic psychoanalytical pattern. As explained by Dr. A. A. Brill: Whenever a person's powerfully repressed fears or desires are suddenly released, the hysterical symptom (in this case, fainting) appears.

The hysterical fainter is one who, finding himself/herself unable to face the consequences of the suddenly revealed inner "problem," seeks escape by falling instantly into a temporary sleep, oblivion, simulated death called "fainting."

13

Wine, dear boy, and truth.

Wine is a peephole on a man.
—Alcaeus, circa 600 B.C.

Some months ago, while charting Freud's actions, movements, and motivations leading up to his fainting attack in Bremen in 1909, I paused to watch a telecast of *Hedda Gabler* starring Miss Janet Suzman.

At first I was completely captivated. But then, during the first act, my attention became sharply divided when I noticed that Hedda Gabler's actions, movements, and motivations were exactly like those of Sigmund Freud at the time of his Bremen fainting fit, an incident that occurred twenty years after *Hedda Gabler* was written.

"Yes," I thought. "In both the earlier fiction and the later real-life happening, there was, detail for detail, the same dense cluster of precisely similar events, places, objects, language, and especially *motives*—all arranged in the same sequence."

A quick comparison had revealed that both Hedda Gabler and Sigmund Freud made the same summer journey, step by step, from the same part of the Austrian Tyrol through Germany and on the same train. Upon arrival at their destinations, each of them staged a similar ulteriorly motivated scene in which she/he manipulated a weaker friend, using the same alcoholic drink as an inhibition-releasing device. In both cases the ulteriorly motivated action boomeranged. Of course Freud's reenactment, if that is what it was, did not end fatally, as did Hedda Gabler's, but even there, there was a physical similarity. And in almost every other respect the two episodes were uncannily alike. How could this be? Do we have here an elaborate network of accidental similarities? No; the quantity and density of the similarities acting in sequence argue against coincidence.

"Did Freud and Ibsen base their respective reality and fiction on an earlier historical or fictional source, a common literary or factual ancestor unknown to me? Most puzzling. Needs further investigating."

14

> KING: What do you call the play?
> HAMLET: "The Mousetrap". . . . this play is the image of a murder done in Vienna. . . . 'Tis a knavish piece of work, but what o' that? Your majesty, and that we have free souls, it touches us not.

To explain this discovered similarity, this *Hamlet*-like "play-within-a-play" "staged" by Freud's "unconscious," I shall first briefly summarize the "Freud-related" parts of *Hedda Gabler:* As the drama begins, we learn that Hedda and George Tesman have just returned from a long wedding trip in Italy, with a stopover in the Austrian Tyrol. From there they crossed the Austro-German border to Munich, where they boarded a train that took them northwest through Germany to a North Sea harbor. They then completed their journey on a steamer to Christiania, now Oslo.

Immediately upon arrival Hedda Gabler learns that her ardent admirer Eilert Lövborg, a reformed alcoholic and whoremonger, has written a phenomenally successful book, and is now the leading contender for the professorship Hedda and her husband had counted on. (She had married this man whom she despised only because she believed he would guarantee her security with the professorship.) The completely selfish and ruthless Hedda resolves to prevent Lövborg from standing in her way.

On the following day she invites a few friends to a homecoming party, among them Lövborg and his mistress, Mrs. Elvsted, who has deserted her husband and children for him.

At the party Hedda separates these two from the others and goes to work on them. Knowing that a single drink will drive Lövborg back to his old self-destructive habits and ruin his chances for the coveted job, she plies him with a strong wine-punch. She also wishes to destroy the Lövborg-Elvsted relationship and, at the same time, to demonstrate her control over him.

Part of the scene reads:

HEDDA: But now, my dearest Thea, you really must have a glass of cold punch.

MRS. ELVSTED: No, thanks—I never take anything of the kind.

HEDDA: Well, then, you, Mr. Lövborg.

LÖVBORG: Nor I, thank you.

MRS. ELVSTED: No, he doesn't either.

HEDDA: But if I say you shall?

LÖVBORG: It would be of no use.

HEDDA: (laughter) Then I, poor creature, have no sort of power over you?

LÖVBORG: Not in that respect.

HEDDA: But seriously, I think you ought to—for your own sake.

MRS. ELVSTED: Why, Hedda—!

LÖVBORG: How so?

HEDDA: Or rather on account of other people.

LÖVBORG: Indeed.

HEDDA: Otherwise people might be apt to suspect that—in your heart of hearts—you do not feel secure—quite confident in yourself.

MRS. ELVSTED: (softly) Oh, please, Hedda—

LÖVBORG: People may suspect what they like for the present.
MRS. ELVSTED: (joyously) Yes, let them!

But these two are no match for this General's daughter. After some further needling of Lövborg, and the malicious use of confidential information given her by Mrs. Elvsted, Hedda succeeds in driving her weak friend to drink. After gulping down several glasses of the strong wine-punch, Lövborg accepts an invitation to a stag drinking party. After that he goes drunkenly to the local whorehouse, where he kills himself with a dueling pistol given him by Hedda. (She keeps the companion gun.)

Hedda Gabler's diabolical actions boomerang on her. When the evil Judge Brack learns that the suicidal gun was given to Lövborg by Hedda, he tries to blackmail her sexually. But Hedda, unable or unwilling to accept any man's domination, chooses to kill herself with the matching pistol. She *falls dead onto a "sofa."*

Here, for ready reference and better visual comparison, is a tabulation of the Hedda Gabler–Sigmund Freud similarities:

Ibsen: On their way home after a prolonged wedding trip to *Italy,* Hedda Gabler Tesman and her husband stop over in the *Austrian Tyrol* for a vacation.

Freud: After vacationing with his family in the *Austrian Tyrol,* Dr. Sigmund Freud leaves his family to go to America. His family then goes to *Italy.*

Ibsen: George Tesman has just been made an honorary *"Doctor."* His aunt Juliana says, "Some *foreign university* has made him a doctor— while he was abroad, you know."

Freud: He is on his way to lecture at Clark University (a *foreign university*) and receive an *honorary doctorate.*

Ibsen: Hedda and her husband leave the *Tyrol* and cross the border to nearby *Munich.* There they take the train that carries them northwest through Germany to a *North Sea harbor.*

Freud: He also leaves the *Tyrol* to cross the border to *Munich.* There he also takes the train that carries him northwest through Germany to

Bremen, a *North Sea harbor*. It is the same train. (Though Bremen is inland, it is a North Sea harbor.)

Ibsen: Hedda Gabler's *ship sails through the North Sea to a foreign country.*

Freud: His *ship sails through the North Sea en route to America.*

Ibsen: Upon arrival in Christiania, Hedda *hosts* an afternoon "homecoming" party attended by a few friends.

Freud: Upon arrival in Bremen, Freud *hosts* a luncheon for his two friends and companions Sandor Ferenczi and Carl Jung.

Ibsen: At this party Hedda Gabler separates *two friends* from the others to act out her little "Machiavellian" scene with them. The other guests, in the background, represent the "public."

Freud: He plays host in a public place to *two friends* so that he may (a) celebrate the forthcoming recognition in America and (b) "act out" his ulteriorly motivated actions toward Carl Jung.

Ibsen: To release her friend-admirer Lövborg's inhibitions, *control* his actions, drive a wedge between him and another person, and gain a victory over him, Hedda offers him a *wine-punch.*

Freud: To gain *control* over Jung, drive a wedge between him and his superior Dr. Bleuler, release his speech inhibitions, and win a psychological victory, Freud offers Jung a *glass of wine.*

Ibsen: At first Lövborg, an abstainer on principle, *refuses.*

Freud: At first Jung, an abstainer on principle, *refuses.*

Ibsen: When Hedda teases and insists, Lövborg is *persuaded* to drink.

Freud: When Freud teases and insists, Jung is *persuaded* to drink.

Ibsen: Hedda Gabler's ulterior motives for plying her friend with inhibition-releasing alcohol have been stated above: she uses the homecoming party as a screen for acting out these motives. (a) She jealously drives a wedge between Mrs. Elvsted and her still passionate admirer Lövborg; (b) an ego-imperialist, she wishes to demonstrate her control over the man; (c) she wants to get him drunk so he will commit antisocial acts which will destroy his chances for the coveted professorship.

Freud: From the evidence, as I interpret it, Freud had ulterior motives. Consciously/unconsciously he plied Jung with wine because he wanted to (a) drive a wedge between Jung and his superior, a fanatic anti-alcoholist; (b) gain greater control over his then-disciple Jung. (c) He also wanted to get Jung drunk so that he would reveal his true underlying attitudes toward Freud and his theories. (Jung had already shown signs of acute restlessness as a follower and potential successor to Freud.)

Ibsen: After first refusing the wine-punch because of his abstaining principles, Lövborg responds to Hedda's tauntings and accepts first one drink, then several more.

Freud: After first refusing wine because of his abstaining principles, Jung responds to Freud's tauntings and drinks several glasses.

Ibsen: Hedda Gabler's *actions boomerang* disastrously. After just two or three drinks, Lövborg embarks on a course of action that ruins him and leads to his suicide. When the evil Judge Brack learns that Lövborg has shot himself with a pistol given him by Hedda Gabler, he tries to blackmail her sexually, but she *kills herself* with the companion dueling pistol.

Freud: Freud's wine-pushing *tactic boomerangs.* After Jung's tongue is loosened, he "chatters" confusedly about some "peat-bog" corpses he transfers from other places to Bremen. When Freud interprets this "chatter" as revealing "death wishes" toward him, he *faints* (symbolic death). Thus the drinking of wine and "death" are linked together in both Ibsen and Freud.

Ibsen: The social conflict in *Hedda Gabler* hinges on the *professorship* issue: both Lövborg and Hedda Tesman desire the crucially needed academic post.

Freud: For many years Freud was refused the *professorship* he wanted. In this respect Dr. Professor Freud equals Dr. Professor Tesman.

Ibsen: The final result, at the end of the play, of Hedda's forcing of wine upon Lövborg finds her *lying prostrate* in death on a "sofa."

Freud: Freud's jocular forcing of wine on Jung ends with Freud *lying prostrate* on the floor in a dead faint. If, as both Freud and Jung said, fainting is a form of symbolic dying, then Freud and Hedda Gabler "ended" similarly. In his memoirs, Jung says that he carried Freud to a "sofa."

Another striking similarity:

Ibsen: During her first scene with Lövborg, before she plies him with the fatal beverage, Hedda shows him the photographic album of her honeymoon stopover in the Austrian *Tyrol*. She says, "Do you see this range of mountains, Mr. Lövborg? Tesman has written the name underneath. Here it is: The Ortler group near *Meran*."

Freud: He must certainly have responded with interest to the name "Meran" spoken by Hedda Gabler because, about a year earlier, he wrote a long and beautiful letter to his daughter Mathilda while she was under a doctor's care in *Meran*, a *Tyrolese* town.

15

Like the great majority of liberal intellectuals in the 1880–1900 period and onward, Freud greatly admired the world-famous Ibsen as dramatist and moral champion.

The strong resemblance between the two men has been commented on: Both fought successfully for moral and sexual enlightenment against similar social, political, and religious reactionaries. Both achieved international fame for ideas that transformed the world's mode of thinking about human behavior and motivation.

His friends and biographers tell us that Freud knew Ibsen's plays intimately, as shown by his deep study of *Rosmersholm's* Rebecca West. While visiting his Vienna home and office, I was especially interested in his personal copy of *Rosmersholm* in which, as I have shown earlier, I had found circumstantial evidence to support the fantasy (or fact) that Freud may have reenacted elements of *Rosmersholm*—with himself as a "Johan-

nes Rosmer," and with a member of his extended household as his
"Rebecca West."

16

Though Freud undoubtedly gave the traumatic fainting incident immediate and full attention in his ongoing self-analysis and in his private
journal, he said nothing about it publicly until the Munich repetition three
years later.

When Jung expressed concern about his health, Freud answered:
"Now I shall be glad to answer your questions. My attack in Munich was no
more serious than the similar one at the Essighaus in Bremen; my condition improved in the evening, and I had an excellent night's sleep.
According to my private diagnosis, it was a migraine (of the M. opthalm.
type), not without a psychic factor, which unfortunately I haven't had the
time to track down. The dining room of [Munich's] Park Hotel seems to
hold a fatality for me. Six years ago I had a first attack of the same kind
there, and four years ago a second. A bit of neurosis I ought really to look
into."*

But Freud really *had* "looked into this bit of neurosis." In a letter
written to Jones about a week later (December 8, 1912), he gave the
diagnosis he had withheld from Jung:

> I cannot forget that six and four years ago I suffered from very similar
> though not such intense symptoms in the *same* room of the Park Hotel. I saw
> Munich first when I visited Fliess during his illness, and this town seems to
> have acquired a strong connection with my relation to that man. *There is some
> piece of unruly homosexual feeling at the root of the matter.* [Italics mine.]
> When Jung in his last letter again hinted at my "neurosis," I could find no
> better expedient than proposing that every analyst should attend to his own
> neurosis more than the other's. After all, I think we have to be kind and
> patient with Jung and, as old Cromwell said, "keep our powder dry."†

The Freud/Jung Letters, edited by William McGuire.
†This is another syndromic instance—in the midst of this severe personal crisis Freud
has done the predictable: he has identified with Oliver Cromwell, one of his personal
heroes, on the eve of conflict. Freud was able to identify with Cromwell for several
reasons. One was: Cromwell was friendly to Jews. Freud named one of his sons Oliver
after the English regicide and revolutionary.

17

OCCULT, hidden (from sight); concealed by
something interposed; not exposed to view . . .
not disclosed or divulged, privy, secret; com-
municated only to the initiated. The supernatural.
—*Oxford Unabridged Dictionary*

The most dramatic confrontation between the Oedipal odd couple prior
to Bremen was staged by Jung in Freud's study just five months before
Bremen. It was a preliminary skirmish which alerted Freud to the
conscious/unconscious hostility of his nominated "crown prince"; and, I
surmise, it contributed to Freud's psychosomatic collapses.

As in the case of the two faintings, the public did not hear of this
confrontation for nearly a half century, until Jones reported it in the third
volume of his Freud biography in 1957. His all-too-brief and typically
played-down version reads:

Jung was steeped in various occult interests and, as is well known, has
remained so. On one of his first visits to Vienna, on March 25, 1909, he
regaled Freud with astonishing stories of his (occult) experiences, and also
displayed his powers as a poltergeist by making various articles in the room
rattle on the furniture. Freud admitted having been very much impressed by
this feat and tried to imitate it after Jung's departure. He then found, however,
obvious physical reasons for any faint noises to be observed, and he remarked
that his credulousness had vanished altogether with the magic of Jung's
personality (presence). He wrote at once to warn his friend to keep a cool head
in the matter.

Four years later (1961) Jung published in his memoirs his own version
of the incident, presenting himself as an occultist-hero triumphing over
the rationalist Freud. In several long paragraphs placed cheek-in-jowl
with his versions of Freud's Bremen and Munich faintings, he recalls the
psychological "victory" he had won fifty-two years earlier:

It interested me to hear Freud's views on prerecognition and parapsychology in general. When I visited him in Vienna in 1909 I asked him what he
thought of these matters. Because of his materialistic prejudices, he rejected
the entire complex of questions as nonsensical, and did so in terms of so

shallow a positivism that I had some difficulty in checking the sharp retort at the tip of my tongue. It was some years before he recognized the seriousness of parapsychology and acknowledged the factuality of "occult" phenomena.

Then it happened: "While Freud was going on in this way, I had a curious sensation. It was

> as if my diaphragm were made of iron and were becoming red-hot—a glowing vault. At that moment there was such a loud report in the bookcase, which stood right next to us, that we both started up in alarm, fearing that the thing was going to topple over on us. I said to Freud: 'There is an example of so-called catalytic exteriorization phenomenon.'
> 'Oh, come,' he exclaimed. 'That is sheer bosh.'
> 'It is not,' I replied. 'You are mistaken, Herr Professor. And to prove my point, I now predict that in a moment there will be another such report!' Sure enough, no sooner had I said the words than the same detonation went off in the bookcase.
> To this day I do not know what gave me this certainty. But I knew beyond all doubt the report would come again."

Jung concludes his recollection of the event: "Freud only stared aghast at me. I do not know what was in his mind, or what the look meant. In any case, this incident aroused his mistrust of me, and I had the feeling that I had done something against him. I never afterward discussed the incident with him."

But he *did* discuss the matter with Freud. A few days after his return to Zurich, he wrote to Freud: "When I left Vienna I was afflicted with some *sentiments d'incomplètetude* because of the last evening I spent with you. It seemed to me that my spookery struck you as altogether stupid and perhaps unpleasant because of the Fliess analogy. (Insanity!)"

Freud's response (April 16), a syndromic eye-opener, deserves reprinting in full:

> It is strange that on the very same evening when I formally adopted you as my eldest son and anointed you—*in partibus infidelium**—as my successor and crown prince, you should have divested me of my paternal dignity, which divesting seems to have given you as much pleasure as I, on the contrary, derived from the investiture of your person. Now I am afraid of falling into the

---

*Translation: "in the land of the unbelievers."

father role with you if I tell you what I feel about the poltergeist business. But I must, because my attitude is not what you might otherwise think. I don't deny that your stories and your experiment made a deep impression on me. I decided to continue my observations after you left, and here are the results: In my first room there is a constant creaking where the two heavy Egyptian steles rest on the oaken boards of the bookshelves. That is too easy to explain. In the second, where we heard it, there is seldom any creaking. At first I was inclined to accept this as proof, if the sound that was so frequent while you were here were not heard again after your departure—but since then I have heard it repeatedly; not, however, in connection with my thoughts and never when I am thinking about you or this particular problem of yours. (And not at the present moment, I add by way of challenge.) My credulity, or at least my willingness to believe, vanished with the magic of your personal presence; once again, for some inward reasons that I can't put my finger on, it strikes me as quite unlikely that such phenomena should exist; I confront the de-spiritualized furniture as the poet confronted Nature after the gods of Greece had passed away.* Accordingly, I put my fatherly spectacles on again and warn my dear son to keep a cool head, for it is better not to understand something than to make such great sacrifices to understanding.†

Freud concluded this section of a long letter: "Consequently, I shall receive further news of your investigations of the spook complex with the interest one accords to a charming delusion in which one does not oneself participate."

(After some years of reading about the alleged "occult" or "supernatural" rappings, tappings, and other similar "poltergeist" manifestations, I still do not understand why the "occultists" insist that they are caused by "spooks" or other former people. The *paltriness*, the *incoherence* of the "visiting spirits' " and their actions makes me feel sorry for them. And even more sorry for those who accept such rude noises as proof of survival after death. But then I'm a rationalist too.)

18

One afternoon, after my third visit to the Freudhaus, an exploratory reverie accompanied me back to my hotel: "Freudhaus . . . he occupied

---

*The clearly syndromic reference is to Schiller, in his poem *"Die Gotter Griechenlands"* ("The Gods of Greece").

†*The Freud/Jung Letters.*

this house from 1891 to 1938. Forty-seven years. For the first seventeen years, until 1908, *he used apartments on two floors.* His living quarters were on the second floor; his professional suite—waiting room, consulting room, and study—was on the lower-floor halfway between the second and ground floors. Historically, that lower floor, corresponding to Freud's analogy of the 'unconscious' as the lower storey of a multi-leveled house, was the more important: psychoanalysis was born in the consulting room and study below. In the small, dark rooms of that lower level (Lobner showed them to me) Freud listened to his first analysands; in the adjoining study he wrote his great seminal books: *The Interpretation of Dreams* (1900), *The Psychopathology of Everyday Life* (1904), and *Wit and Its Relation to the Unconscious* (1905). The lower-floor waiting room also held the early meetings of the seminar group that later grew into the international psychoanalytical movement. Freud's visitors during the early years reported the extraordinary differences between Freud's 'two worlds': the upstairs living quarters, they agree, were utterly bourgeois, with conventional furniture, pictures, and decorative objects. But Freud's lower-floor rooms looked like a museum, with the beginnings of his large collection of ancient Egyptian tomb art and Greek and *Roman* figures and artifacts.

"I am reviewing all this for reasons related to the end of the Freud-Jung relationship. . . . Freud's occupancy of *two floors of a house* has reminded me of one of the dreams Jung reported in the 'Sigmund Freud' chapter of his memoirs . . . the vivid dream in which he took over an already furnished multi-level house. Though Freud is not mentioned in the dream, one may see from its details and the context of his relationship to Freud that Jung's dream may be interpreted as his unconscious desire to dispossess Freud from the 'house of psychoanalysis.' "

I base this tentative conclusion on my observation that Jung positioned his account and interpretation of this dream *immediately after* his lengthy account of Freud's faintings during (a) his "death wish" quarrel with Freud about the "peat-bog" mummified bodies found in Bremen *cellars,* and (b) his heated argument with Freud about the Ikhnaton-Amenhotep Oedipal conflict. (More mummies and "death wishes" implied.)

Furthermore: As any reader of Jung's memoirs may see, Jung's "house dream" is followed *immediately* by a more self-serving discussion of his tortured relationship with Freud and with an account of yet another "wish-fulfilling" dream (already reported in this book) in which he saw the still-alive Freud as the ghost of a long-dead customs official guarding the Swiss-Austrian border. (Obviously trying to keep Jung and his heretical ideas from entering Austria.)

Jung's dream begins: "The trip to the United States which began in Bremen in 1909 lasted for seven weeks. [Freud] and I were together every day, and analyzed

each other's dreams. At the time I had a number of important ones, but Freud could make nothing of them. I did not regard that as any reflection upon him, for it sometimes happens to the best analyst that he is unable to unlock the riddle of a dream. . . . They were dreams with collective contents containing a great deal of symbolic material. One in particular was important to me, for it led me for the first time to the concept of the 'collective unconscious' and thus formed a kind of prelude to my *Wandlungen und Symbole der Libido** [1912].

This was the dream. *I was in a house I did not know, which had two storeys.* It was "my house." I found myself in the upper storey, where there was a kind of salon with fine old pieces in rococo style. On the walls hung a number of precious old paintings. *I wondered that this should be my house.* But then it occurred that I did not know what the lower floor looked like. Descending the stairs, I reached the ground floor. There everything was much older, and I realized that this part of the house must date from the fifteenth or sixteenth century. The furnishings were medieval; the floors were of red brick. Everywhere it was rather dark. I went from one room to another, thinking, 'Now I must really explore the whole house.' I came upon a heavy door and opened it. Beyond it I discovered a stone stairway that led down into the cellar. Descending again, I found myself in a beautifully vaulted room which looked exceedingly ancient. Examining the walls, I discovered layers of brick among the ordinary stone blocks. . . . As soon as I saw this I knew the walls dated from Roman times."

Jung's dream continues:

My interest was now intense; I looked more closely at the floor. It was of stone slabs, and in one of these I discovered a ring. When I pulled it, the stone slab lifted, and again I saw a stairway of narrow stone slabs leading down into the depths. These too I descended, and entered into a low cave cut into the rock. Thick dust lay on the floor, and in the dust were scattered bones

---

Psychology of the Unconscious.

and broken pottery, like remains of a primitive culture. I discovered two human skulls, obviously very old and half disintegrated. Then I awoke.

What chiefly interested Freud in this dream were the two skulls. He returned to them repeatedly, and urged me to find a *wish* in connection with them. What did I think about these skulls? And whose were they? I knew perfectly well what he was driving at: that secret death wishes (toward him) were concealed in the dream. "But what does he really expect from me?" I thought to myself. Towards whom would I have death wishes? I felt violent resistance to any such interpretation. I also had some intimation what the dream might really mean. But I did not then trust my own judgment, and wanted to hear Freud's opinion. I wanted to learn from him. Therefore I submitted to his intention and said, "My wife and sister-in-law"—after all, I had to name someone whose death was worth the wishing!

Jung then seeks to justify his fantasy-murder of his wife and sister-in-law:

I was newly married at the time and knew perfectly well that there was nothing within myself which pointed to such wishes. But I would not have been able to present to Freud my own ideas on the interpretation of the dream without encountering incomprehension and vehement resistance. I did not feel up to quarreling with him, and I also feared that I might lose his friendship if I insisted on my own point of view. On the other hand, I wanted to know what he would make of my answer, and what his reaction would be if I deceived him by saying something that suited his theories. And so I told him a lie.

I was quite aware that my conduct was not above reproach, but *à la guerre, comme la guerre!* It would have been impossible for me to afford him any insight into my mental world. The gulf between it and his was too great.

After pausing for a moment to wonder futilely why Jung fantasy-murdered his new bride and her sister, and what Freud thought when he heard this improvised explanation, we continue with the part of Jung's interpretation that had led me to suspect that his dream-house was mainly Freud's "house of psychoanalysis":

It was plain to me that the house represented a kind of image of the psyche. . . . Consciousness was represented by the [upper-floor] salon . . . the ground floor stood for the first level of the unconscious. The deeper I went, the more alien and darker the scene became [Freud's lower flat is much darker than the one above]. In the cave, I discovered remains of a primitive culture . . .

Certain questions had been much on my mind during the days preceding this dream. They were: *On what premises was Freud's psychology founded?* . . . *My dream thus constituted a kind of structural diagram of the human psyche.* [My italics and interpolation.]

19

Woe is me! I am faint before murderers.
—The prophet Jeremiah, *Old Testament*

When thinking about dramatic events (like the Freud-Jung confrontations), we invariably focus on the leading actors and dismiss the others onstage as "cardboard figures" or "innocent bystanders." This is certainly true in the events we've been discussing. The medical witnesses— Ferenczi in Bremen; and Jones, Ophuijsen, Riklin, Seif, and Abraham in Munich—have been almost completely ignored.

Yet we can easily imagine the great interest (understatement) with which these psychoanalysts observed the quarrels and faintings: surely they reacted not only as deeply concerned friends but also as disciple-colleagues whose careers depended on Freud. "If he should be defeated by Jung or, heaven forbid, die . . ."

But they were also professionals trained by Freud to diagnose such hysterical happenings objectively; we may assume that the implications of the two "dramas," especially the sexual, did not escape them.

Yet, when Freud "passed out" while quarreling with Jung, a kind of mutually protective aphasia seized them, compelling public silence. To my knowledge, *forty years* elapsed before one of them, Ernest Jones, broke the spell. In 1953, as authorized biographer, Jones felt constrained to mention the "fainting attacks" (the last word continues to interest me), but he did so in a minimal, soft-pedaling manner, and without his usual analytical vigor or penetration. (Would he have written about them if Freud were still alive? I doubt it.) In 1961 Jung, the alleged "aggressor" on both occasions, perhaps wishing to respond to Jones defensively, published his version in his memoirs, adding some important details unknown to or omitted by Jones.

My thoughts about the "Bremen fainting" and its sole witness, Sandor Ferenczi, Freud's closest friend in the post-Jung period, went something like this: "If, as Jones tells us, this man was able to accurately predict Freud's second 'attack,' obviously he had diagnosed it correctly. But, as far as I have been able to learn, Ferenczi never made public that diagnosis. But, since he was a prolific writer, he may have made a reference to *fainting* in one of his technical monographs—that may throw some light on the event he witnessed."

With this in mind I searched through all of Ferenczi's translated papers—and, as expected, I found no direct mention of Freud's blackouts. But, tucked away in his 1920 monograph about his "active intervention" in the therapy of several patients,* I did find his summary of a *fainting male patient* which appears to have been written with Freud in mind.

Ferenczi begins his paper with several references to Freud, including a reference to his "case of Infantile Neurosis." He then offers a brief summary of his work with a pretty Croatian concert pianist who came to him because she was unable to play public solos or even "finger exercises"; when crowds were present she made many acutely embarrassing mistakes.

This patient responded well to treatment. Soon, says the doctor, she was able to play his piano flawlessly and sing arias "in an unusually beautiful soprano." Sometimes, for encores, she leaped from the couch "to conduct symphonies, imitating all the orchestral sounds."

But the "fun phase" of this diverting analysis ended when doctor and patient discovered that her public musical fiascos were caused by her guilt feelings: her piano *fingering* had gotten all mixed up in her subconscious mind with her secret masturbatory *fingerings* and with her latent homosexuality as well.

After this antic prelude, Ferenczi presents a brief summary of the "man of bucolic appearance who visited my consulting room at the workers' polyclinic complaining of attacks of loss of consciousness. I considered the attacks to be hysterical and took him to my house to examine him more closely.

He told me a long-winded family history of trouble with his father, who would have nothing to do with him on account of his unsuitable marriage, so that he had to work as a canal cleaner, while . . . at these words he became

---

*Further Contributions to the Theory and Technique of Psychoanalysis. (New York, Basic Books, 1952.)

pale, swayed and would have fallen had I not caught him. He seemed to have lost consciousness and muttered incomprehensible stuff. I did not let myself be misled, however, but shook him quite severely, repeated the sentence he had begun and demanded forcibly that he finish his sentence.

He then said in a feeble voice that he had to work as a canal cleaner while his younger brother saw to the tillage; he would see him walking along behind the plow with its span of six beautiful horses and then going home after work was done and having his meals with his father, etc.

He was going to faint a second time, too, when he spoke of the dissension between his wife and his mother. I forced him to tell this to an end also."

Ferenczi comments: "In a word this man had the knack of hysterical fainting which he did whenever he wanted to escape from the unhappy reality into the beautiful world of fantasy, or from painful trains of thought. This actively compelled thinking out of the hysterical fantasies to their completion affected the patient like a miraculous cure; he could not get over his astonishment that I could cure him thus 'without medicine.' "

I now offer a tentative reconstruction and comparative summary: Dr. Sandor Ferenczi witnessed Freud's possumlike simulation of death (one interpretation) in Bremen; four years later he learned the details of the second attack he had accurately predicted. Like the other witnesses he never commented publicly on either of the historic events.

However, like all suppressed or censored responses which finally find outlets, Ferenczi's vital reactions approached the surface in a technical paper on the question "Should an analyst break the rules and force the 'truth' out of the patient *physically?*"

The following progression of ideas may be observed in Ferenczi's monograph: Roughly, after mentioning Freud several times, particularly in connection with the paper "A Case of Infantile Neurosis," Ferenczi recalls the cases of two patients seemingly unrelated to Freud (except as recipients of his therapy). One was the entertaining "Croatian pianist" whose public performances were spoiled by her secret sexual and homosexual hangups. The other was the Oedipal Hungarian peasant-turned-muckraker who staged hysterical public faintings whenever he thought of his lost inheritance or when he "saw" his brother plowing his father's fields. Or orally enjoying his mother's hot food at the parental table.

Then, to show that Freud and Jung were still in his thoughts, Ferenczi speaks of his theoretical disputations with Jung during the time when Jung was still trying to wrest control of the psychoanalytical movement from Freud.

Summary of a summary: Ferenczi's essay, though supposedly about "active intervention in therapy," is *really* his oblique commentary about Freud's public faintings as told through two comparable cases, especially that of the Hungarian muckraker.

Though the world-renowned Freud and the anonymous Hungarian peasant are as far apart as any two men could possibly be, they seem to have fainted for the same basic reason: their hysterical responses to a "father-son" quarrel over the control of an "estate." Though Freud's "estate" was incomparably grander and richer, to each of them the contemplation of his loss was utterly unbearable.

And Ferenczi's diagnosis of the "man of bucolic appearance" seems to describe the Sigmund Freud of Bremen and Munich perfectly: *"In a word, this man had the knack of hysterical fainting, which he did whenever he wanted to escape from the unhappy reality into the beautiful world of fantasy, or from painful trains of thought."*

Of course none of the psychoanalysts present at Freud's two "embarrassments" would have dared perform an "active intervention" like the one imposed on the bucolic Hungarian. But I wonder: If Ferenczi, treating Freud as he did his humble patients, had "shaken him quite severely" and "demanded forcibly that he finish his sentences," what would Freud have added to the words he mumbled when he recovered consciousness?

20

. . . nor is there any doubt that all weapons and tools are symbols of the male organ, e.g., the plough . . . in the same way landscapes . . . clearly may be recognized as the (female) genitals.
—Freud, *The Interpretation of Dreams*

If [Marina] were a thornier piece of ground than she is, she shall be ploughed.*
—Shakespeare, *Pericles, Prince of Tyre*

---

*To Shakespeare and other Elizabethans, "ploughed" meant "fucked."

I continued to study Ferenczi's tantalizingly brief résumé of the fainting attacks experienced by the "canal cleaner" whenever he "saw" his brother plow his father's fields. I wondered: "Why doesn't Ferenczi probe the classical Freudian sexual symbols told him by his patient? If he did recognize them (and how could he miss?), why doesn't he tell us about them?"

The key symbols I refer to are contained in the words ". . . he had to work as a canal cleaner," and the words added when Ferenczi shook him severely: ". . . while his younger brother saw to the tillage . . . and then going home and having meals with his father." "Canal cleaning," or the dredging up of unseen muck and objects from the canal bottom in order to keep the channel navigable, is a perfect paradigm of psychoanalysis. (And his constant insertion of his pole into the muck could be a fair description of his paternally disapproved marriage.)

But the Freudian symbolism goes much deeper. To Freud and Abraham the *plowing of a field* does sometimes signify incestuous intercourse; in his "dream-work" quoted above, Freud, speaking of "inter-uterine fantasies," offers as an example, "The dream of a young man who, in his imagination, had taken advantage of an inter-uterine opportunity to watch his parents copulating."

In this dream, says Freud, "He was in a deep pit with a window in it like the one in the Semmering Tunnel (under the Alps). At first he saw an empty landscape through the window, but he then invented a picture to fit the space . . . the picture represented a field which was being ploughed up deeply with some implement. He then saw a book upon educating children open in front of it, and was impressed to see how much attention was devoted to the sexual feelings of children."

As seen above, Freud's great idol Shakespeare consciously used the plow as a male sexual symbol; again, in his *Antony and Cleopatra*, referring to their celebrated fornications, Shakespeare's character Agrippa exclaims pre-Freudianly:

> O royal wench!
> She made great Caesar put his sword to bed,
> *He ploughed her and she reaped.*

In recent American male-chauvinist slang a man *plowed* a woman when he assaulted her sexually. Is this cruel word still being used?

21

Climax in Munich: 1912

Freud's dramatic repetition of the Bremen fainting "in Jung's presence" began, we learn, when Freud asked Jung, titular head of the Psychoanalytical Association, to convene a "Congress" in Munich on November 24, 1912.* Purpose of the meeting: to help rid Freud of Dr. Wilhelm Stekel, a once-valuable disciple who had become obnoxious.

Seven psychoanalysts arrived in Munich: Freud, Jung, Abraham, Jones, Riklin, Ophuijsen, and Seif. On the morning of the fateful luncheon at which Freud fainted, he and Jung left the others to discuss Jung's badly injured feelings—arising from a visit Freud had made to the ailing Ludwig Binswanger near Zurich without also visiting Jung. During this heated discussion Freud persuaded Jung that he had distorted an innocent situation in order to express his accelerating Oedipal hostility toward Freud. "Jung became extremely contrite," says Jones, "and admitted the difficult traits in his character. But Freud also had steam to let out and did not spare him a fatherly lecture. Jung accepted the criticism and promised to reform." They then walked back to the Park Hotel to rejoin the others.

Ernest Jones, accepting Freud's version of the heart-to-heart argument and Jung's reactions, says it brought the two men together; but hindsight tells us that it really had the opposite effect: a few minutes later the argument and its "fatherly" bawling-out contributed to an explosion that blew the relationship to bits.

Jones describes the argument's aftermath: "Freud was in high spirits at the luncheon, doubtless elated at winning Jung around again. There was a little discussion about Abraham's recent paper about the Egyptian

---

*An example of the high comedy among these pioneer psychoanalysts is seen in Jones's witty report of Jung's hostility directed at him. Though Jung notified the others that the date of the Munich meeting was November 24, he sent Jones the wrong date, "November 25," which meant that Jones would have arrived a day after the others were gone. "In the meantime," says Jones, "I heard the correct date from my wife in Vienna, and so arrived on time. The look of astonishment on Jung's face told me that the mistake belonged in the class called 'parapraxes,' but when I told Freud of Jung's unconscious mistake, he replied: 'A gentleman should not do such things even unconsciously.' " I mention the little incident because of its bearing on what followed.

(Pharaoh) Amenhotep, with some differences of opinion, and then Freud started to criticize the Swiss for their recent publications in Zurich where his work and even his name were ignored. This incident, including the fainting attack, I have already narrated and need not repeat here. . . ."

Replay: Jones is referring here to his incomplete account of the historic event in his previous volume of the biography. To refresh the reader's memory, I, always willing to be helpful, quote it:

> An aftermath [of Freud's break with his beloved Wilhelm Fliess] appeared some eight years later. Freud asked five of us to meet him in Munich, on November 24, 1912. He wished to consult us about his editorial difficulties with Stekel and to secure our support for a proposal he had in mind. That matter was quickly and amicably settled, but as we were finishing luncheon (in the Park Hotel) he began reproaching the two Swiss, Jung and Riklin, for writing articles expounding psychoanalysis in Swiss periodicals without mentioning his name. Jung replied it was unnecessary to do so, it being so well known, but Freud had sensed already the dissension that was to follow. . . . He persisted, and I remember thinking he was taking the matter rather personally. Suddenly, to our consternation, he fell to the floor in a dead faint. The sturdy Jung carried him to a couch in the lounge, where he was soon revived. His first words as he was coming to were strange: "How sweet it must be to die"—another indication that the idea of dying has some esoteric meaning for him.

Jones then ties the fainting attack to Freud's "passionate friendship" with Wilhelm Fliess: "Not long afterward he confided to me his explanation of his attack. It was a repetition. In a letter of December 8 he wrote to me: 'I cannot forget that six and four years ago I suffered from very similar though not such intense symptoms in the *same* room of the Park Hotel. I saw Munich first when I visited Fliess during his illness, and this town seems to have acquired a strong connection with . . . that man. There is some piece of unruly homosexual feeling at the root of the matter.' " In yet another version of the same event, Jones added, "The incident must have been occasioned by the intuition that he would have to face parting with Jung, of whom he had been so fond." (As he had previously been "fond" of Wilhelm Fliess, with whom he had also parted traumatically.)

Though all this may seem to some a "tempest in a teapot," the "steam"

Freud had to "let off" was, we learn, under dangerously high pressure. There had been five years of harmonious intellectual collaboration highly beneficial to the cause of mental-emotional healing (Jones calls them the "Golden Years"), but now the unceasing subsurface father-son shenanigans became more and more unpleasant. In 1912 Freud reluctantly admitted to close friends his fear that Jung could not be trusted to continue his most important ideas; that the relationship was rapidly approaching its end.

He based this on several obvious indications. First, reports from New York that Jung, during his lectures at Fordham University, had downgraded Freud and his more controversial theories. Then, upon his return to Zurich, Jung wrote a letter to Freud in which he boasted of his American success in terms calculated to bring their impending separation one giant step closer: "Everywhere I met with great interest and was favorably received. Thus I had rich soil and was able to do a great deal for the spread of the movement. I gave nine lectures at the Jesuit [!] University of Fordham, New York—a critical account of the development of the theory of psychoanalysis. . . . Naturally I also made room for those of my views which deviate from the hitherto existing conceptions [Freud's], particularly in regard to the libido theory. . . . I find my version of psychoanalysis won over many people who had until now been put off by the problem of sexuality in neurosis. . . . I feel no need to let you down, provided you can take an objective view of our common endeavors. I regret it very much if you think that the modifications in question have been prompted solely by resistances to you. I assure you that I have objective reasons for my views."*

To this Freud answered: "Many thanks for your news of the state of affairs in America. But we know that the battle will not be decided over there. You have reduced a great deal of resistance with your modifications, but I shouldn't advise you to enter this in the credit column, because, as you know, the farther you remove yourself from what is new in psychoanalysis, the more certain you will be of applause and the less resistance you will meet."†

*The Freud/Jung Letters.
†Ibid.

22

Jones's comment that Freud's "first words when he was coming to were strange: 'How sweet it must be to die,' " incited another analytical reverie: "Were these 'strange words' murmured by the syndromic actor Freud his own, or were they from another of his reenactments from his inner repertory theater? . . . 'Steppenwolf,' who also staged perverse dramas within his mind, comes to *my* mind. . . . The words 'how sweet' and 'die' in the context of Freud's avowed 'homosexual feelings' for the long-departed Fliess seem distinctly Shakespearean. Freud constantly quoted Shakespeare in his books, letters, and lectures. In his *Interpretation of Dreams* there are eighteen references and quotations from the plays, especially *Hamlet*, and his elaborate theories about that play are well known. Also: Freud recognized the 'Brutus' in himself, and he identified syndromically with Caesar, The Duke of Gloucester, and King Lear. Yes, look for the words 'how sweet it must be to die' in Shakespeare, starting with *Hamlet*. But a sound-alike is not enough. To fulfill the syndromic requirement, the matching Shakespearean line, if there is indeed one, must arise out of the same context, as described by Ernest Jones: *an expressed desire to die a sweet death because of a painful parting with a beloved man*."

Later, feeling like Sherlock Holmes after a successful bit of sleuthing, I wrote, "Yes, Freud's words 'how sweet . . . to die' are Shakespearean, but not from *Hamlet* or any of the other plays mentioned by Freud in his writings. I believe they come from the sonnet sequence 80–92, dealing with precisely the same emotional problem which Jones, quoting Freud, says triggered Freud's faintings. The sonneteer, lamenting the terrible loss of his 'master-mistress,' cries 'O, *how I faint* when I of you do write' (Sonnet 80), and, in Sonnet 92, completes the image. Yes, I do believe that Freud did reenact a 'scene' from his beloved Shakespeare. *This time as Shakespeare himself.* Or so it seems."

Here, with my italics underscoring the Shakespeare-Freud similarities, are the relevant lines. While reading them, please note the amazing pre-Freudian sexual metaphor of the poet and his rival as ships *riding* on the fickle youth transformed metaphorically into a body of water.

O, how I faint when I of you do write,
Knowing a better spirit doth use your name,
And in the praise thereof spends all his might,
To make me tongue-tied, speaking of your fame!
But since your worth, wide as the ocean is,
The humble as the proudest sail doth bear,
My saucy bark, inferior far to his,
On your broad main doth wilfully appear.
Your shallowest help will hold me up afloat,
*Whilst he upon your soundless deep doth ride;**
Or, being wrecked, I am but a worthless boat,
He of tall building and of goodly pride.
   Then if he thrive, and I be cast away,
   The worst was this: my love was my decay.

The sonnet sequence, which begins with this metaphorical "fainting"
at the thought of losing his lover, ends with the thought quite similar to
Freud's "How sweet it must be to die" when faced by what Jones calls "the
intuition that he would have to face parting with Jung, of whom he had
been so fond." Sonnet 92:

> *But do thy worst to steal thyself away,*
> For term of life thou art assured mine,
> And life no longer than thy love will stay,
> For it depends upon that love of thine.
> Then need I not to fear the worst of wrongs
> When in the least of them my life doth end;
> I see a better state to me belongs
> Than that which on thy humour doth depend;
> Thou canst not vex me with inconstant mind,
> Since that *my life on thy revolt doth lie.*
> O, what a happy title do I find,
> *Happy to have thy love, happy to die!*
>   But what's so blessed-fair that fears no blot?
>   Thou mayst be false, but I know it not.
>   [My emphases.]

---

*Wow!

Here, for the reader who wishes to review the alleged "similarities" quickly, I—uh—lay them side by side:

Shakespeare: The speaker is an older man addressing his young friend.
Freud: When Freud uttered his little "recovering" speech he was fifty-six, Jung was thirty-seven.

Shakespeare: The poet speaks of his young friend's "revolt."
Freud: Freud's fainting and speech were performed in the context of Jung's impending revolt against Freud and his basic ideas.

Shakespeare: In Sonnet 80, at the beginning of the "lost love" sequence, the older man speaks of being "faint" when he thinks of another man's usurpation of his love.
Freud: He actually fainted when, as Jones puts it, he intuited his impending loss of a younger man "of whom he had been so fond."

Shakespeare: His ultimate response to this loss of love is: *"happy to die!"*
Freud: His "strange words" while coming out of his faint: *"How sweet* it must be *to die."*

A question arises: Were the words quoted by Jones as spoken by Freud in German or English? The image would be the same when translated, but the words would of course be different. It may be that Jones unconsciously used *Shakespeare's* words to translate Freud's words. . . .

23

Strange thoughts cluster around Freud's diagnostic words to Jones: "The dining room of the Park Hotel . . . seems to hold a fatality for me." The first is that of *cannibalism.* The second is the disturbing surreal image of the dignified Dr. Sigmund Freud, then a bearded man in his mid-fifties, lying helplessly supine on the dining room floor surrounded by human carnivores devouring the flesh of slaughtered beef and pigs. The third image links these animals to the "totemic ancestors" worshipped by ancient people. These words join this free-association cluster, I guess, because I know that shortly before Munich, Freud published his *Totem and Taboo*, an explanation of the Oedipus complex's origin. In this book, based on his readings of Charles Darwin, Robertson Smith, and Sir James Frazer, Freud postulated a primordial family tyrannized over by a father who was slain and *cannibalized* by his sons because he kept all the women for himself.

Need I say that once again, when in a state of crisis, Freud identified with a mythic figure, this time with the "primordial father" whose existence is now denied by anthropologists and sociologists? Or so it seems.

As I read about Freud's relations to his disciples during the years 1909–1913, I deduced that, apart from his impersonal scientific reasons for writing *Totem and Taboo*, Freud wished to describe unconsciously his own personal situation: he was also a "primordial father" who felt he was being attacked and (intellectually) cannibalized by his rebellious "sons," who challenged his domination of psychoanalytical thought and of the burgeoning international psychoanalytical movement. Wilhelm Stekel, one of the leading "heretics," read *Totem and Taboo* and said: "Freud has the 'primitive horde' complex. *He* is the Old Man afraid of his disciples."

Carl Jung went further. In a pugnacious, even insolent letter written shortly after the book appeared, he wrote: "Dear Professor Freud . . . your technique of treating your pupils like patients is a *blunder*. In that way you produce either slavish sons or impudent puppies (Adler-Stekel and the whole insolent gang now throwing their weight about in Vienna). I am objective enough to see through your little tricks. You go about sniffing out the symptomatic actions in your vicinity, thus reducing everyone to the level of sons . . . *meantime you remain on top as the father, sitting pretty*. . . . *If you should ever rid yourself of your complex and stop playing the father to your sons*, and, instead of aiming continually at their weak spots, take a good look at your own for a change, then I will mend my ways and at one stroke uproot the vice of being in two minds about you."*
(My emphases.)

The Freud/Jung Letters.

24

In 1959–60, a half century after Bremen and Munich, the eighty-five-year-old Jung, wishing perhaps to offset Jones's pro-Freudian versions of the psychosomatic fainting attacks, wrote his version. In the first part of this long-range recollection, quoted earlier, he said: "In Bremen the much discussed incident of Freud's fainting fit occurred. It was provoked—indirectly—[Jung omits the "wine-pushing" scene] by my interest in 'peat-bog corpses.' I knew that in certain districts of Northern Germany these so-called bog corpses were to be found. They were the bodies of prehistoric men who either drowned in the bogs or were buried there. . . . Having read about these peat-bog corpses, I recalled them when we were in Bremen. But, being a bit muddled [the wine Freud forced on him], confused them with the mummies in the lead cellars of the city. This interest of mine got on Freud's nerves. 'Why are you so concerned with these corpses?' he asked me several times. He was inordinately vexed by the whole thing, and during one such conversation, while we were having dinner together, he suddenly fainted. Afterward he said to me that he was convinced that all this chatter about corpses meant that I had death-wishes toward him. I was more than surprised by this interpretation. I was alarmed by the intensity of his fantasies—so strong that, obviously, they could cause him to faint."

Jung then recalled the "high-noon showdown" at Munich. The alert reader will note that here in his memoirs Jung omits the immediate cause of Freud's collapse: his bitter complaint that Jung had Ikhnatonically "erased" his name from his writings about psychoanalysis in Swiss papers.

In a similar connection Freud once more suffered a fainting fit in my presence. This was during the Psychoanalytic Congress in Munich in 1912. Someone had turned the conversation to Amenophis IV (Ikhnaton). The point was made that as a result of his negative (Oedipal) attitude toward his father, he had destroyed his father's cartouches on the steles, and that at the back of his great creation of a monotheistic religion there lurked a father complex. This sort of thing irritated me, and I attempted to argue that Amenophis (Ikhnaton) had been a creative and profoundly religious person whose acts could not be explained by personal resistances to his father. On the contrary, I said, he had held the memory of his father in honor, and his zeal for destruction had been directed only against the name of the god Amon, which he had everywhere annihilated; it was also chiseled out of the cartouches of his father Amon-hotep. Moreover, other pharaohs had replaced the names of their actual or divine forefathers on monuments or statues by their own, feeling they had the right to do so, since they were reincarnations of the same god. Yet they, I pointed out, had inaugurated neither a new style nor a new religion.

Then it happened: "At that moment Freud slid out of his chair in a faint. Everyone clustered helplessly around him. I picked him up, and carried him into the next room, and laid him on a sofa. As I was carrying him, he half came to, and I shall never forget the look he cast at me. In his weakness he looked at me as if I were his father. Whatever other causes may have contributed to this faint—the atmosphere was very tense—the fantasy of father-murder was common to both cases. . . . At this time Freud made allusions indicating that he regarded me as his successor. These hints were embarrassing to me, for I knew that I would never be able to uphold his views properly, that is to say, as he intended them."

25

WHODUNIT (hoo dun' it), *n. Informal.* a narrative dealing with a murder or series of murders, a detective story. Jocular formation from the question: *Who did it?*
—*Random House Dictionary*

. . . stop playing the father to your sons, and, instead of aiming continually at their [my] weak spots, take a good look at your own for a change.
—Jung, in a letter to Freud, December 18, 1912

A psychological "whodunit"? Yes, the various accounts of Freud's mysterious "attacks," including Jung's, repeated the words "in the presence of Jung," and though on both occasions others—all professional psychoanalysts—were present, these expert witnesses are treated like operatic spear-carriers. The constantly reiterated words "in the presence of Jung" imply that in these bitter "father-son" showdowns, Jung was solely responsible for Freud's blackouts. And this is the consensus.

But my accumulated "detective" probings tell me that it was not nearly that simple. I now believe that in his "Oedipal" attack in Munich, *Jung had two secret accomplices.* (This idea was suggested to me by the facts in the case, by Freud's teachings about the multiple causes of even simple behavior; it was also suggested by Agatha Christie's *Murder on the Orient Express,* in which Hercule Poirot detects and exposes the twelve individually motivated men and women who separately killed "Mr. Ratchett.")

The *visible* cause of Freud's Munich attack was of course his verbal fight with Jung. Jung did hold the "smoking pistol"; he did publicly challenge and defy Freud's "papal" authority to become a kind of psychoanalytical Martin Luther or Huldreich Zwingli (Swiss Protestant rebel). (Freud licensed this analogy: When asked why his leading disciples Adler and Jung had defected, Freud answered half-jokingly, "Precisely because *they too* wish to be Popes.") To Freud, who knew, as we all do, that "Pope" (*papa* in Italian) means "father," this was a wordplay that also meant "because they wish to eliminate me to make way for their succession to my throne."

Jung's first "accomplice" in this psychoo dun'it? Freud himself. As we have seen, Freud did not publicly blame Jung for his humiliating displays of weakness. Instead, consistent with his theories, he said in letters and conversations that though the quarrels with Jung were contributory, his faintings were caused by the sudden surfacing of strongly suppressed memories of his latent (?) homosexual relationship and break with Wilhelm Fliess. They, in turn, dredged up unresolved Oedipal neuroses dating back to early childhood.

Thus, to Freud, the secret undetected "criminal" who twice felled him was the segment of his unconscious mind which had eluded his lifelong self-analysis and strenuous sublimations.

Also, a pretty good case may be made for the conjecture that the dramatistic *Freud used Jung,* that he joined the Munich quarrel about the remote Ikhnaton because he wanted to end his ever-worsening relationship with Jung. He may even have driven toward that final showdown, anticipating that it would end with the psychosomatic moment known as a "fainting attack." Psychoanalysts have taught us that many of us frequently incite or collaborate in attacks upon ourselves.

(Though all this is relevant when applied to Freud, this kind of reasoning reminds me, uncomfortably, of the sophistical Becket-slaying ruffians in *Murder in the Cathedral* who try to persuade audiences that they were really Becket's victims, that he had forced them to kill him so that he could fulfill his egomaniacal ambition to become a martyred saint!)

26

My deduction that Freud, or his inner "villain" who played the "Satan," "Hagen," or "Brutus" role, may have preselected Jung to perform as his "Judas" is based on Freud's remarkable confession in his *Interpretation of Dreams:* "My emotional life has always insisted that I should have an intimate friend and a hated enemy. I have always been able to provide myself afresh with both, and it not infrequently happened that . . . friend and enemy have come together in the same individual." It would seem that like Wilhelm Fliess before him, Jung fulfilled Freud's "emotional" requirements quite nicely.

Recently, while seeking verification of my deduction that Freud's faintings were in part a response to his hostile feelings toward Jung, feelings that boomeranged disastrously, I found a letter Freud wrote to Ludwig Binswanger* which read in part:

> My fainting attack in Munich was surely provoked by psychogenic elements, which received strong somatic reinforcements (a week of troubles, a sleepless night, the equivalent of a migraine, the day's tasks). I had several such attacks; in each case there were similar contributory causes, often a bit of alcohol [as in Bremen when he reenacted *Hedda Gabler*], for which I have no tolerance. Among the psychic elements there is the fact that I had quite a similar seizure in the same place in Munich, on two different occasions, four and six years ago. In the light of a most careful diagnosis, it seems scarcely possible to attribute my attacks to a more serious cause, for instance, a weak heart.

Freud then adds: *"Repressed feelings, this time directed against Jung, as previously against a predecessor [Fliess], naturally played the main part."* (Italics mine.)

---

*Ludwig Binswanger, *Sigmund Freud, Reminiscences of a Friendship.*

27

Replay: KING: What do you call the play?
HAMLET: "The Mousetrap" . . . this
play is the image of a murder done in
Vienna.
—Shakespeare's "play-within-a-play," *Hamlet*

I nominate as the "criminal" third man in this whodunit reconstruction scenario a man who has never been mentioned as a leading actor in the "Munich incident": Dr. Karl Abraham. I know this will startle those who know him as Freud's brilliant, loyal, trustworthy, and dutiful disciple and friend—who was never known to act in an underhanded way.

But, taking my investigative cue from Freud, who, as we have seen, never hesitated to expose the villainous "Hagen" or "Brutus" or "Satan" aspects of his (or anyone's) personality, I now offer my reasons for suspecting Karl Abraham as a secret instigator of Freud's Munich surrender.

I first began to suspect Abraham of conscious or unconscious mischief during my repeated readings of the dramatic scene at Munich's Park Hotel. As I ran my Sherlockian eye down Jones's list of witnesses: ". . . [himself], Jung, Jones, Abraham, Ophuijsen, Riklin, and Seif," wondering how several of these highly trained analysts had reacted to the drama and why they had never published their diagnoses of the historic event, my eye kept returning to the name "Abraham."

I thought: "Something strange here. Though it was his Egyptological paper that started the momentous quarrel between the two great antagonists, there's no mention of Abraham's part in the verbal battle. He seems to have been silent. But, come to think of it, how did he *happen* to write that inflammatory essay? I suspect some psycho-monkey-business here. Needs looking into."

Later, after reviewing Abraham's triangular relationship with Freud and Jung, including the incident of the "Egyptian things hidden by Freud in his briefcase," I wrote the following: "Yesterday, while browsing through a book of quotations, I found one from Hesiod (700 B.C.) that applies nicely to Karl Abraham and his Egyptian monograph, the *only* one he wrote about Ikhnaton or any Pharaoh. 'Right timing,' said Hesiod, 'is in all things the most important element.' " Yes, the *timing* of Abraham's essay provokes some very interesting questions. Such as: Was the writing of that paper at that time merely coincidental? No, psychoanalysts don't believe in such "coincidences" and assign hidden motives to all psychological events. Was the appearance of that paper, quite unrelated to Abraham's other writings at that time, born only of his desire to perform an exercise in applied psychoanalysis? And, speaking of "timing," were the publication and circulation of that "parable" at that moment of time merely the covert warning of a faithful disciple worried about Jung's increasingly disruptive role in the psychoanalytical movement? And, a heavily loaded question: Was this Abraham's retaliative act against a Jacob-like father figure who had unwisely bestowed his greater love upon an undeserving sibling rival?

Here in scenario form, with some strategic repetitions, are my reasons for thinking that Karl Abraham's motives for writing the Ikhnaton essay were ambivalent in the highest degree.

As we have seen, Karl Abraham was accepted by Freud to become one of his most brilliant theoreticians and loyal colleague-disciples. But during his first meeting with Freud, or shortly thereafter, he warned him that Jung, whom he had observed closely, was not only a mystic and a believer in spiritualism, but was far too powerful to remain anyone's disciple. He seems also to have warned Freud that Jung was a latent anti-Semite who would inevitably turn against Freud.

These warnings created serious problems for Freud. Though he shared Abraham's misgivings about Jung as a potentially rampant anti-Semite, he had already chosen him as his heir apparent. The severe anxiety aroused by the conflict between these two formidable disciples then caused Freud to react syndromically. First, as we have seen, he mentally transferred the present conflict to the ancient past: he dramatized the triangular relationship by restaging the "Egyptian objects secretly hidden in his brother's sack" incident, an action that Abraham, keen analyst of symbolic action, did not fail to comprehend. With this reenactment Freud implied in part: "Sorry, I have already bestowed the parental 'multi-colored robe' upon your 'sibling rival.' Remember what happened after that in the Biblical story, O brother of Joseph. Let's end such rivalries for the good of the cause and live together happily in our diasporic 'exile.' "

Some months after this symbolic reenactment (in which "death wishes" toward Abraham were subtly suggested by the planting of objects found in tombs), Freud wrote Abraham a candid, tactful, disciplinary letter: "Now I believe the rivalry between you to be inevitable; in dealing with the question at issue I do not hesitate to say that you are in the right and to attribute Jung's sensitiveness to his vacillations. But I should be most unwilling to see serious dissension between you two. There are still so few of us that disagreements, based perhaps on personal 'complexes,' ought to be excluded among us. Another thing to weigh with us is that Jung should find his way back to the views he has now abandone l and you have stood by so consistently. I believe there are prospects of this. . . ."

Then, referring to Jung as the editor of the journal to which Abraham contributed theoretical papers, Freud continued:

Thus you will actually be doing me a great personal favor if you inform him in advance of what you are going to write and ask him to discuss with you the objection that he then makes, which you wish to take into account. Such an act of courtesy would certainly nip dissension in the bud, would give me great pleasure, and would show we are all capable of drawing practical benefit for ourselves from the practice of psychoanalysis. Do not make too heavy going of the small self-sacrifice demanded.

And then, in the part of the same letter which I have quoted before but repeat here for emphasis, Freud concluded: "Please be tolerant and do not forget that it is easier for you than it is for Jung to follow my ideas, for in the first place you are closer to my intellectual constitution because of racial kinship, while he as a Christian and a [Lutheran] pastor's son finds his way to me only against great inner resistance. His association with us is all the more valuable for that. I nearly said that it was only by his appearance on the scene that psychoanalysis escaped the danger of becoming a Jewish national affair. I hope you will do what I ask and send my cordial greetings."

Freud's recognition of Jung's seething ambivalences toward him and his Viennese and other Jewish followers was clearly expressed in another letter to Abraham written in 1908. Referring to a theoretical monograph submitted to him and Jung for publication, Freud said, "You must know what it is that mars my pleasure in your paper. It makes manifest your latent quarrel with Jung. You certainly had every justification for writing that way, but it would have shown greater delicacy of feeling not to have made use of it. . . . Please do not misunderstand me: I have nothing to reproach you with. I nurse the suspicion that the anti-Semitism of the

Swiss [he means Jung] that spares me is deflected in reinforced form upon you. But I think that we Jews, if we wish to join in, must develop a bit of masochism, be ready to suffer some wrong. Otherwise there is no hitting it off. Rest assured that if my name were Oberhuber, in spite of everything my innovations would have met with far less resistance."

Believing he had effected a truce between his two disciples, Freud went on to other things. He may even have dismissed it from his mind. But Abraham, finding himself a low man on the Freudian totem pole (could anything be more "Freudian"?), did not. He obeyed dutifully and bided his time.

But this less-favored son never stopped playing his assigned role. More than fifteen years after the Munich showdown ended with Jung's departure, Abraham, an unlistened-to Cassandra, felt constrained to warn Freud against yet another close friend and disciple who was about to defect. Opening his never-healed wounds, Abraham wrote:

> You know, dear Professor, that . . . I find myself once more in the same position as on several different occasions. In almost twenty years we have had no difference of opinion except where personalities were concerned whom I, very much to my regret, had to criticize. The same sequence of events repeated itself each time you indulgently overlooked everything in the behavior of the persons concerned—while all the blame—which you subsequently recognized as unjustified—was directed at me. In Jung's case your criticism was that of "jealousy." In the case of Rank, "unfriendly behavior." Could the sequence of events not be the same again? *I advanced the position which is basically yours as well but which you did not wish to admit to consciousness.* All the displeasure linked to the relevant facts is then turned against the person who has drawn attention to them.
>
> It gives me pain to have aroused your displeasure once again, although I am certain that this time, as on previous occasions, you will one day reconsider your judgment of me; but I on my part wanted to do everything to get the facts clear. . . . [Italics mine.]

As I read the above I thought: Though Abraham was a first-rate psychoanalyst, he seems not to have read (or understood) Freud's already quoted confession in *The Interpretation of Dreams:* "My emotional life has always insisted that I should have an intimate friend and a hated enemy. I have always been able to provide myself afresh with both, and it has not infrequently happened that . . . friend and enemy have come together in the same individual."* Freud's "emotional insistence" may have been stronger than the need to excommunicate "heretics" detected by Abraham. It would seem also that Abraham excluded himself from close friendship with Freud by being too much of a "friend" and not enough "enemy."

My scenario continues: Then, in 1912, three more indications of Jung's impending departure became known to Freud, Abraham, and the other psychoanalysts.

First: During his lectures at New York's Fordham University (Jesuit), Jung not only had belittled Freud and his "sexual theories" but had replaced them with his own theories.

Second: News reached Freud and his inner circle, including Abraham, that Jung and his Zurich associates, yielding to the intense Swiss antagonism to Freud's disquieting theories, had omitted Freud's name from their published writings and lectures.

Third: Early in the year Jung published his clearly "heretical" *Psychology of the Unconscious*, in which, among many other topics, he wrote about Pharaoh Ikhnaton as the founder of monotheism. But, significantly, he said nothing about Ikhnaton's best-known action: his ruthless suppression of his father Amenhotep III's religion and his erasure of his father's name from all public records and monuments.

Abraham, keen psychoanalyst, recognized these three "Oedipal" actions as parables of Jung's inner feelings toward Freud; he then wrote his orthodox essay about the Pharaonic father-son conflict and sent it to Freud, who, of course pleased with it, sent it to *Imago*, the journal of applied psychoanalysis. If Freud recognized the parallel between the ancient father-son story and his own relationship to Jung (and he seems not to have), he said nothing about it. (Did he write about the resemblance in his unpublished journals?)

Then, in November 1912, the Munich Congress was convened. There, as we know, "someone" (was it Abraham?) mentioned the "Ikhnaton" paper, and, as predicted, Jung, rebellious son, sided with Ikhnaton, while

---

*Repeated for the fourth time because of its great importance.

Freud heatedly defended Abraham's (and his own) interpretation of the ancient affair.

At first these bourgeois gentlemen tried hard to control their burgeoning mutual hostility, but as each debated point brought them closer to the Oedipal core of the quarrel between Ikhnaton and his dead father, the Freud-Jung confrontation grew hotter.

Surprisingly, neither of these great analysts seemed to realize that Karl Abraham's Hamletic "play-within-a-play" had brought on this long-delayed obligatory scene. Would they have started this verbal battle in a crowded hotel dining room if they had divined Abraham's conscious/ unconscious intention? One answer to this question might be: "No, they would not." Another answer: "Both men were seeking a pretext for a public showdown, and this was a dandy."

Yes, this was high comedy. Freud, identifying with Amenhotep III, agreed with Abraham's orthodox Freudian opinion that Ikhnaton's principal motive for eliminating his father's religion and erasing his name was Oedipal, an act of symbolic murder. But Jung-Ikhnaton hotly defended the son as a great man who loved his dad but loved God more. Obviously Jung was describing his own position, since we know now that his primary theoretical reason for leaving Freud was a religious one. Jung's greatest influence today is upon religious intellectuals.

Finally, characteristically, Freud brushed aside the façade argument to reveal what was really on his mind: his anger at the news that Jung and the Zurich group had omitted Freud's name from their Swiss publications. He then fainted.

28

That Karl Abraham actually related his Amenhotep III–Ikhnaton monograph to his first visit to Freud—with its provocative gift of Josephian Egyptian objects—may be inferred from the letter he wrote Freud some months before the same monograph triggered the events leading to Freud's Munich fainting:

Dear Professor: . . . I have just completed the preparatory work on my paper for the new journal. I know that its theme will interest you: It is about

Amenhotep IV and the Aton Cult. *The subject has a peculiar attraction for me*—to analyze the manifestations of repression and substitute-formation in a person who lived 3,300 years ago, the Oedipus complex, sublimation, and substitute-formation, all exactly as in a neurotic of the present day. I did the preparatory work in the Egyptian department of the Berlin Museum and *was reminded more than once of the first introduction to Egyptology that I enjoyed in Vienna in December, 1907.* [Italics mine.]

Wondering: What was it he saw in the Berlin Museum's Egyptian department that reminded him of his first Vienna visit? Did he see there objects like those Freud hid in his briefcase?

Freud's response shows no sign of recognition of any ulterior motive on Abraham's part:

Just think of it, Amenhotep IV in the light of psychoanalysis. That's surely a great advance in orientation. Do you know that you are now the *bête noire* of psychoanalysis of whom I have been warned? That is what is apparent after your Sagantini [paper], and now what will it be after Amenhotep? But you will not let that worry you.

Then, referring to his own work on *Totem and Taboo,* dealing with the origins of the Oedipus complex in the murder and the devouring of the "primal father" by his sons, Freud added: "The reason I am in such a good mood is that I have just finished a paper for *Imago* on the ban on incest among savages."

After mentioning the Amenhotep monograph in various letters written throughout the year, Freud wrote to Abraham just a few weeks before they met in Munich: "I like the Amenhotep in its revised form very much better. It is an ornament to our *Imago,* which continues to count on you."

Here, together with some additional exploratory suggestions, is a provisional summary of the "Case of the Fallen Psychoanalyst." I am sure that you, reader, will add your own interpretations to the list:

Item: Freud fainted because he suddenly realized, traumatically, that his long-suppressed fears had been fulfilled: he had lost Jung, just as he had lost Jung's predecessor Fliess, whom he had loved a decade earlier.

Item: Freud fainted because he realized that in Jung he had lost the Joshua-like successor who would bring psychoanalysis to the "Promised Land."

Item: Freud fainted because, as he confessed earlier, he had once again come face to face with his self-image as a kind of psychological Minotaur in the act of devouring a man who was both "intimate friend" and "hated enemy." If this was so, then we ask: Was Freud's conscience (superego) aghast at this revelation, or did it grieve over the loss of the "single individual" so necessary emotionally?

Item: Freud fainted because his lifelong syndromic compulsions forced him to identify with the dead Pharaoh Amenhotep III, and dying for a moment (fainting). This may be interpreted as an act of homeopathic magic like those in Frazer's *The Golden Bough*. His sudden histrionic fall to the ground seemed to say in effect: "I outwit your death wishes by *voluntarily* simulating death. But by recovering quickly, as one does in hysterical faintings, I am resurrected."

Item: Perhaps the most important. Freud fainted because he suddenly had to face the enormity of his emotional and intellectual errors about Jung. Others present, especially Abraham, had been right all along about Jung, while he, presumably the greatest of all analysts of men's motives and behavior, had been dead wrong.

Item: Freud fainted because he felt the need to relive Hedda Gabler's actions toward self-destruction. Hedda Gabler was a fictional person. So was the Sigmund Freud who fainted.

Item: During a wine-drinking celebration, Philip of Macedonia fell to the floor in a drunken stupor when he tried to attack his son Alexander. Later, as we know, Alexander probably took part in the murder of his father. The reader will recall that Sigmund Freud, aged ten, persuaded his parents to name his little brother Alexander.

29

The deduction that Freud thought of fainting as a histrionic simulation of death is verified in a paper published fifteen years after Munich: "Dostoevsky and Patricide." After noting that the Russian novelist's epileptic fainting spells began immediately after his father's death (Freud related his own similar attacks in part to his guilt feelings toward his dead father), Freud wrote:

244 / WHY FREUD FAINTED

[Dostoevsky's] attacks had the significance of death. . . . *We know the meaning and intention of such deathlike attacks. They signify an identification with a dead person, either with someone who is really dead or with someone who is still alive but whom the subject wishes dead. The latter is more significant. The attack then has the value of a punishment. One has wished another dead, and now one is that other person and is dead oneself.* [Italics mine.]

Though this is Freud's objective analysis of Dostoevsky's illness, it may also be read as a precise diagnosis of his own faintings. For "subject" or "Dostoevsky" read "Freud"; for "someone who is really dead" read "Amenhotep III" or "Freud's father"; for "someone whom the subject [Freud] wishes dead" read "Carl Jung."

Dr. Paul Roazen, to whose book *Freud and His Followers** I am indebted for this Dostoevsky quotation, says: "In fainting in Jung's presence, then, Freud may have been atoning for his murderous hate (of Jung), with which he responded to the death wishes toward himself he detected in his disciple."

30

and on the other hand . . .

In his last controversial book, *Moses and Monotheism*, published twenty years after his bitter argument with Jung about Ikhnaton, Freud mysteriously changed the position he had held at the time. He did so in a manner suggesting that he had fainted for an additional or supplementary reason: his underlying desire to identify with Jung and, through Jung, with the Pharaoh who symbolically "killed" his already dead father. If this seems confused, contradictory, farfetched, it may not be *my* fault. As Freud might be the first to agree, his psyche—anybody's psyche—is a labyrinth very difficult to traverse. Even with a Freudian-Ariadne thread.

Look at this *volte-face* statement from *Moses and Monotheism:*

---

*(New York, Knopf, 1975.)

I begin by abstracting the results of my second—the purely historical—essay on Moses. . . . The historical background of the events which have aroused our interest is as follows: Through the conquests of the Eighteenth Dynasty, Egypt had become a world empire. The new Imperialism was reflected in the development of certain religions; if not those of the whole people, then in those of the governing and intellectually active upper stratum. Under the influence of the priests of the Sun God at On (Heliopolis), possibly strengthened by suggestions from Asia, there arose the idea of a universal God Aton—no longer restricted to one people and one country.

Freud now reveals a different attitude toward the young Pharaoh whom he had formerly charged with Oedipal reasons for erasing his father's name from public monuments and records:

With the young Amenhotep IV (who later changed his name to Ikhnaton), a Pharaoh succeeded to the throne who knew no higher interest than in developing the idea of such a God. He raised the Aton religion to the official religion and thereby the universal God became the *only* God; all that was said of the other gods became deceit and guile. With a superb implacability he resisted all the temptations of magical thought and discarded the illusions, so dear to the Egyptians, of a life after death. With an astonishing premonition of later scientific knowledge, he recognized in the energy of the sun's radiation the source of all life on earth, and worshipped the sun as the symbol of God's power. He gloried in his joy in the creation and in his life in Maat (truth and justice). . . . It is the first case in the history of mankind, and perhaps the purest, of monotheistic religion.

Freud then reveals why he has come to see Ikhnaton in a new light. It is Ikhnaton's influence on Moses, the greatest identification figure in Freud's life:

This is what has been established historically, and now at this point our work of hypothesis begins. Among the intimates of Ikhnaton was a man perhaps called Thotmes, as so many others were at the same time—the name does not matter, but its second part must have been -mose. He held high rank and was a convinced adherent of the Aton religion, but in contradistinction to the brooding King he was forceful and passionate. For this man the death of Ikhnaton and the abolishing of his religion meant the end of all his hopes.

Only proscribed or recanting could he remain in Egypt. If he were governor of a border province, he might well have come in touch with a certain Semitic tribe which had immigrated several generations ago. He chose them as his people and tried to realize his own ideals through them. After he left Egypt with them—accompanied by his immediate followers—he hallowed them by the custom of circumcision, gave them laws and introduced them to the Aton religion, which the Egyptians had just discarded. Perhaps the rules Moses imposed on his Jews were even harder than those of his master and teacher Ikhnaton; perhaps he also relinquished the connection with the Sun God of On, to whom the latter had adhered.

Before publishing his *Moses and Monotheism*, Freud thought he should have called it a "novel." The above quotation may help explain why he thought so.

31

The last entry in my Vienna notebook reads: "December 9, aboard the Swissair flight to New York, 11:00 A.M. The return trip is entirely different: the horizon-to-horizon 'yogurt' that hid the Atlantic Ocean during my flight over has vanished, and the cloudless sky, the water six miles below are a deep Raoul Dufy blue." After devouring all the magazines aboard the plane (I must take a *slow* reading course for long boring trips like this), I resumed my ruminations about my exploratory journey through "Freud's Vienna," and the fitting climax experienced last night.

At midnight, too stimulated to sleep, I lay in bed . . . my thoughts returning over and over again to my first walk from the hotel to the Freudhaus . . . and the unfulfilled self-instruction to explore the interior and exterior imagery of the "false-Gothic" Votive Church.

"So dominant an image," I thought, "*must* have played an important role in the psyche of so ultra-responsive a man. . . . Freud saw this church and its sculptural adornments many thousands of times while on his way to his lectures at the nearby University, at the beginning of his compulsive daily marches around the Ring, and while walking to the museum that housed the Egyptian collection. Yes, thousands of times.

"As for me, though I've passed the church more than a dozen times, and have seen it every time I left the hotel, I've never walked across the wide Währinger Strasse to inspect it closely. And my all-too-brief visit will end early tomorrow morning."

Now my vagrant thoughts wandered to other Gothic and Romanesque cathedrals I'd seen and photographed while working in France: Chartres, Notre Dame, Vézelay, Autun, Arles, and Strasbourg. On one of them—I can't remember which it was—there stood a *minyon* (congregation) of stone figures: Christ, flanked by his leading disciples and five Hebrew patriarchs—one of whom was a horned Moses angrily displaying the first edition of God's Commandments to his people, whom he had caught perversely worshipping the unspeakable Golden Calf. As in the engraving in Freud's waiting room, Moses is about to smash the sacred tablet.

My curiosity ignited, I leaped from my bed, dressed, left the hotel, and walked the three short blocks to the Votive Church. There, by the feeble light of distant streetlamps, I saw that, like the remembered French cathedral, the Votive Church's front façade displayed the figure of Christ, flanked by his disciples and the leading Old Testament patriarchs—led by a powerful Moses, angrily holding aloft the tablet of the Ten Commandments.

And of course this midnight spectator responded with the expected question: Did Sigmund Freud, who responded syndromically to the hot mythic images in his immediate environment—Medusa, Melusina, Pomona, Satan, Diana-Demeter, the falcon-headed Re, and Ramses II—respond to and identify with the Moses who stood at the portal of the Christian church just a few hundred feet from Berggasse 19?

If he did, then this might help explain Freud's curious, controversial hypothesis of the Moses who was a Jew yet not a Jew, but instead an Egyptian nobleman (*goy*) whose mother pretended to have found him in a floating basket. (This hypothetical "identification" also links Freud to the Moses who, according to Freud, based his new religion on the monotheism of the "father-erasing" Ikhnaton.)

The resemblance between Freud and his neighbor Moses goes further: Like Moses, Freud held aloft a set of implied moral commandments for all Vienna to see—and ignore.

Coda:

In the great garden before the historic Belvedere Palace, about two miles from Freud's house, there stand ten gigantic stone figures of the mythic Sphinx, the monstress destroyed by the question-answering Oedipus. Each of these great figures has the body of a male lion and the face of a Viennese housewife. One of these days I will explore the possible connections between these Viennese Sphinxes and the Viennese poet-doctor Sigmund Freud. The search for the inner Freud continues.

Index